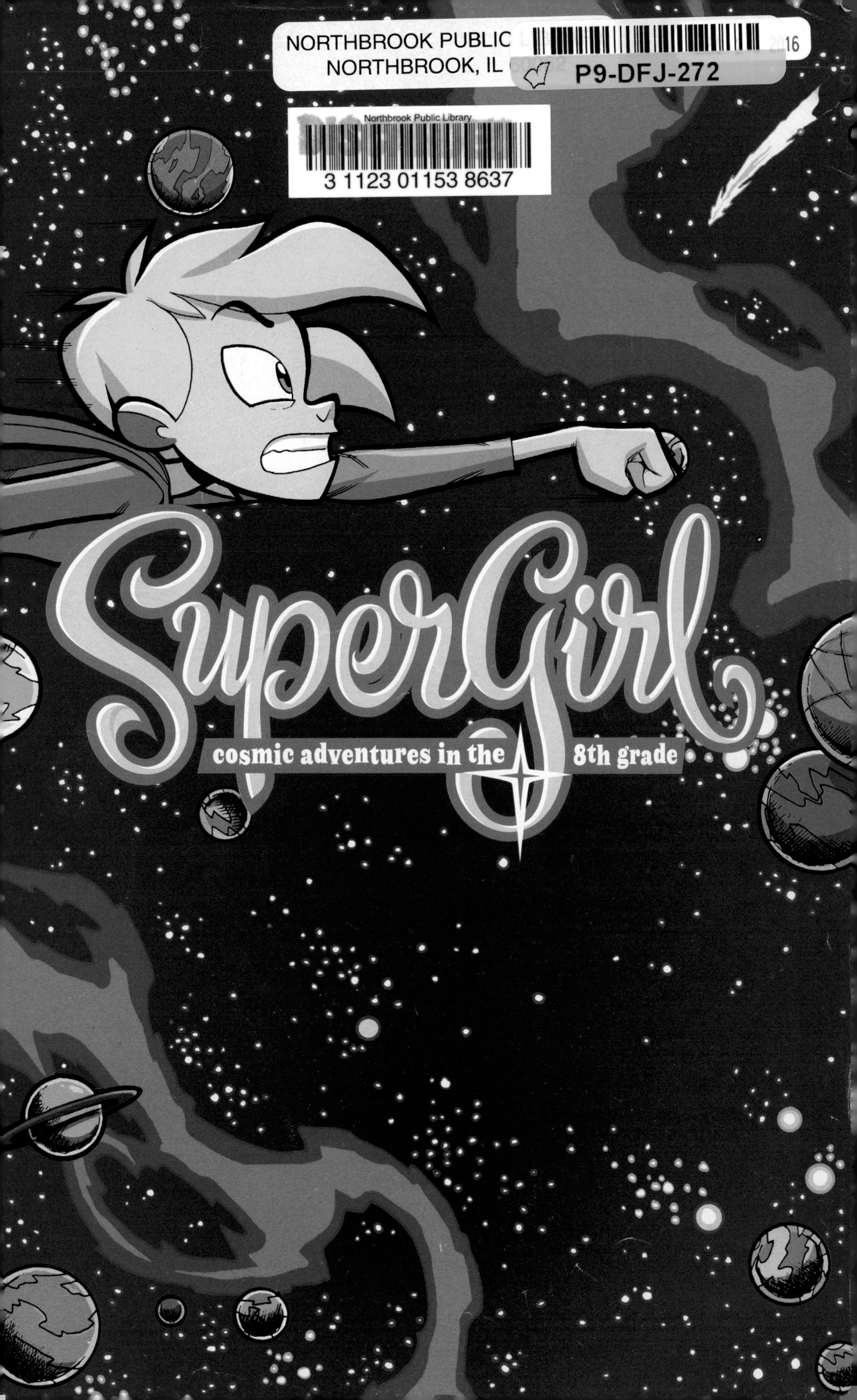
SuperGirl
cosmic adventures in the 8th grade

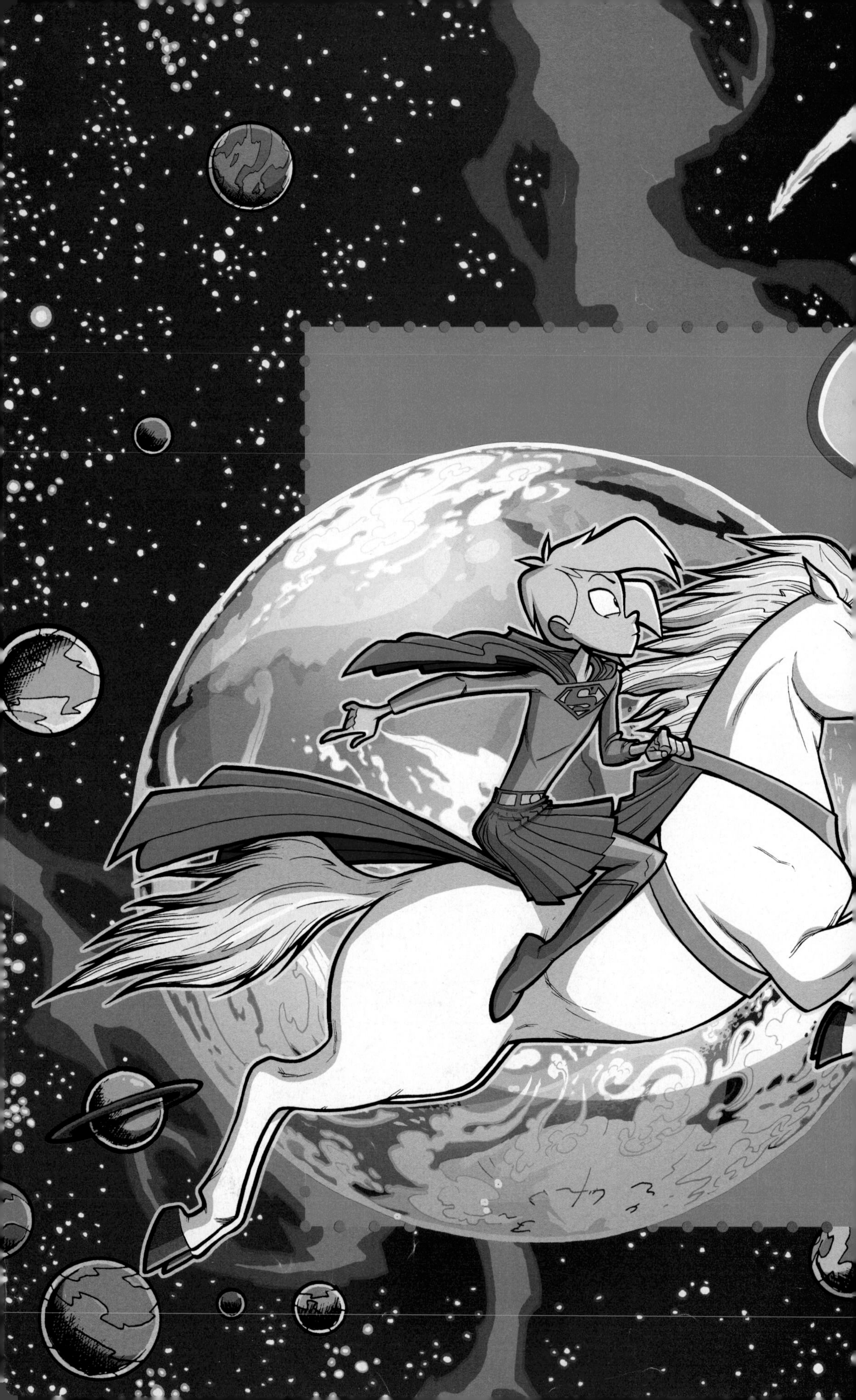

SuperGirl

cosmic adventures in the 8th grade

Landry Q. Walker
Writer

Eric Jones
Artist

Joey Mason
Colorist

Pat Brosseau
Travis Lanham
Sal Cipriano
Letterers

Jann Jones Elisabeth V. Gehrlein Editors-original series
Adam Schlagman Associate Editor-original series
Simona Martore Assistant Editor-original series
Jeb Woodard Group Editor-Collected Editions
Sean Mackiewicz Editor-Collected Edition
Steve Cook Design Director-Books

Bob Harras Senior VP – Editor-in-Chief, DC Comics
Diane Nelson President
Dan DiDio and Jim Lee Co-Publishers
Geoff Johns Chief Creative Officer
Amit Desai Senior VP – Marketing & Global Franchise Management
Nairi Gardiner Senior VP – Finance
Sam Ades VP – Digital Marketing
Bobbie Chase VP – Talent Development
Mark Chiarello Senior VP – Art, Design & Collected Editions
John Cunningham VP – Content Strategy
Anne DePies VP – Strategy Planning & Reporting
Don Falletti VP – Manufacturing Operations
Lawrence Ganem VP – Editorial Administration & Talent Relations
Alison Gill Senior VP – Manufacturing & Operations
Hank Kanalz Senior VP – Editorial Strategy & Administration
Jay Kogan VP – Legal Affairs
Derek Maddalena Senior VP – Sales & Business Development
Jack Mahan VP – Business Affairs
Dan Miron VP – Sales Planning & Trade Development
Nick Napolitano VP – Manufacturing Administration
Carol Roeder VP – Marketing
Eddie Scannell VP – Mass Account & Digital Sales
Courtney Simmons Senior VP – Publicity & Communications
Jim (Ski) Sokolowski VP – Comic Book Specialty & Newsstand Sales
Sandy Yi Senior VP – Global Franchise Management

Cover illustration by Eric Jones with Joey Mason

DC Comics, 2900 W. Alameda Avenue, Burbank, CA 91505
Printed by RR Donnelley, Salem, VA, USA. 4/1/16.
First Printing. ISBN: 978-1-4012-6320-1

PEFC Certified
Printed on paper from sustainably managed forests and controlled sources
PEFC
PEFC/29-31-75
www.pefc.org

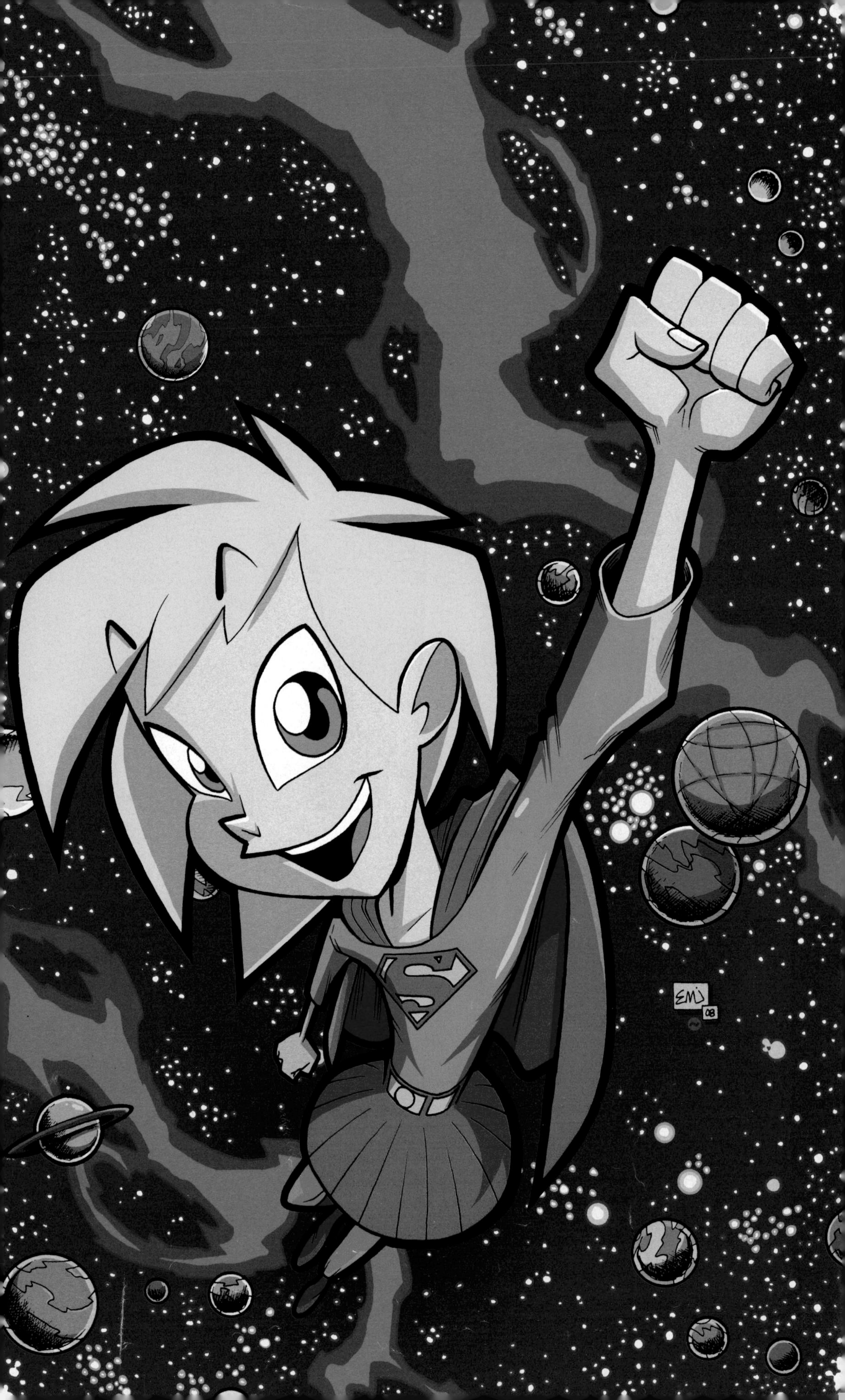

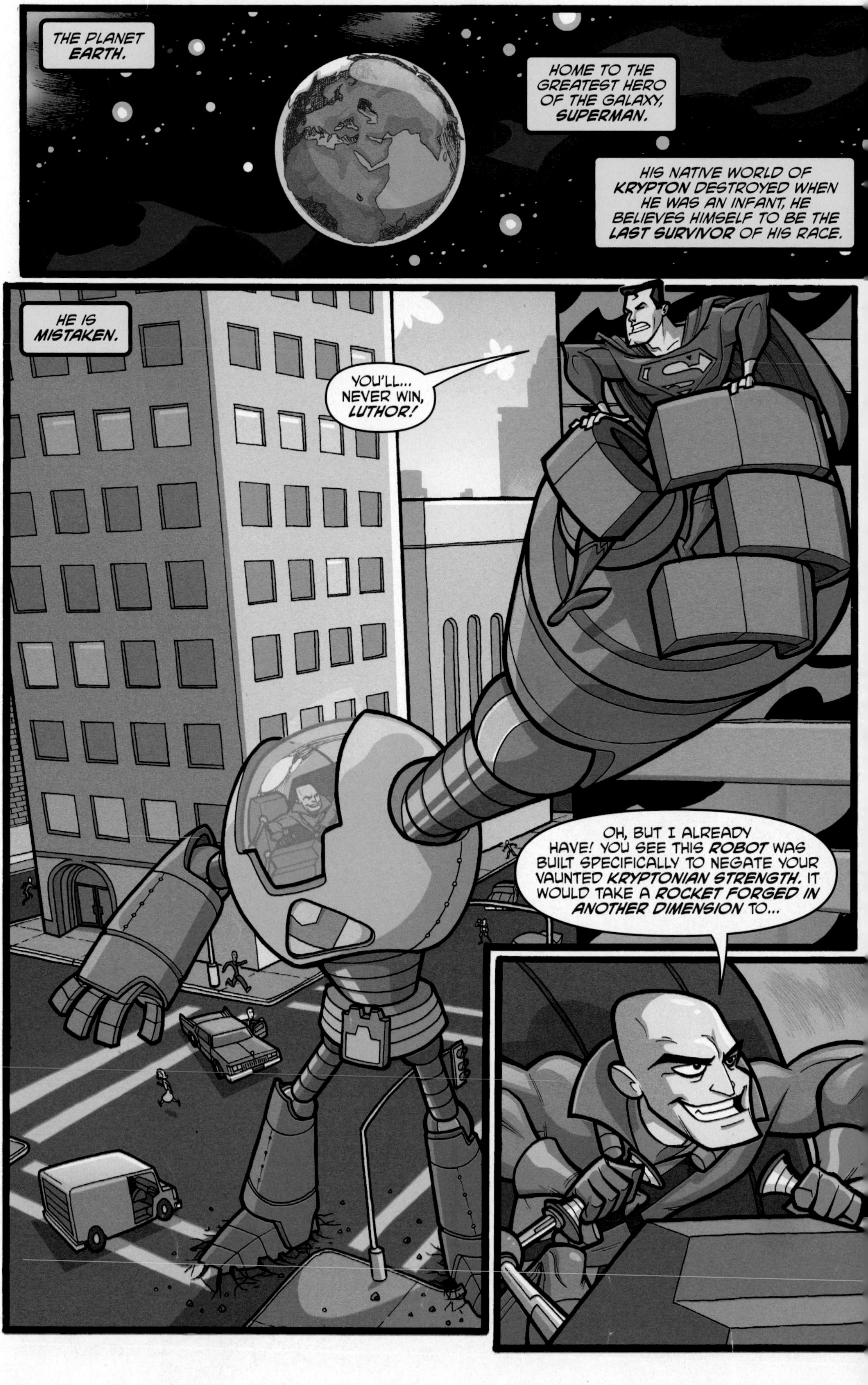
THE PLANET EARTH.
HOME TO THE GREATEST HERO OF THE GALAXY, SUPERMAN.
HIS NATIVE WORLD OF KRYPTON DESTROYED WHEN HE WAS AN INFANT, HE BELIEVES HIMSELF TO BE THE LAST SURVIVOR OF HIS RACE.
HE IS MISTAKEN.
YOU'LL... NEVER WIN, LUTHOR!
OH, BUT I ALREADY HAVE! YOU SEE THIS ROBOT WAS BUILT SPECIFICALLY TO NEGATE YOUR VAUNTED KRYPTONIAN STRENGTH. IT WOULD TAKE A ROCKET FORGED IN ANOTHER DIMENSION TO...

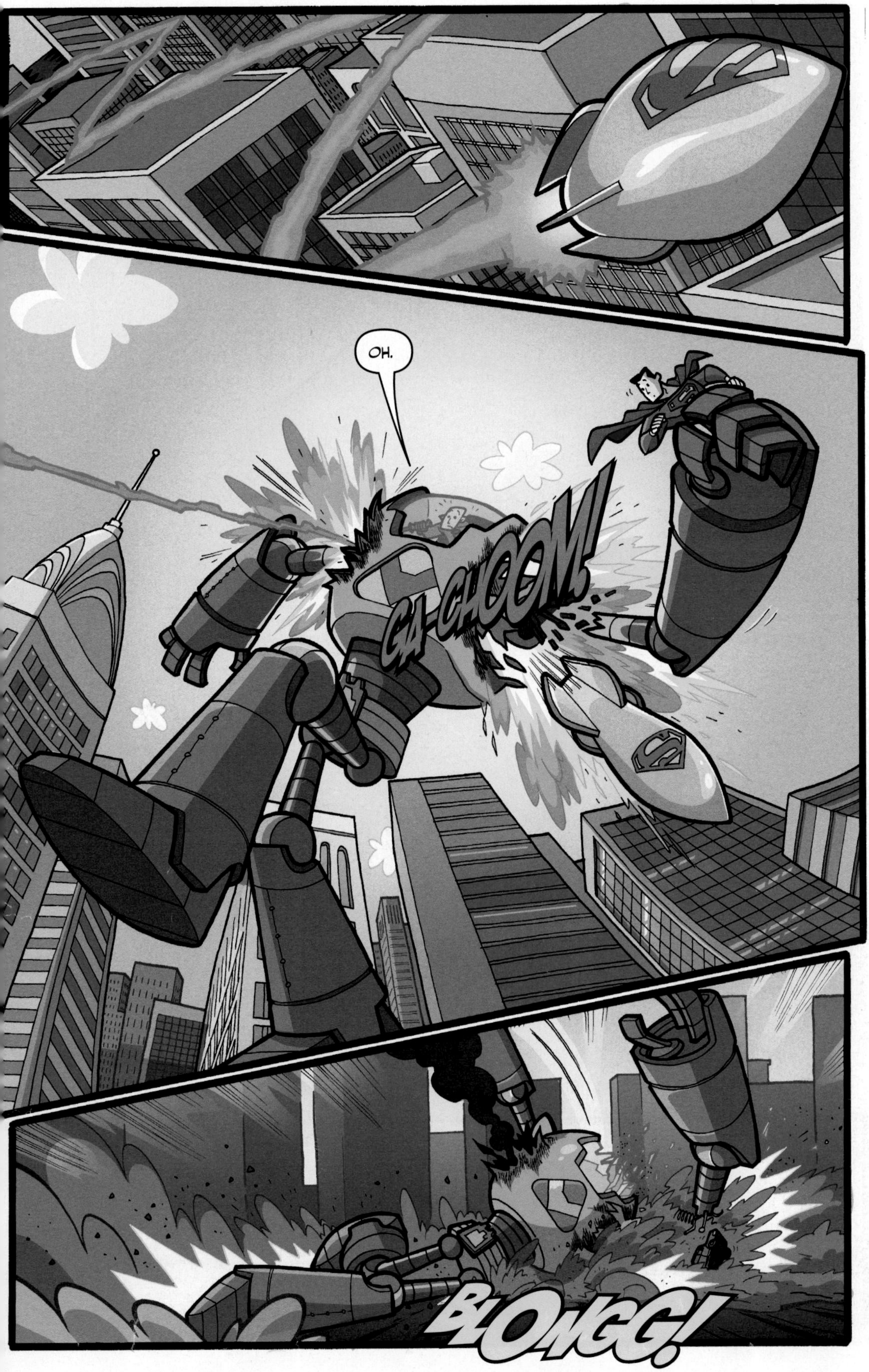
OH.
GA-CHOOM!
BLONGG!

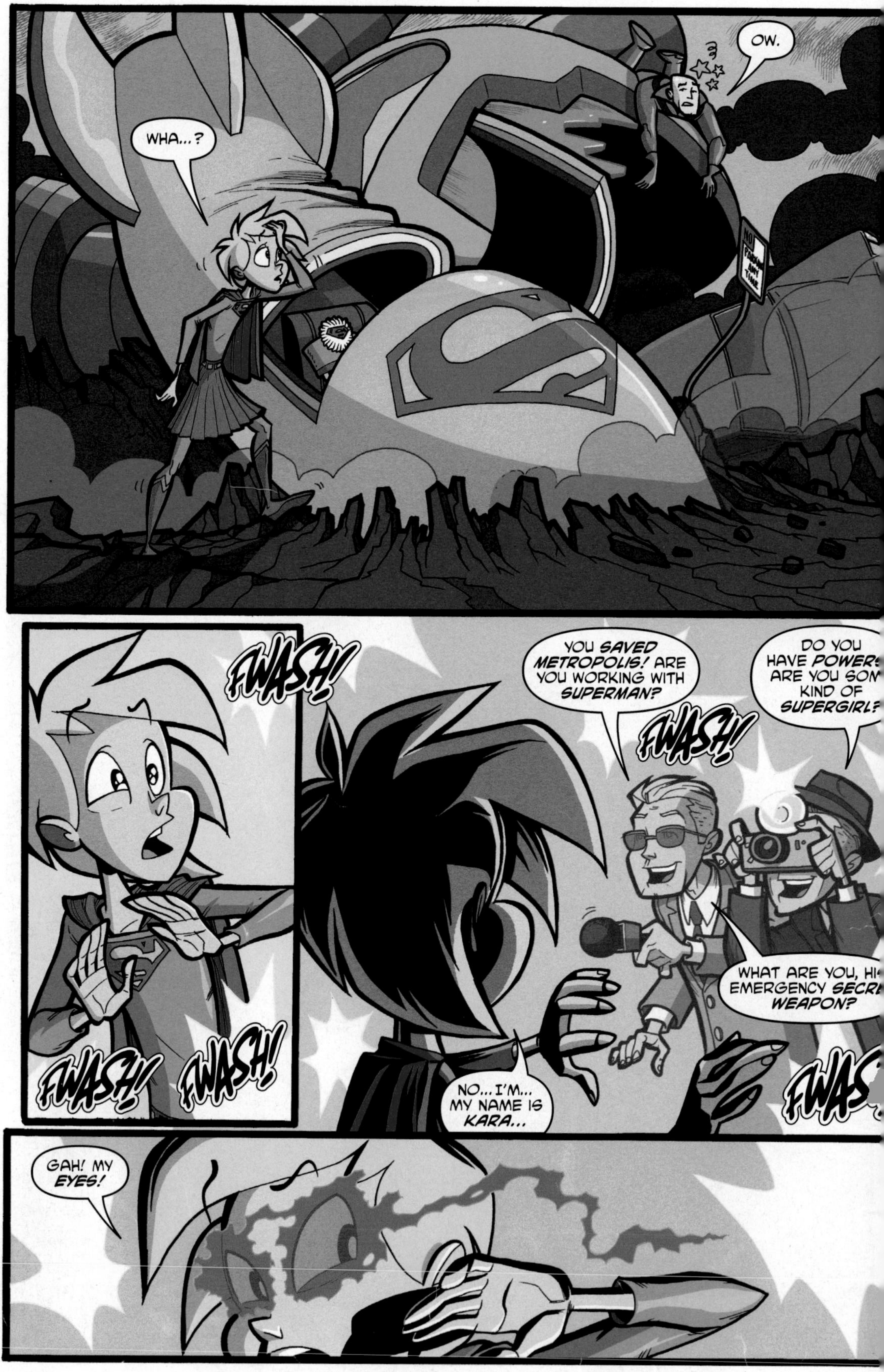
WHA...?
OW.
FWASH!
YOU SAVED METROPOLIS! ARE YOU WORKING WITH SUPERMAN?
DO YOU HAVE POWER ARE YOU SOM KIND OF SUPERGIRL
FWASH!
WHAT ARE YOU, HI EMERGENCY SECR WEAPON?
FWASH! FWASH!
NO... I'M... MY NAME IS KARA...
FWAS
GAH! MY EYES!

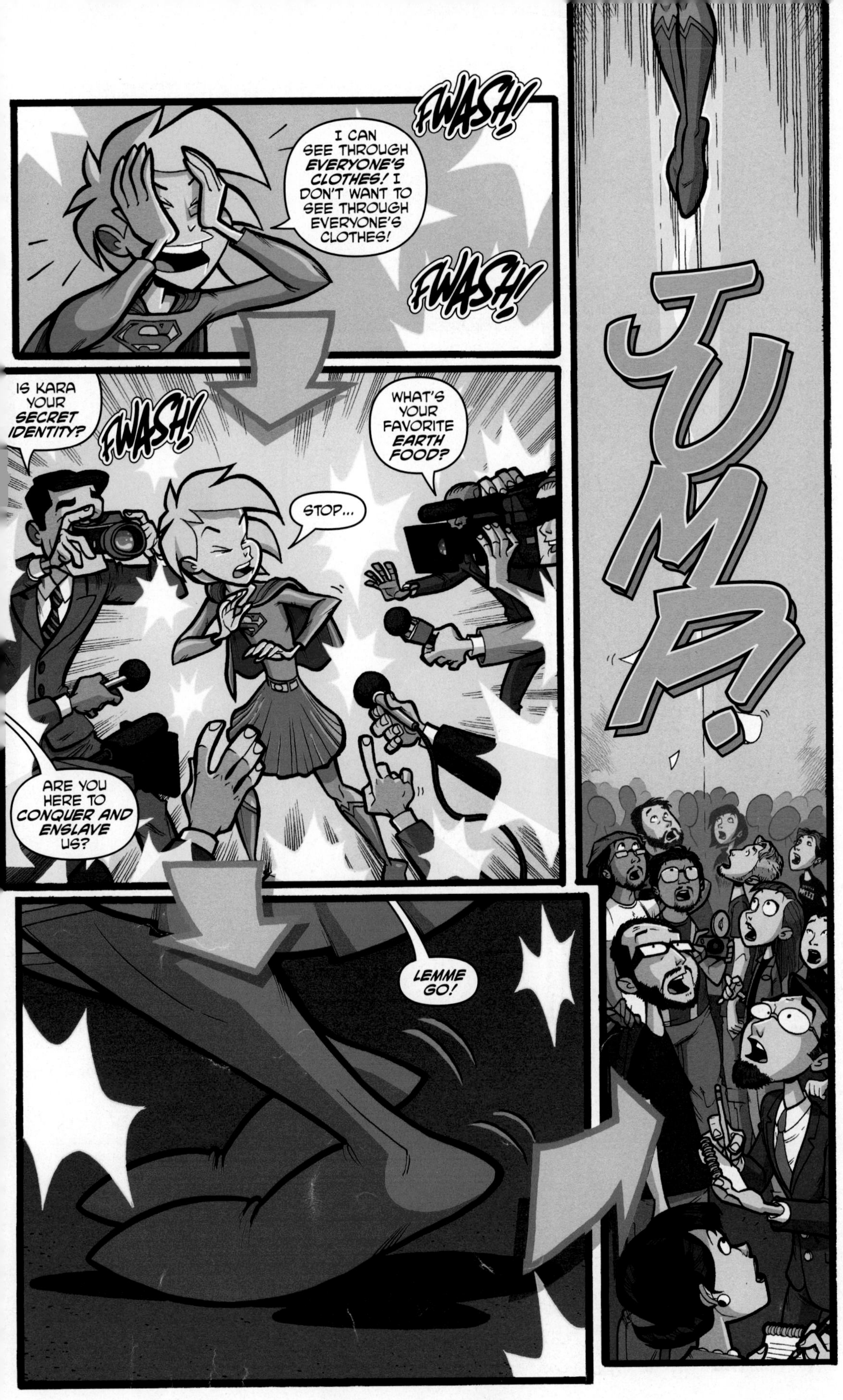

FWASH!
I CAN SEE THROUGH EVERYONE'S CLOTHES! I DON'T WANT TO SEE THROUGH EVERYONE'S CLOTHES!
FWASH!
IS KARA YOUR SECRET IDENTITY?
FWASH!
WHAT'S YOUR FAVORITE EARTH FOOD?
STOP...
ARE YOU HERE TO CONQUER AND ENSLAVE US?
LEMME GO!
JUMP!

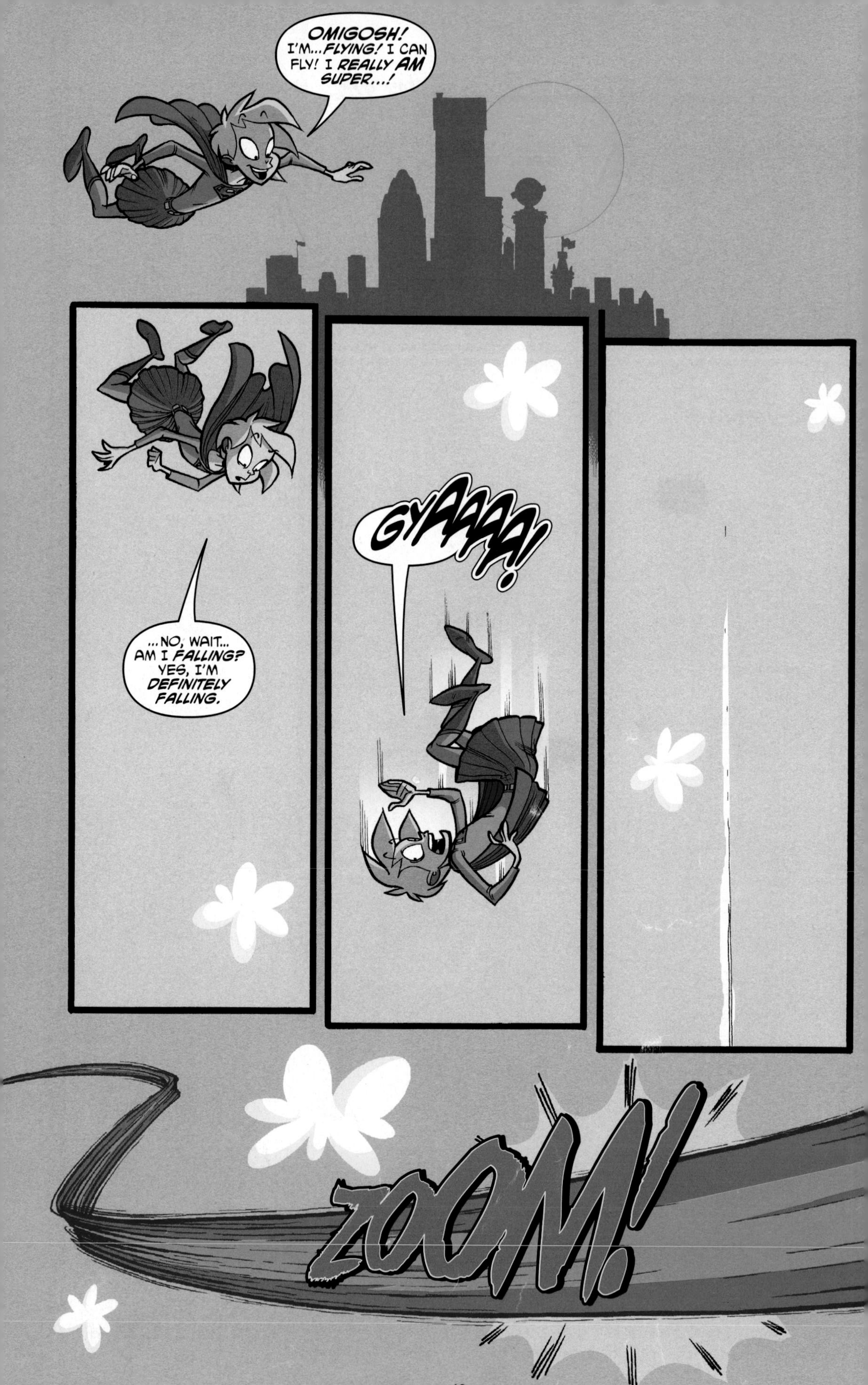
OMIGOSH! I'M...FLYING! I CAN FLY! I REALLY AM SUPER...!
...NO, WAIT... AM I FALLING? YES, I'M DEFINITELY FALLING.
GYAAAA!
ZOOM!

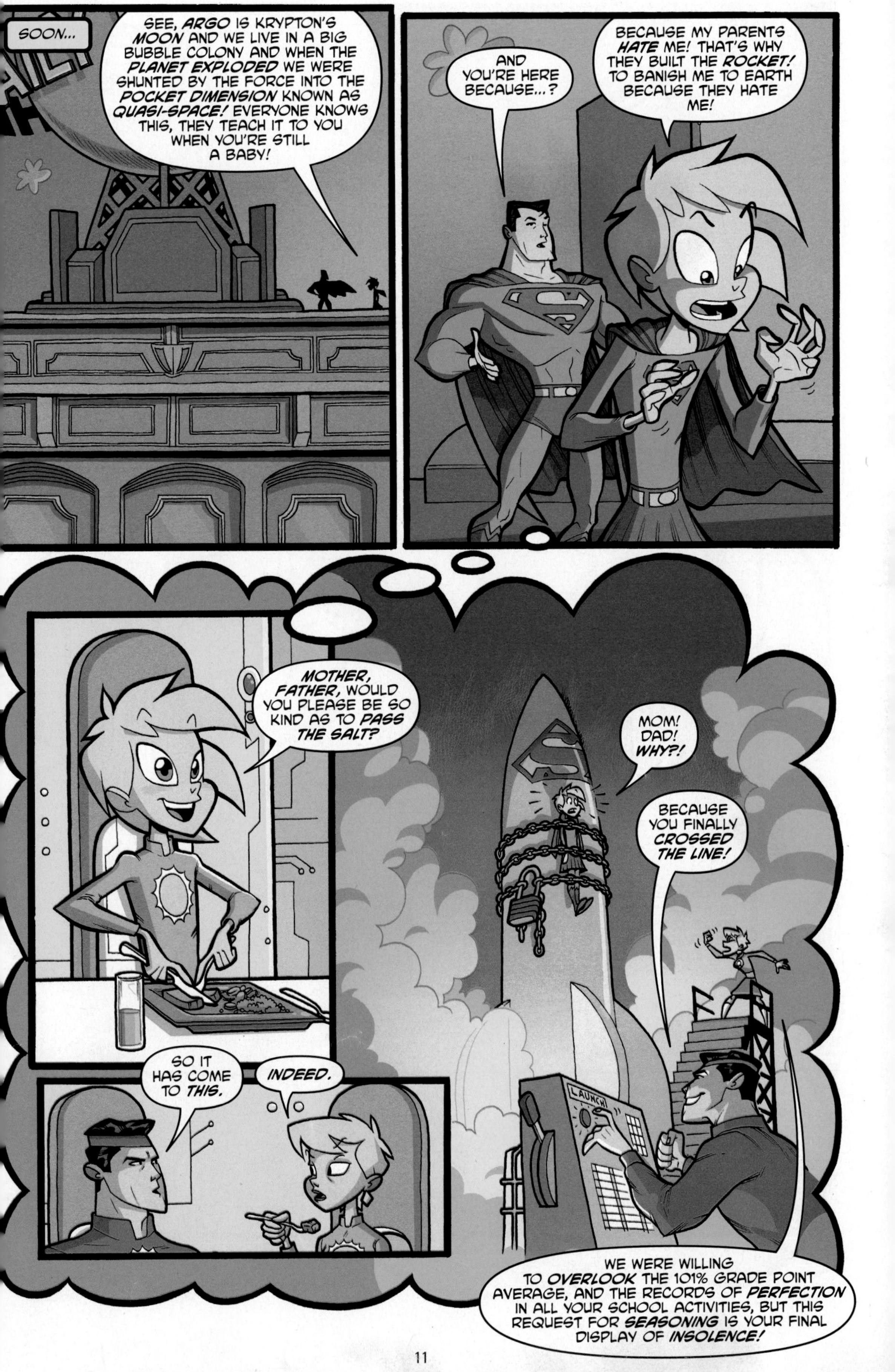
SOON...
SEE, ARGO IS KRYPTON'S MOON AND WE LIVE IN A BIG BUBBLE COLONY AND WHEN THE PLANET EXPLODED WE WERE SHUNTED BY THE FORCE INTO THE POCKET DIMENSION KNOWN AS QUASI-SPACE! EVERYONE KNOWS THIS, THEY TEACH IT TO YOU WHEN YOU'RE STILL A BABY!
AND YOU'RE HERE BECAUSE...?
BECAUSE MY PARENTS HATE ME! THAT'S WHY THEY BUILT THE ROCKET! TO BANISH ME TO EARTH BECAUSE THEY HATE ME!
MOTHER, FATHER, WOULD YOU PLEASE BE SO KIND AS TO PASS THE SALT?
SO IT HAS COME TO THIS.
INDEED.
MOM! DAD! WHY?!
BECAUSE YOU FINALLY CROSSED THE LINE!
LAUNCH
WE WERE WILLING TO OVERLOOK THE 101% GRADE POINT AVERAGE, AND THE RECORDS OF PERFECTION IN ALL YOUR SCHOOL ACTIVITIES, BUT THIS REQUEST FOR SEASONING IS YOUR FINAL DISPLAY OF INSOLENCE!

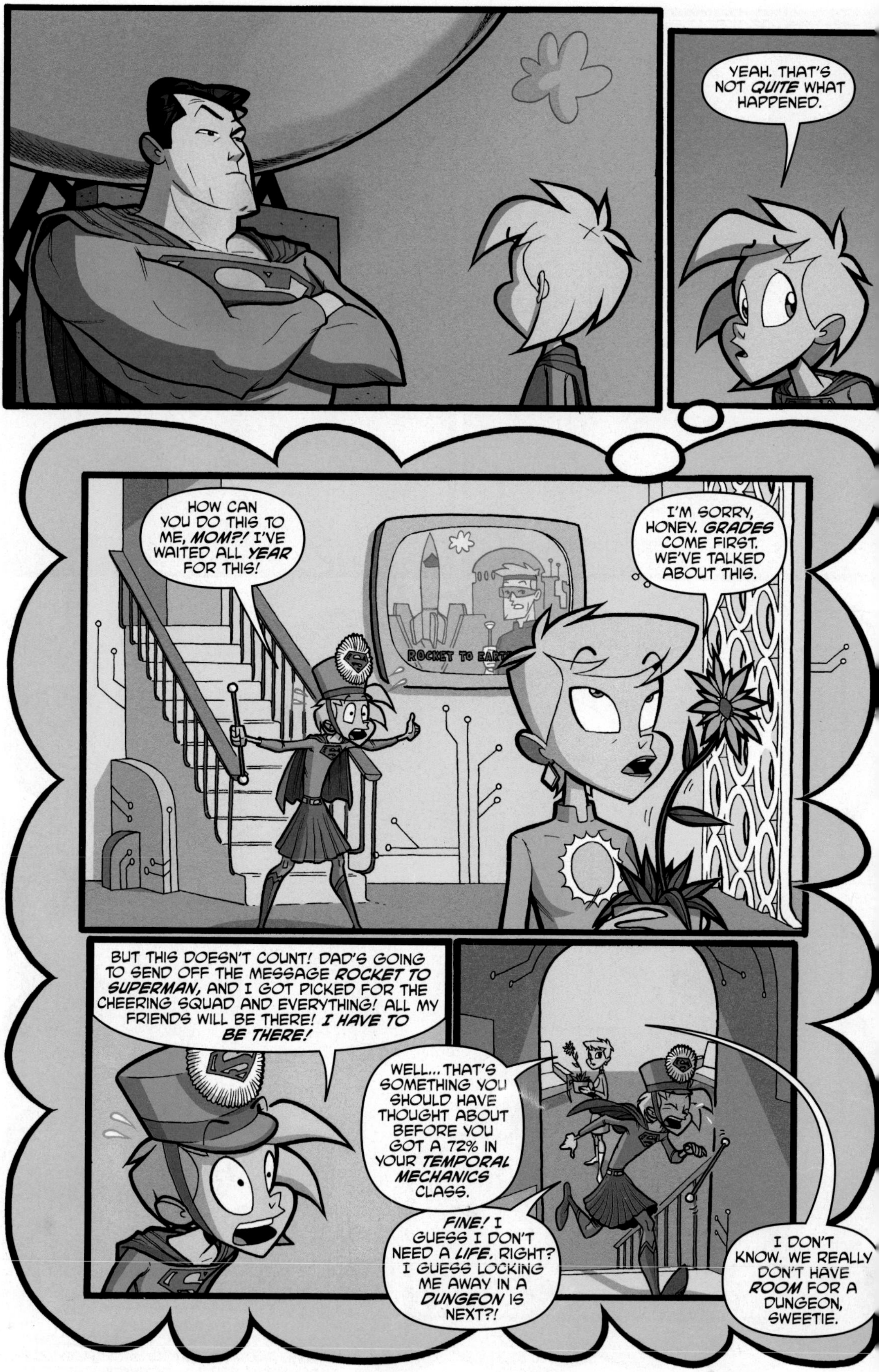
YEAH. THAT'S NOT *QUITE* WHAT HAPPENED.
HOW CAN YOU DO THIS TO ME, *MOM?!* I'VE WAITED ALL *YEAR* FOR THIS!
I'M SORRY, HONEY. *GRADES* COME FIRST. WE'VE TALKED ABOUT THIS.
BUT THIS DOESN'T COUNT! DAD'S GOING TO SEND OFF THE MESSAGE *ROCKET TO SUPERMAN,* AND I GOT PICKED FOR THE CHEERING SQUAD AND EVERYTHING! ALL MY FRIENDS WILL BE THERE! *I HAVE TO BE THERE!*
WELL... THAT'S SOMETHING YOU SHOULD HAVE THOUGHT ABOUT BEFORE YOU GOT A 72% IN YOUR *TEMPORAL MECHANICS* CLASS.
FINE! I GUESS I DON'T NEED A *LIFE.* RIGHT? I GUESS LOCKING ME AWAY IN A *DUNGEON* IS NEXT?!
I DON'T KNOW. WE REALLY DON'T HAVE *ROOM* FOR A DUNGEON, SWEETIE.

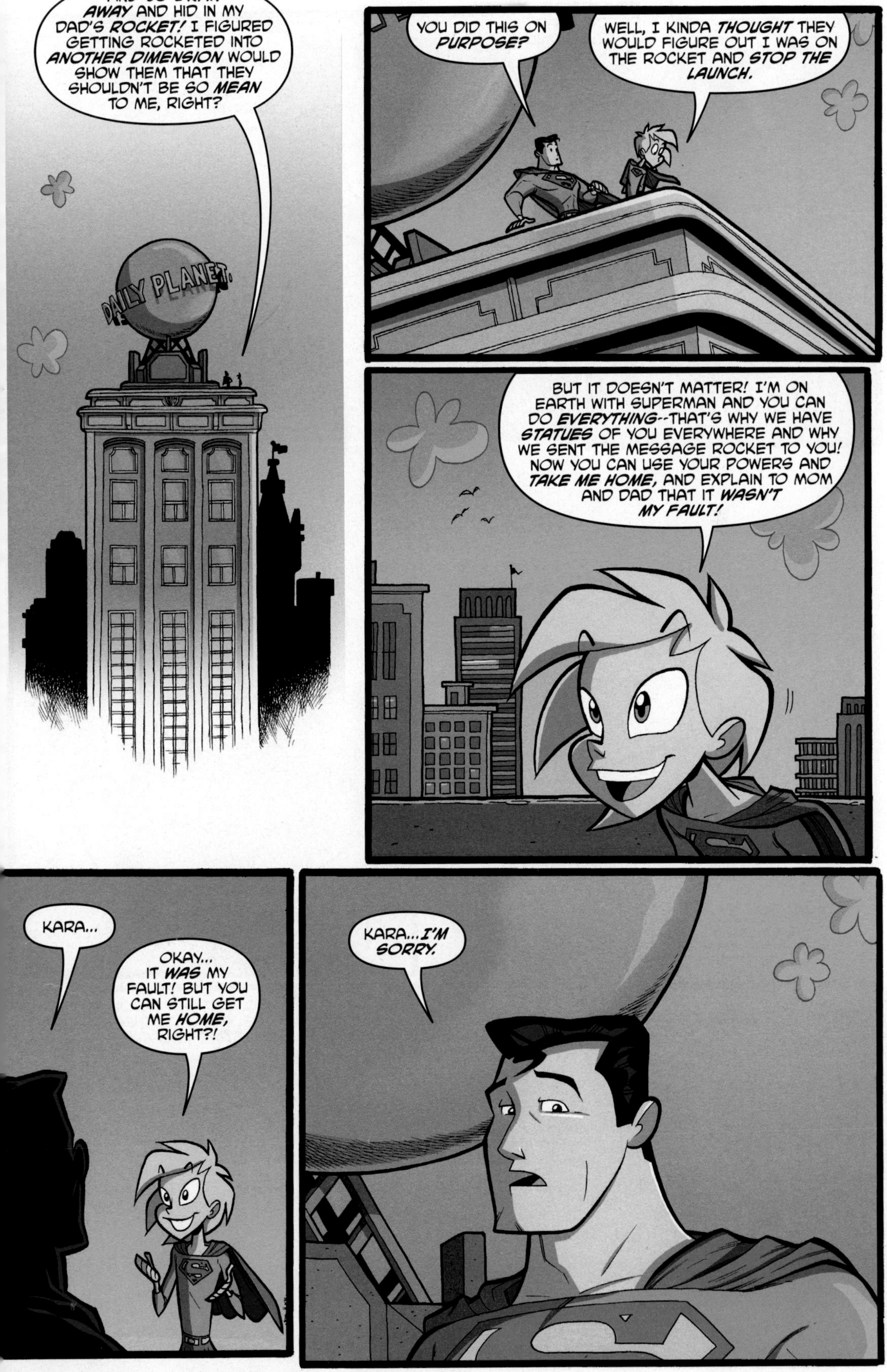
AND SO I RAN AWAY AND HID IN MY DAD'S ROCKET! I FIGURED GETTING ROCKETED INTO ANOTHER DIMENSION WOULD SHOW THEM THAT THEY SHOULDN'T BE SO MEAN TO ME, RIGHT?
DAILY PLANET
YOU DID THIS ON PURPOSE?
WELL, I KINDA THOUGHT THEY WOULD FIGURE OUT I WAS ON THE ROCKET AND STOP THE LAUNCH.
BUT IT DOESN'T MATTER! I'M ON EARTH WITH SUPERMAN AND YOU CAN DO EVERYTHING--THAT'S WHY WE HAVE STATUES OF YOU EVERYWHERE AND WHY WE SENT THE MESSAGE ROCKET TO YOU! NOW YOU CAN USE YOUR POWERS AND TAKE ME HOME, AND EXPLAIN TO MOM AND DAD THAT IT WASN'T MY FAULT!
KARA...
OKAY... IT WAS MY FAULT! BUT YOU CAN STILL GET ME HOME, RIGHT?!
KARA...I'M SORRY.

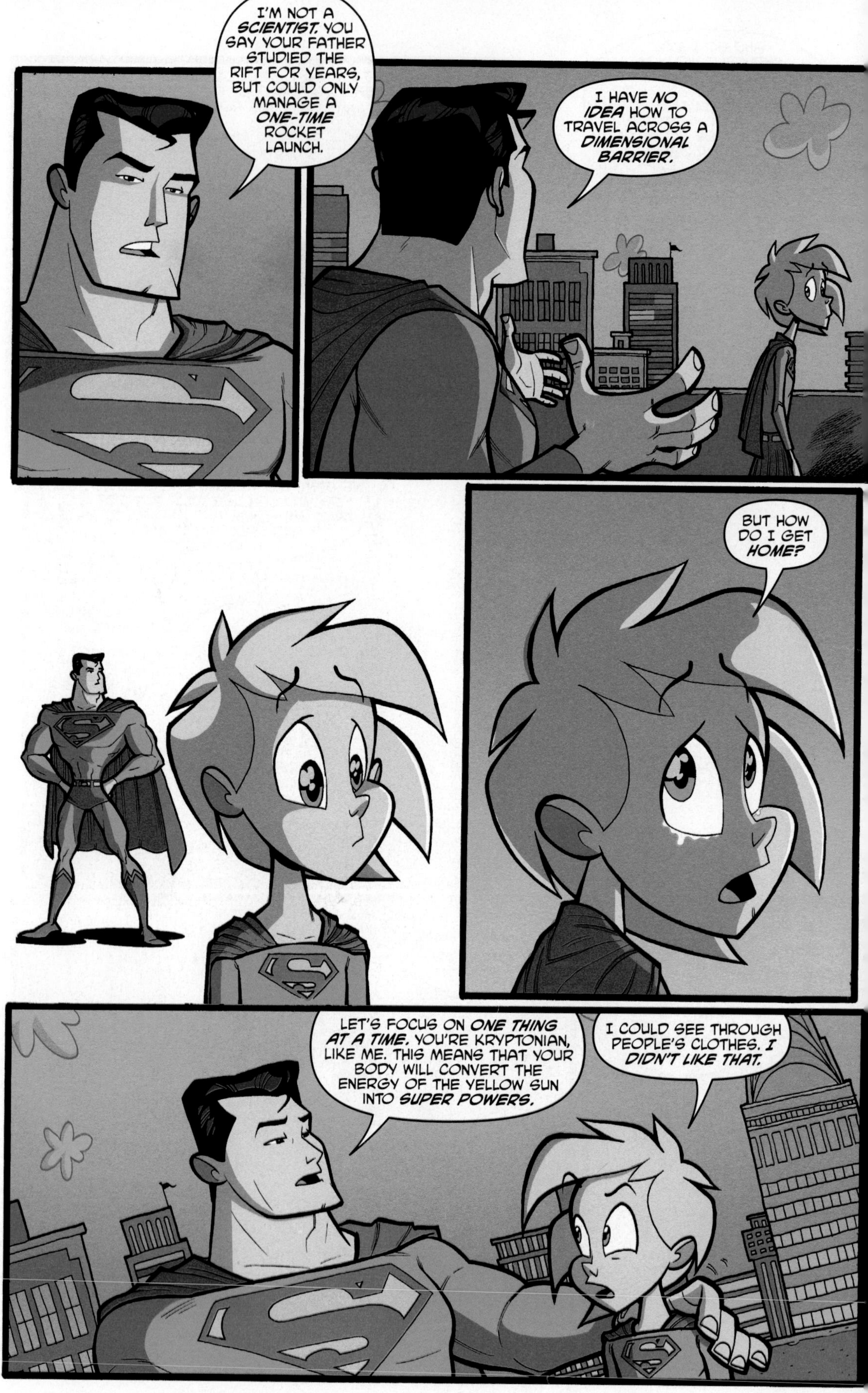
I'M NOT A SCIENTIST. YOU SAY YOUR FATHER STUDIED THE RIFT FOR YEARS, BUT COULD ONLY MANAGE A ONE-TIME ROCKET LAUNCH.
I HAVE NO IDEA HOW TO TRAVEL ACROSS A DIMENSIONAL BARRIER.
BUT HOW DO I GET HOME?
LET'S FOCUS ON ONE THING AT A TIME. YOU'RE KRYPTONIAN, LIKE ME. THIS MEANS THAT YOUR BODY WILL CONVERT THE ENERGY OF THE YELLOW SUN INTO SUPER POWERS.
I COULD SEE THROUGH PEOPLE'S CLOTHES. I DIDN'T LIKE THAT.

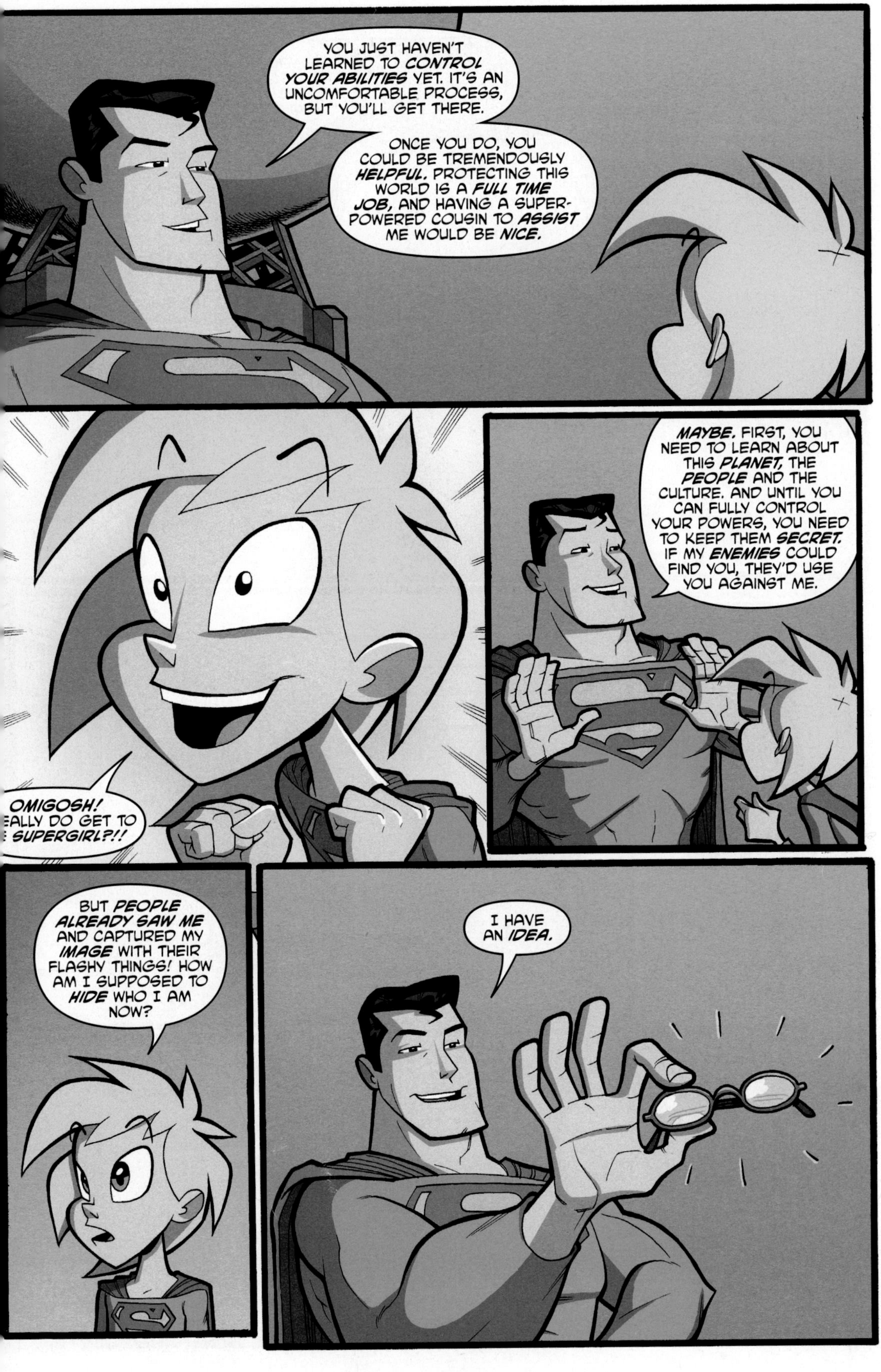
YOU JUST HAVEN'T LEARNED TO CONTROL YOUR ABILITIES YET. IT'S AN UNCOMFORTABLE PROCESS, BUT YOU'LL GET THERE.
ONCE YOU DO, YOU COULD BE TREMENDOUSLY HELPFUL. PROTECTING THIS WORLD IS A FULL TIME JOB, AND HAVING A SUPER-POWERED COUSIN TO ASSIST ME WOULD BE NICE.
OMIGOSH! EALLY DO GET TO SUPERGIRL?!!
MAYBE. FIRST, YOU NEED TO LEARN ABOUT THIS PLANET, THE PEOPLE AND THE CULTURE. AND UNTIL YOU CAN FULLY CONTROL YOUR POWERS, YOU NEED TO KEEP THEM SECRET. IF MY ENEMIES COULD FIND YOU, THEY'D USE YOU AGAINST ME.
BUT PEOPLE ALREADY SAW ME AND CAPTURED MY IMAGE WITH THEIR FLASHY THINGS! HOW AM I SUPPOSED TO HIDE WHO I AM NOW?
I HAVE AN IDEA.

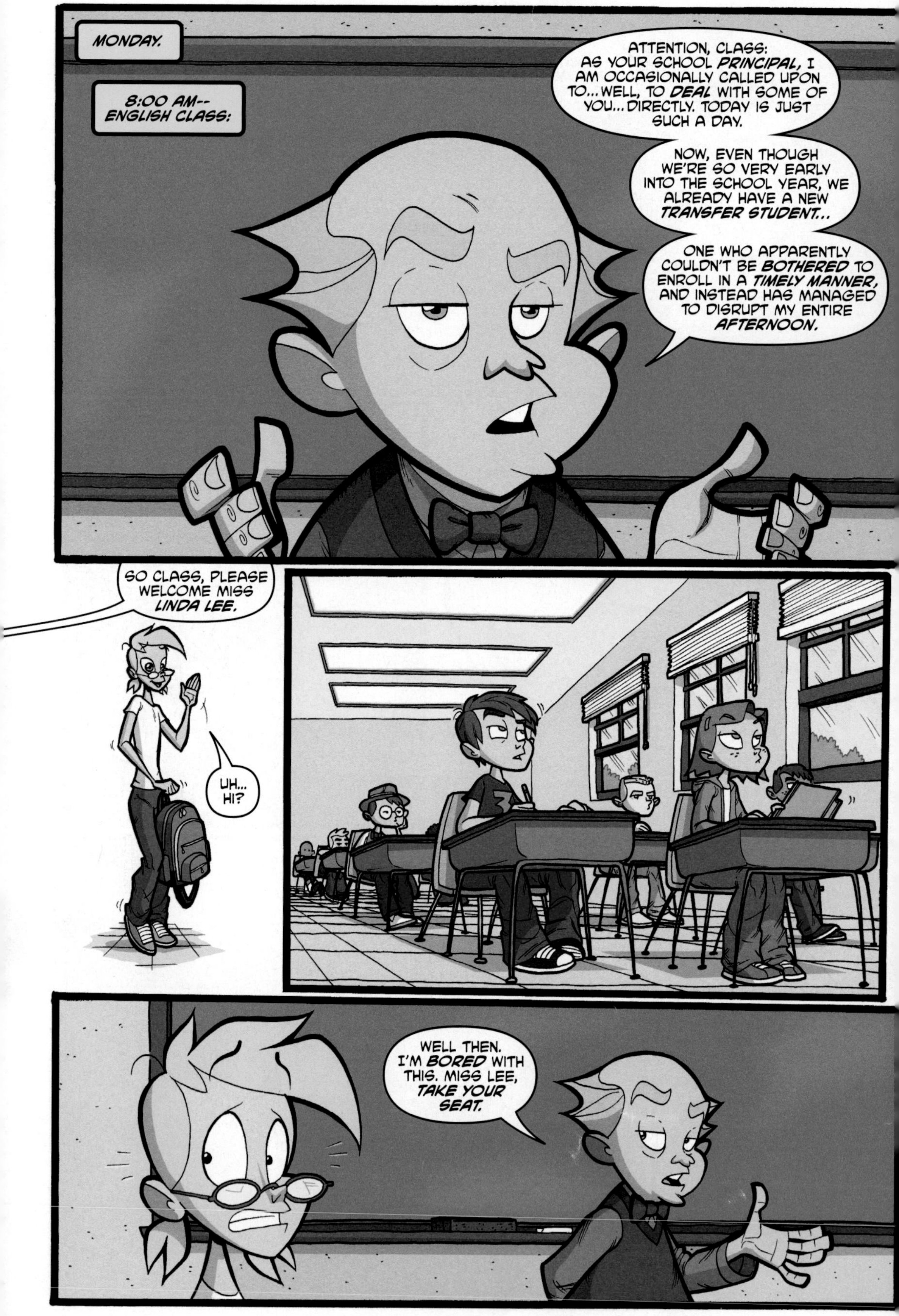
MONDAY.
8:00 AM-- ENGLISH CLASS:
ATTENTION, CLASS: AS YOUR SCHOOL PRINCIPAL, I AM OCCASIONALLY CALLED UPON TO... WELL, TO DEAL WITH SOME OF YOU... DIRECTLY. TODAY IS JUST SUCH A DAY.
NOW, EVEN THOUGH WE'RE SO VERY EARLY INTO THE SCHOOL YEAR, WE ALREADY HAVE A NEW TRANSFER STUDENT...
ONE WHO APPARENTLY COULDN'T BE BOTHERED TO ENROLL IN A TIMELY MANNER, AND INSTEAD HAS MANAGED TO DISRUPT MY ENTIRE AFTERNOON.
SO CLASS, PLEASE WELCOME MISS LINDA LEE.
UH... HI?
WELL THEN. I'M BORED WITH THIS. MISS LEE, TAKE YOUR SEAT.

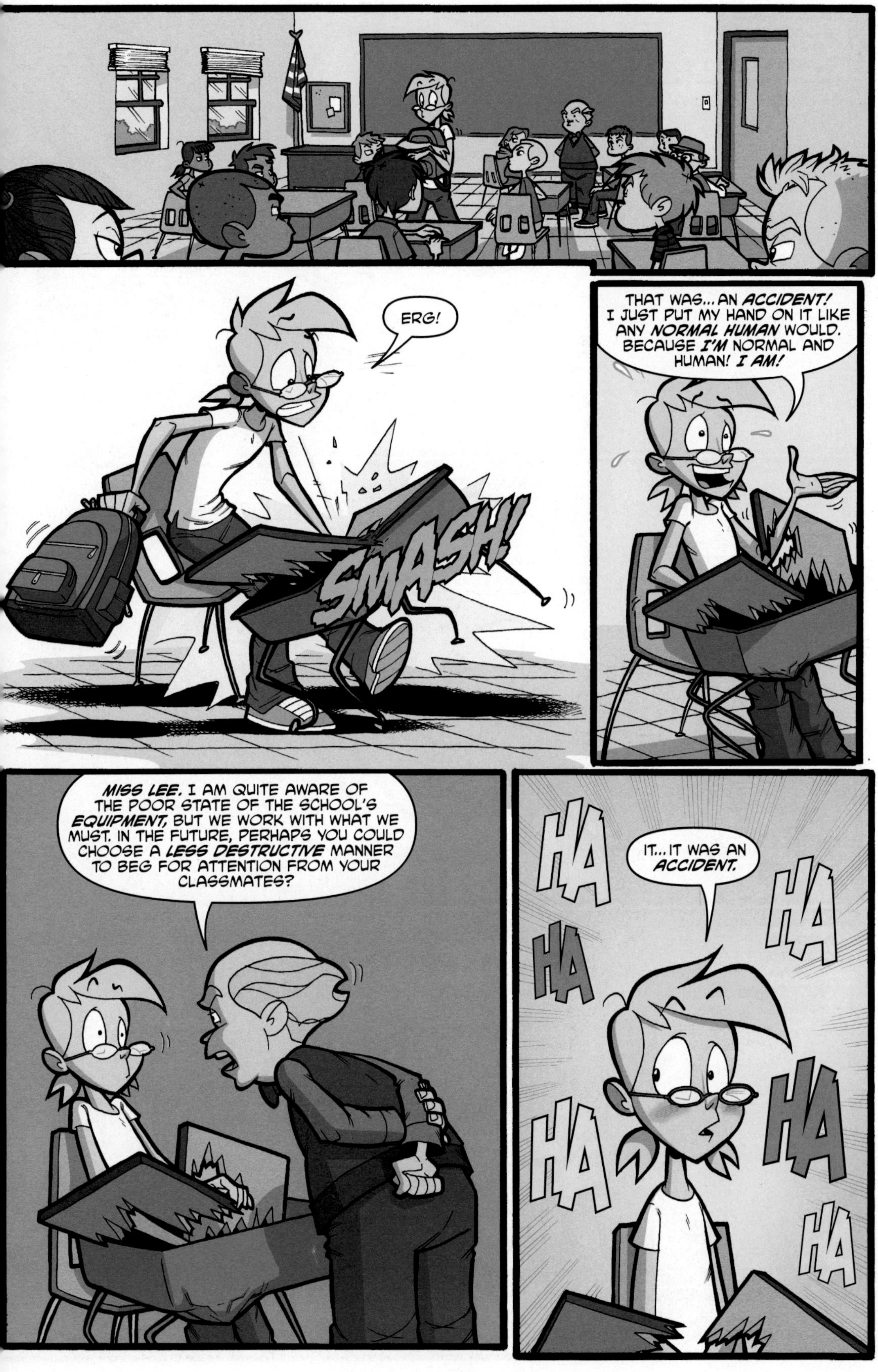
ERG!
SMASH!
THAT WAS... AN ACCIDENT! I JUST PUT MY HAND ON IT LIKE ANY NORMAL HUMAN WOULD. BECAUSE I'M NORMAL AND HUMAN! I AM!
MISS LEE. I AM QUITE AWARE OF THE POOR STATE OF THE SCHOOL'S EQUIPMENT, BUT WE WORK WITH WHAT WE MUST. IN THE FUTURE, PERHAPS YOU COULD CHOOSE A LESS DESTRUCTIVE MANNER TO BEG FOR ATTENTION FROM YOUR CLASSMATES?
HA
IT... IT WAS AN ACCIDENT.
HA
HA
HA
HA
HA

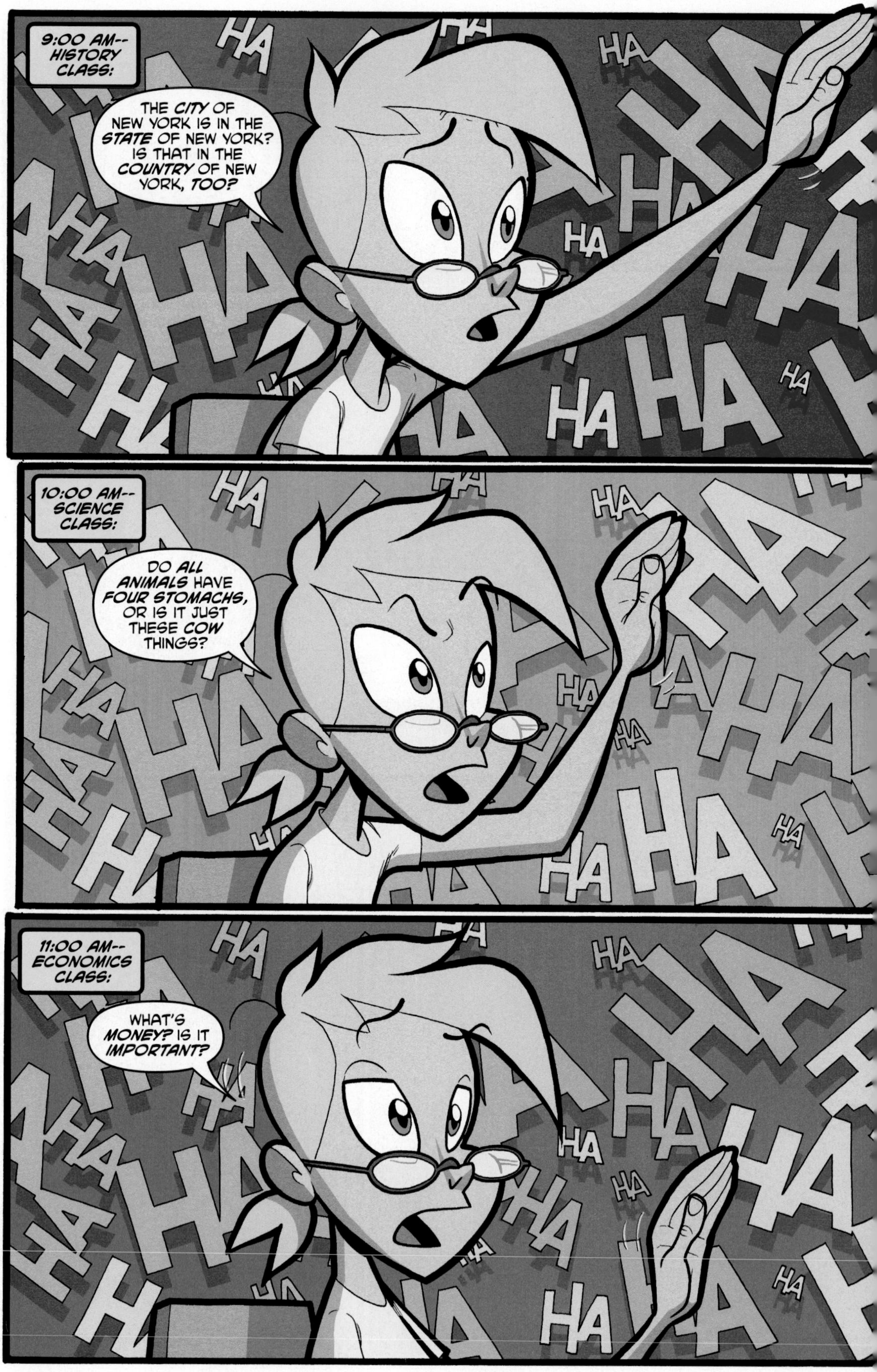
9:00 AM-- HISTORY CLASS:
THE CITY OF NEW YORK IS IN THE STATE OF NEW YORK? IS THAT IN THE COUNTRY OF NEW YORK, TOO?
10:00 AM-- SCIENCE CLASS:
DO ALL ANIMALS HAVE FOUR STOMACHS, OR IS IT JUST THESE COW THINGS?
11:00 AM-- ECONOMICS CLASS:
WHAT'S MONEY? IS IT IMPORTANT?

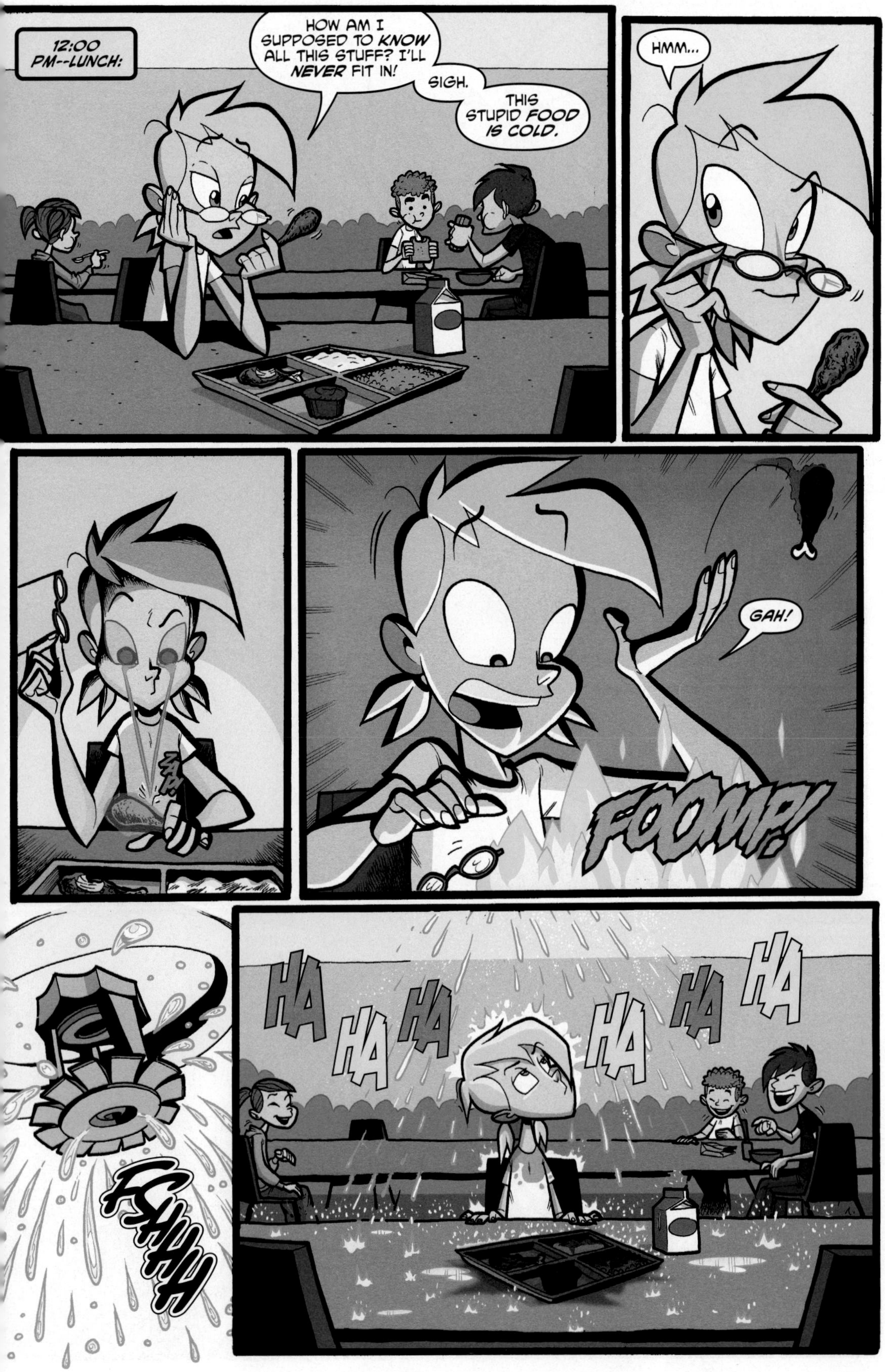
12:00 PM--LUNCH:
HOW AM I SUPPOSED TO KNOW ALL THIS STUFF? I'LL NEVER FIT IN!
SIGH.
THIS STUPID FOOD IS COLD.
HMM...
GAH!
FOOMP!
FSHHH
HA
HA
HA
HA
HA
HA

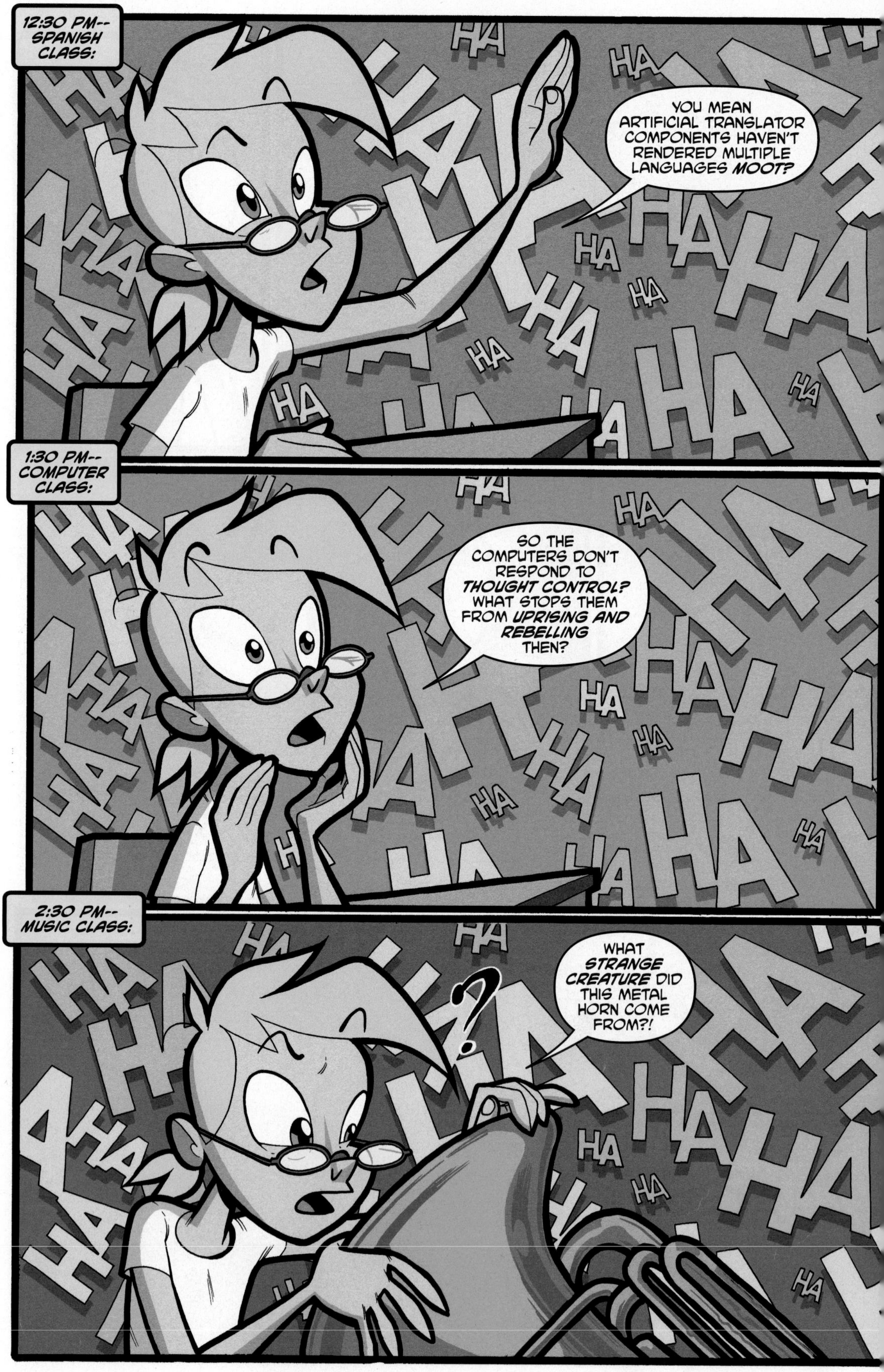
12:30 PM-- SPANISH CLASS:
YOU MEAN ARTIFICIAL TRANSLATOR COMPONENTS HAVEN'T RENDERED MULTIPLE LANGUAGES *MOOT?*
1:30 PM-- COMPUTER CLASS:
SO THE COMPUTERS DON'T RESPOND TO *THOUGHT CONTROL?* WHAT STOPS THEM FROM *UPRISING AND REBELLING* THEN?
2:30 PM-- MUSIC CLASS:
WHAT *STRANGE CREATURE* DID THIS METAL HORN COME FROM?!

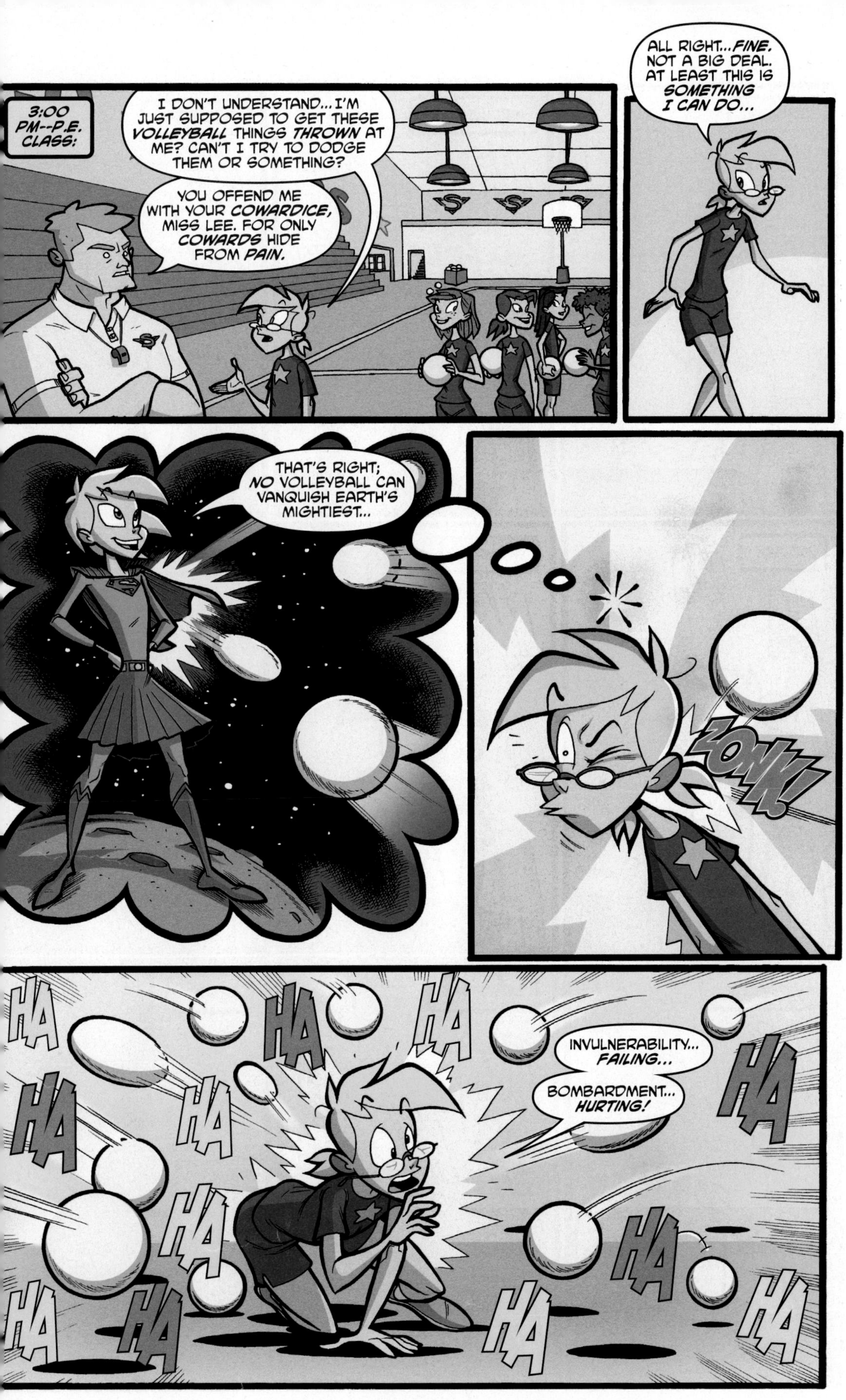
3:00 PM--P.E. CLASS:
I DON'T UNDERSTAND... I'M JUST SUPPOSED TO GET THESE VOLLEYBALL THINGS THROWN AT ME? CAN'T I TRY TO DODGE THEM OR SOMETHING?
YOU OFFEND ME WITH YOUR COWARDICE, MISS LEE. FOR ONLY COWARDS HIDE FROM PAIN.
ALL RIGHT... FINE. NOT A BIG DEAL. AT LEAST THIS IS SOMETHING I CAN DO...
THAT'S RIGHT; NO VOLLEYBALL CAN VANQUISH EARTH'S MIGHTIEST...
ZONK!
HA HA HA HA HA HA HA HA HA HA HA HA HA HA HA
INVULNERABILITY... FAILING...
BOMBARDMENT... HURTING!

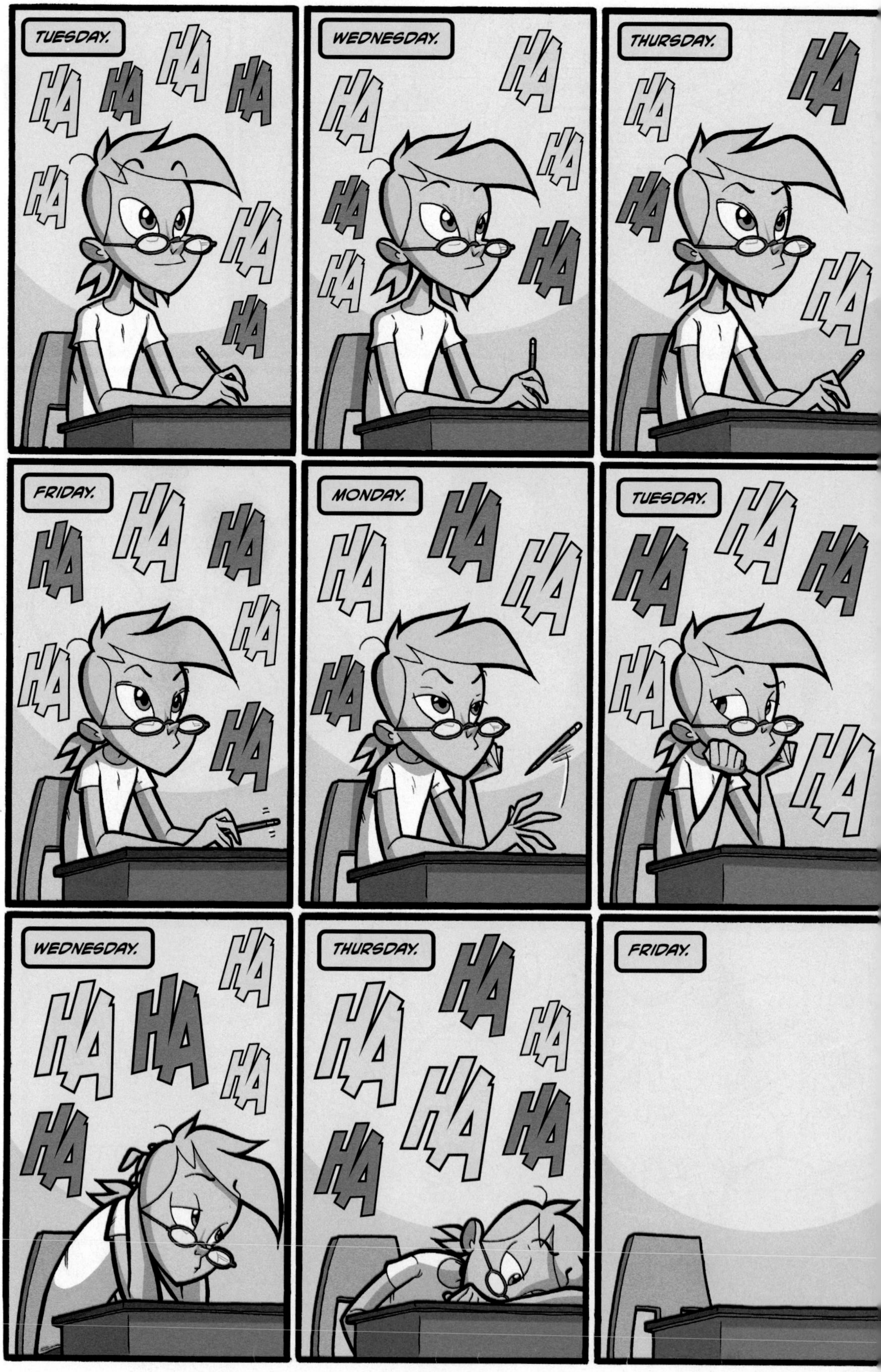
TUESDAY.
HA
HA
HA
HA
HA
HA
HA
WEDNESDAY.
HA
HA
HA
HA
HA
HA
THURSDAY.
HA
HA
HA
HA
FRIDAY.
HA
HA
HA
HA
HA
HA
MONDAY.
HA
HA
HA
HA
TUESDAY.
HA
HA
HA
HA
HA
WEDNESDAY.
HA
HA
HA
HA
HA
THURSDAY.
HA
HA
HA
HA
HA
HA
FRIDAY.

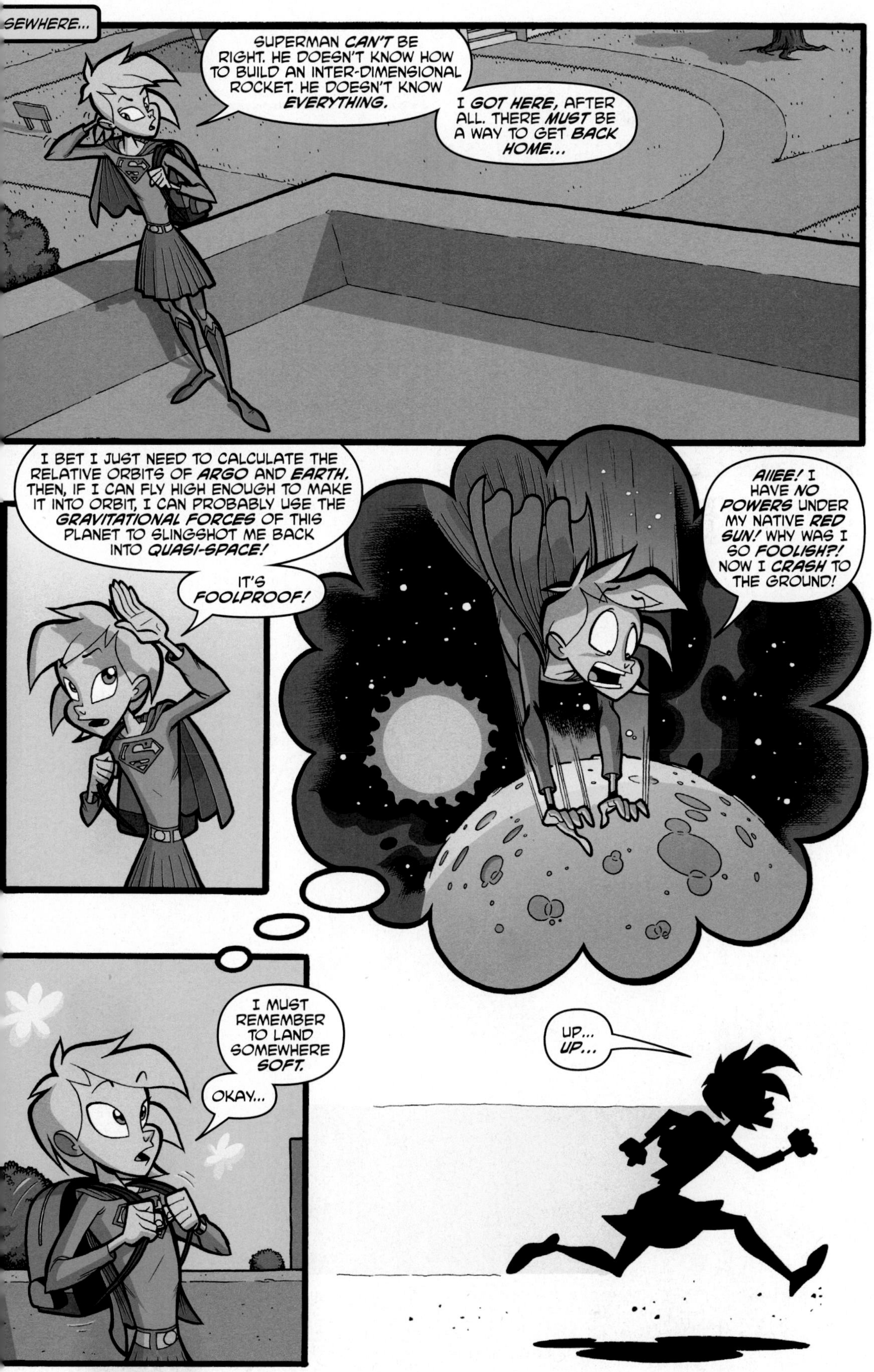
SEWHERE...
SUPERMAN CAN'T BE RIGHT. HE DOESN'T KNOW HOW TO BUILD AN INTER-DIMENSIONAL ROCKET. HE DOESN'T KNOW EVERYTHING.
I GOT HERE, AFTER ALL. THERE MUST BE A WAY TO GET BACK HOME...
I BET I JUST NEED TO CALCULATE THE RELATIVE ORBITS OF ARGO AND EARTH. THEN, IF I CAN FLY HIGH ENOUGH TO MAKE IT INTO ORBIT, I CAN PROBABLY USE THE GRAVITATIONAL FORCES OF THIS PLANET TO SLINGSHOT ME BACK INTO QUASI-SPACE!
IT'S FOOLPROOF!
AIIEE! I HAVE NO POWERS UNDER MY NATIVE RED SUN! WHY WAS I SO FOOLISH?! NOW I CRASH TO THE GROUND!
I MUST REMEMBER TO LAND SOMEWHERE SOFT.
OKAY...
UP... UP...

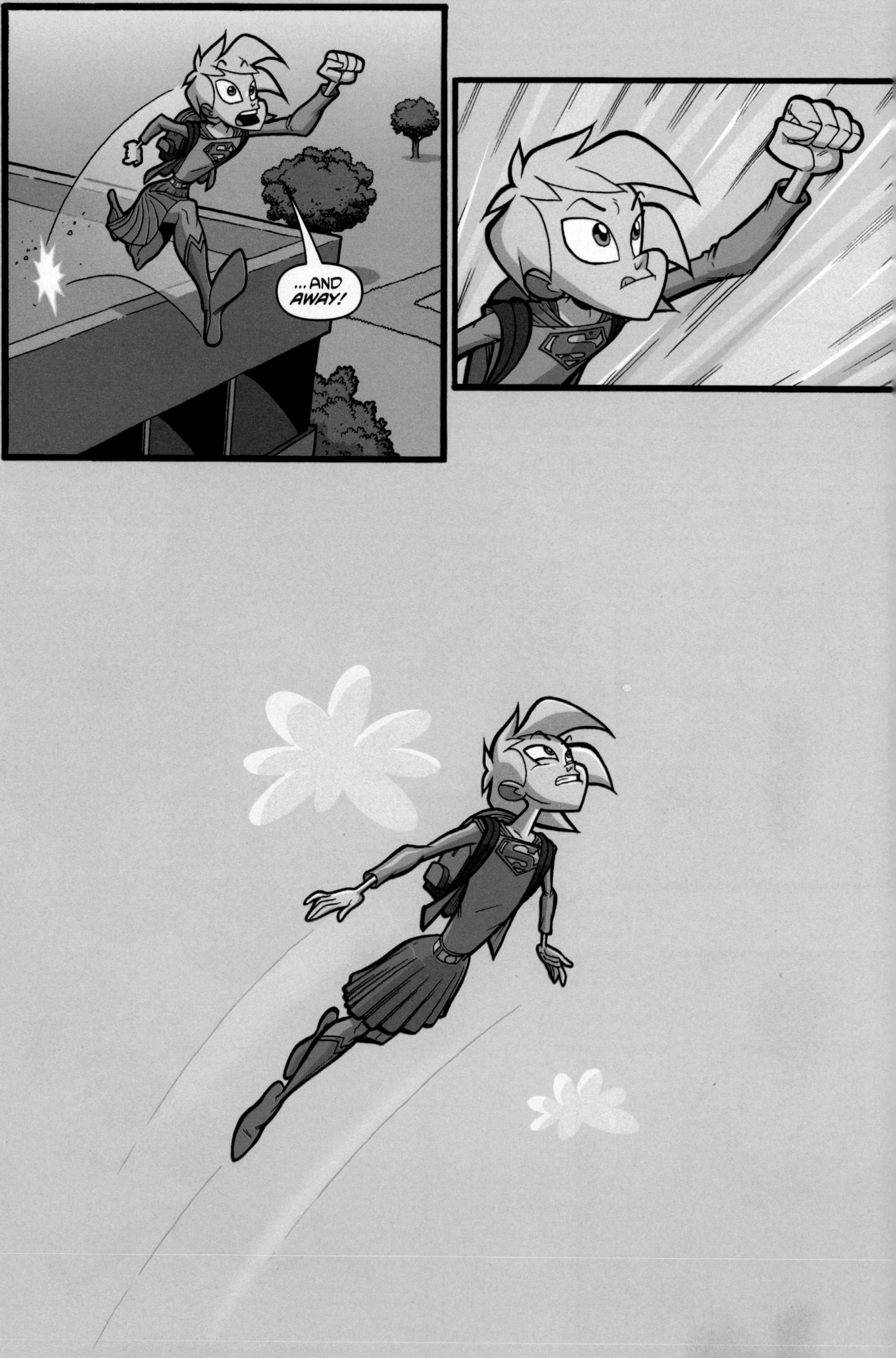
...AND AWAY!

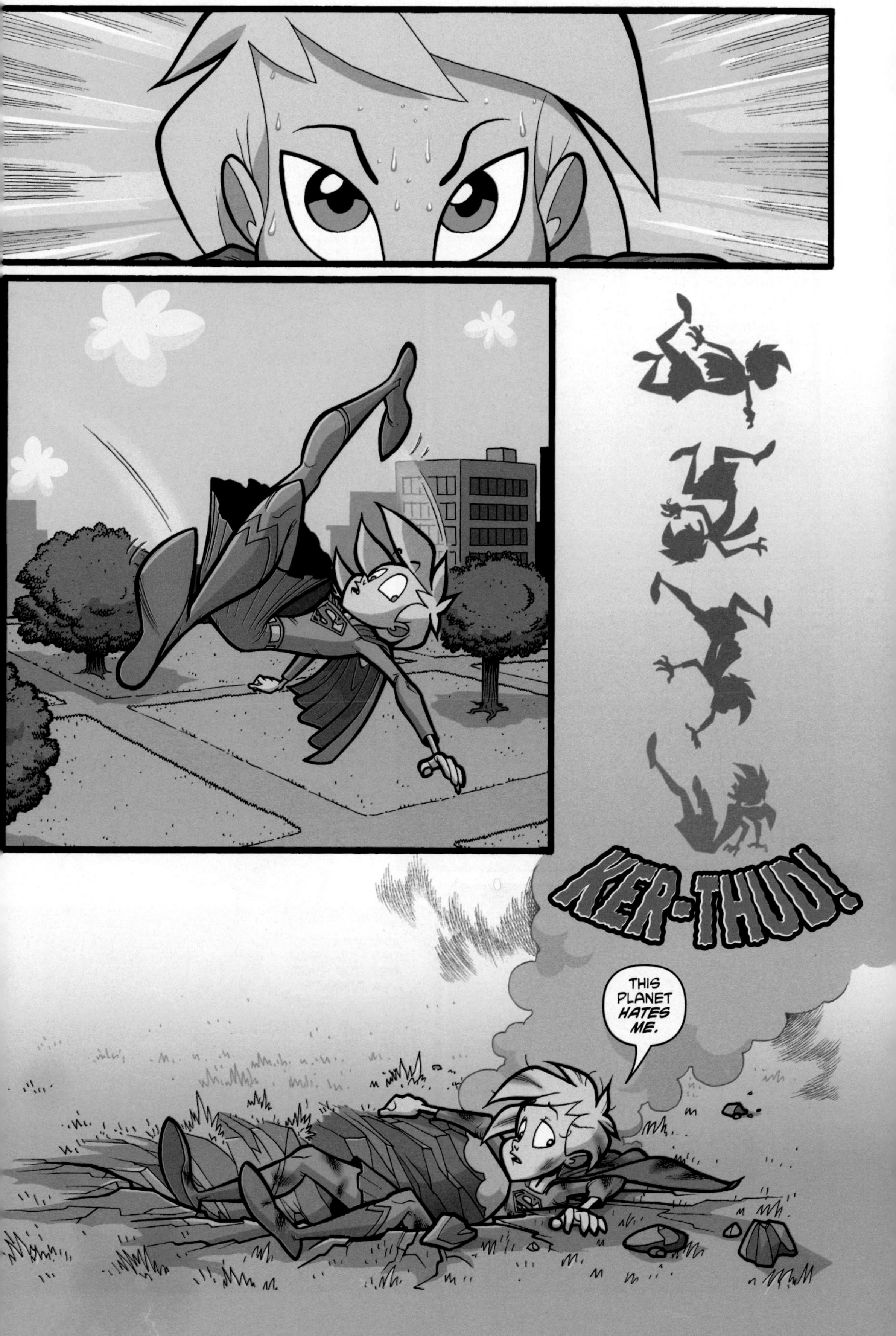
KER-THUD!
THIS PLANET *HATES* ME.

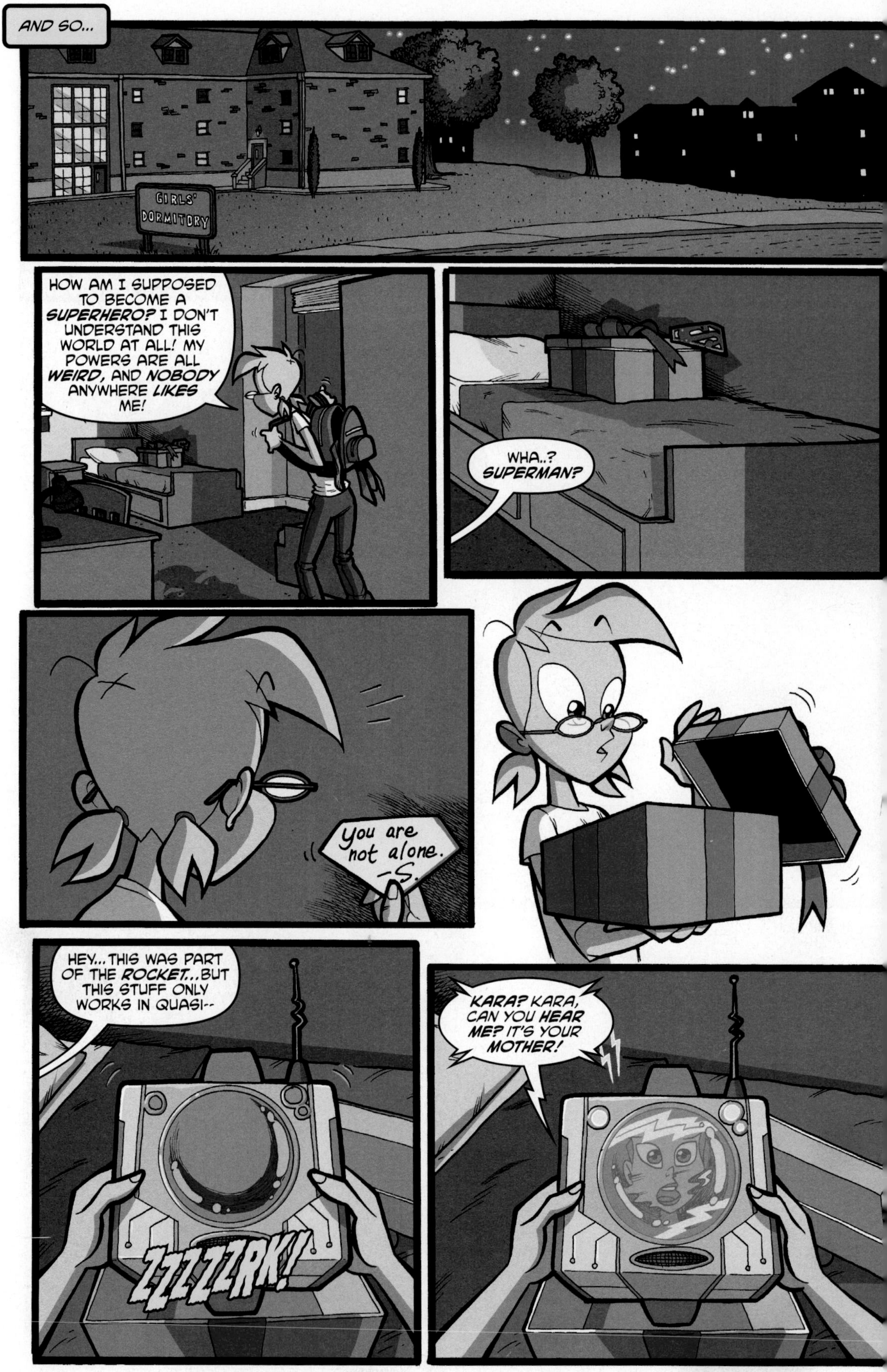
AND SO...
GIRLS' DORMITORY
HOW AM I SUPPOSED TO BECOME A SUPERHERO? I DON'T UNDERSTAND THIS WORLD AT ALL! MY POWERS ARE ALL WEIRD, AND NOBODY ANYWHERE LIKES ME!
WHA..? SUPERMAN?
you are not alone. -S.
HEY... THIS WAS PART OF THE ROCKET... BUT THIS STUFF ONLY WORKS IN QUASI--
ZZZZZRK!
KARA? KARA, CAN YOU HEAR ME? IT'S YOUR MOTHER!

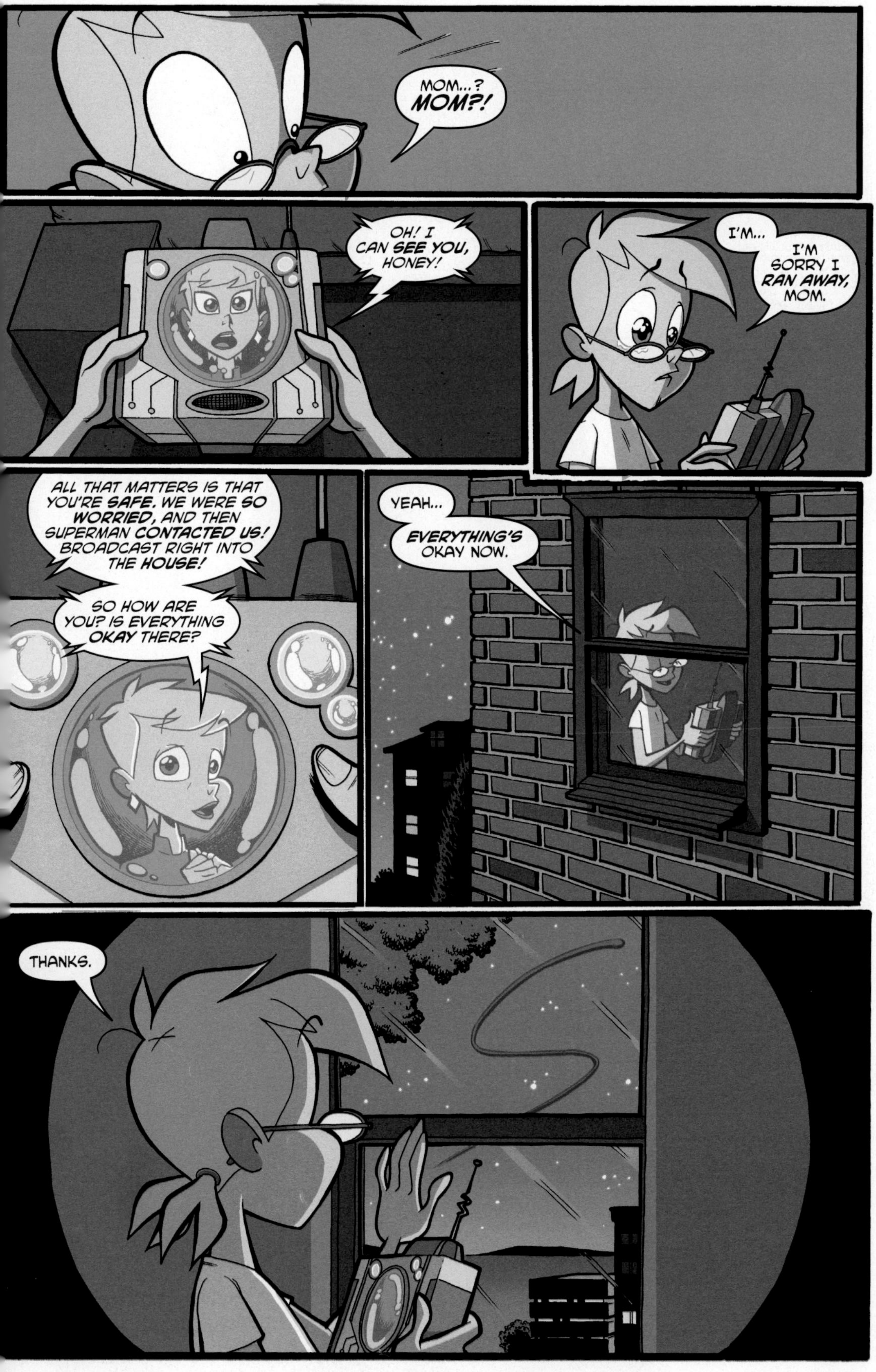
MOM...? MOM?!
OH! I CAN SEE YOU, HONEY!
I'M...
I'M SORRY I RAN AWAY, MOM.
ALL THAT MATTERS IS THAT YOU'RE SAFE. WE WERE SO WORRIED, AND THEN SUPERMAN CONTACTED US! BROADCAST RIGHT INTO THE HOUSE!
SO HOW ARE YOU? IS EVERYTHING OKAY THERE?
YEAH...
EVERYTHING'S OKAY NOW.
THANKS.

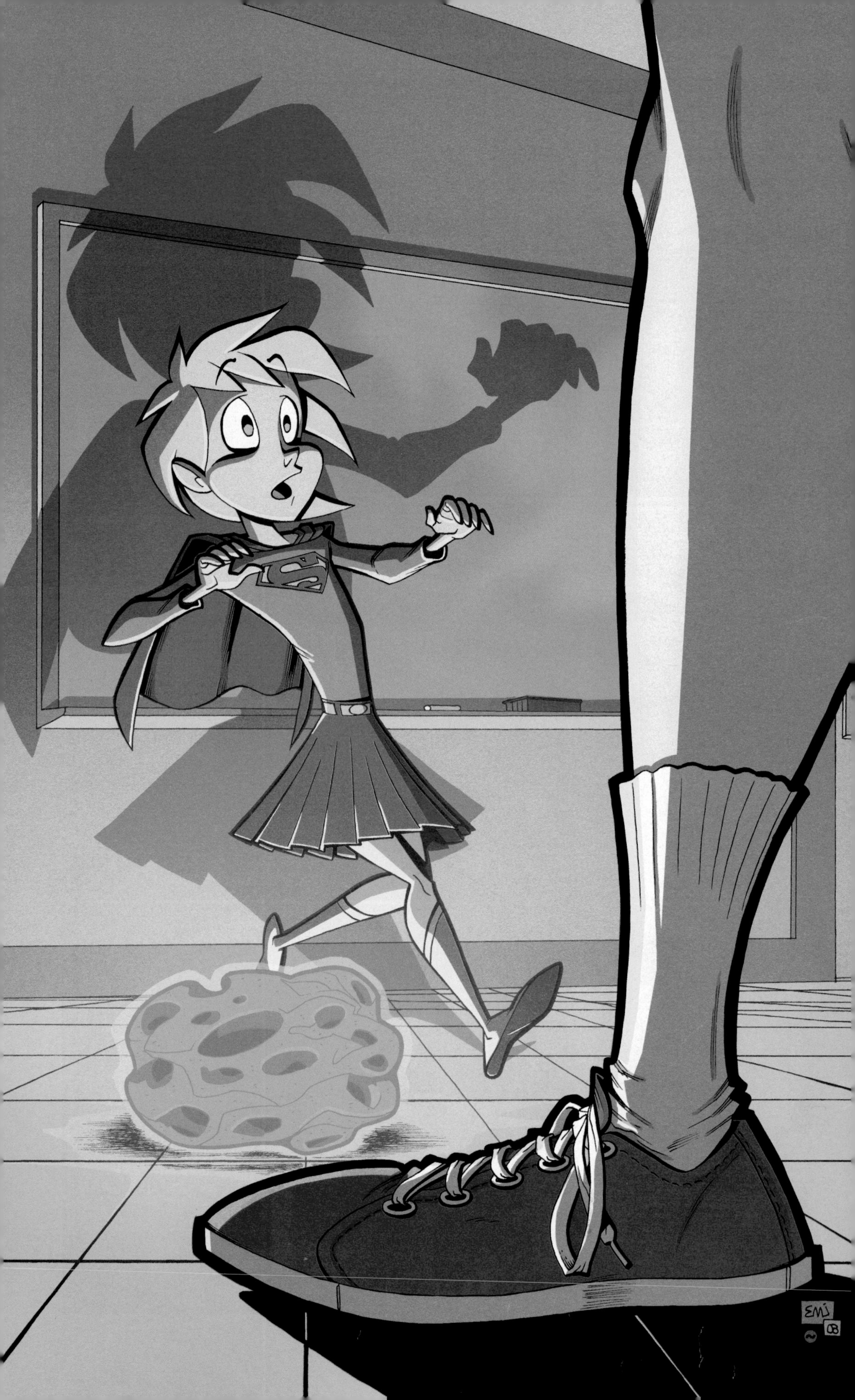

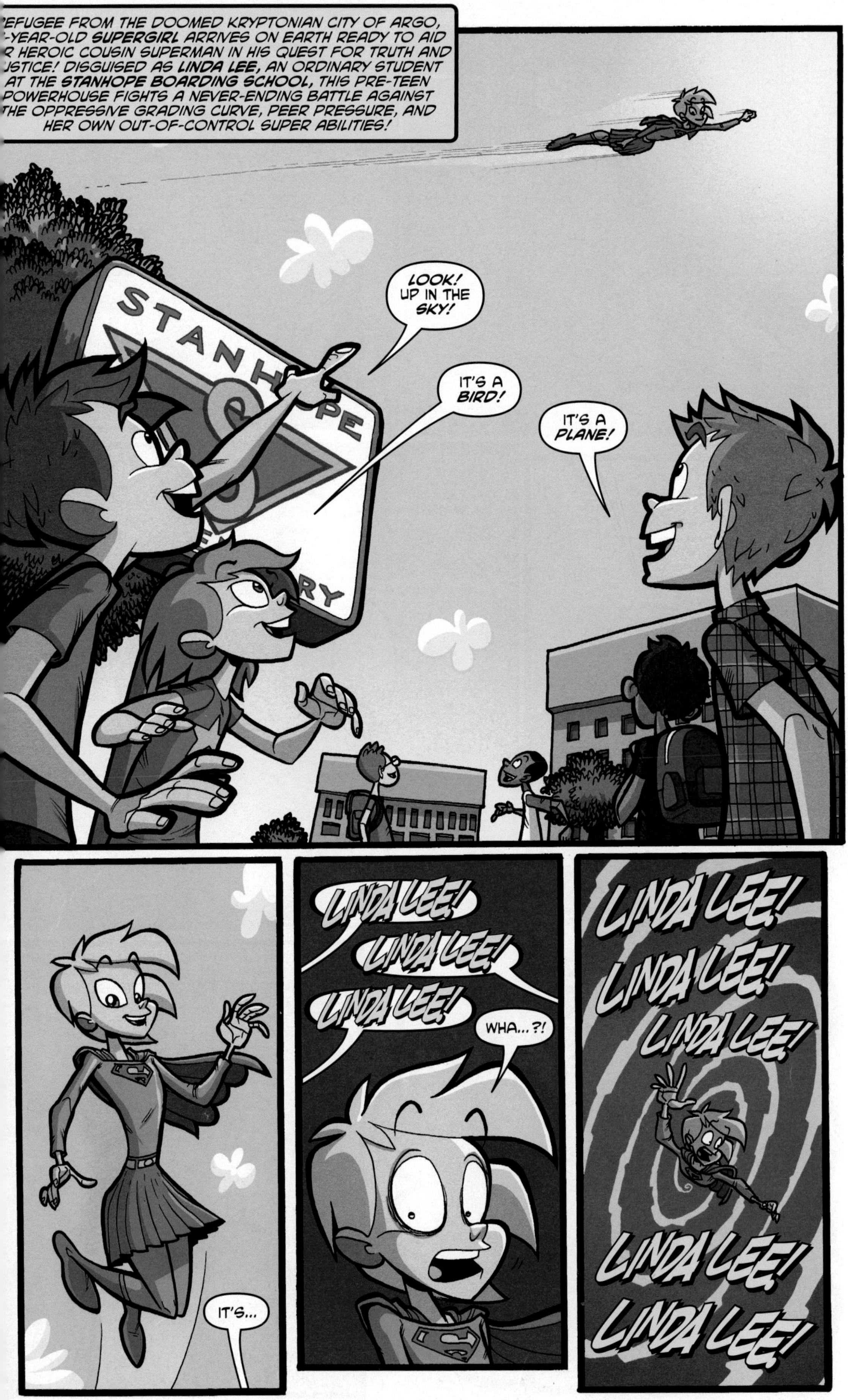
EFUGEE FROM THE DOOMED KRYPTONIAN CITY OF ARGO, -YEAR-OLD SUPERGIRL ARRIVES ON EARTH READY TO AID R HEROIC COUSIN SUPERMAN IN HIS QUEST FOR TRUTH AND USTICE! DISGUISED AS LINDA LEE, AN ORDINARY STUDENT AT THE STANHOPE BOARDING SCHOOL, THIS PRE-TEEN POWERHOUSE FIGHTS A NEVER-ENDING BATTLE AGAINST THE OPPRESSIVE GRADING CURVE, PEER PRESSURE, AND HER OWN OUT-OF-CONTROL SUPER ABILITIES!
LOOK! UP IN THE SKY!
IT'S A BIRD!
IT'S A PLANE!
IT'S...
LINDA LEE!
LINDA LEE!
LINDA LEE!
WHA...?!
LINDA LEE!
LINDA LEE!
LINDA LEE!
LINDA LEE!
LINDA LEE!

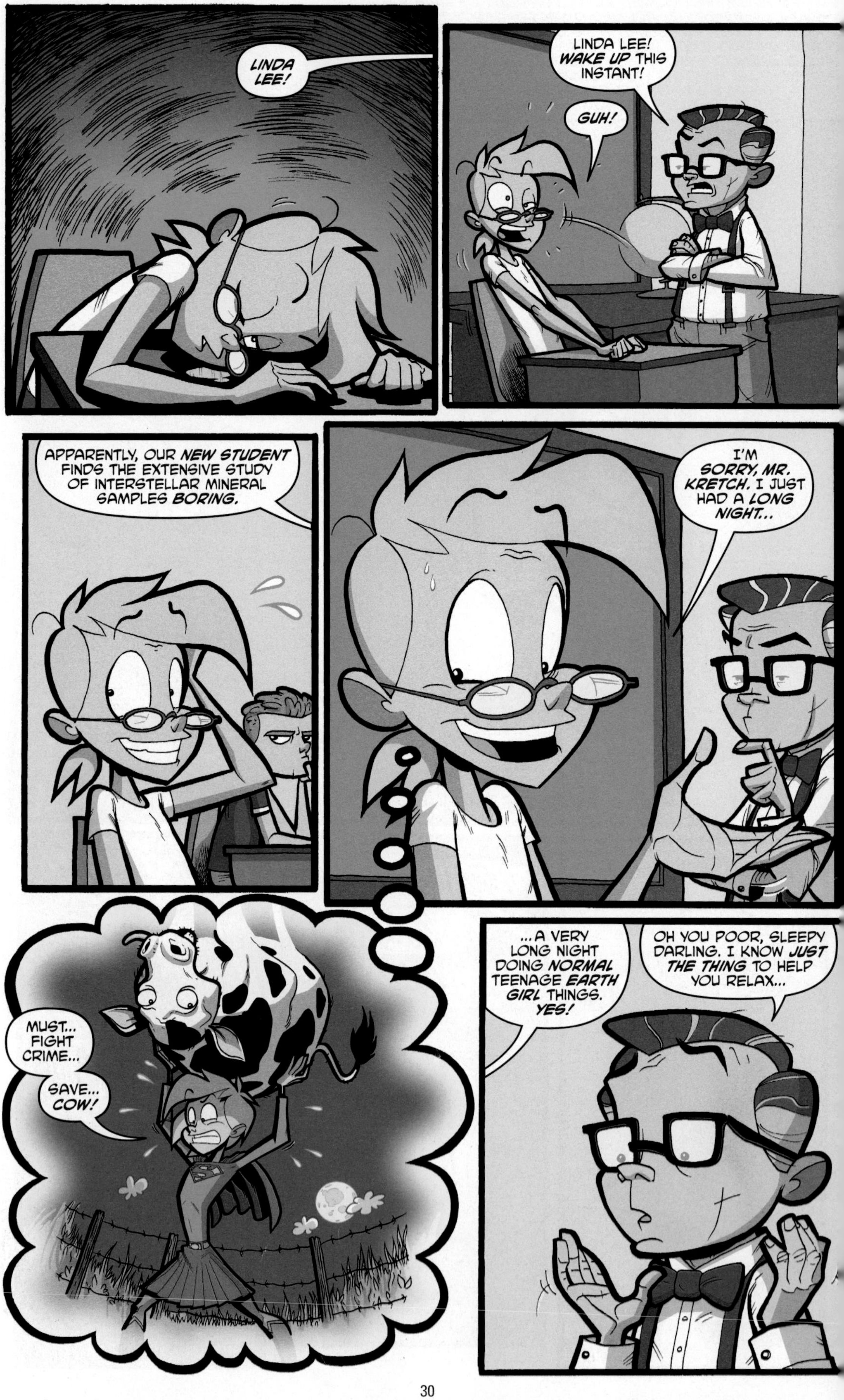
LINDA LEE!
LINDA LEE! WAKE UP THIS INSTANT!
GUH!
APPARENTLY, OUR NEW STUDENT FINDS THE EXTENSIVE STUDY OF INTERSTELLAR MINERAL SAMPLES BORING.
I'M SORRY, MR. KRETCH. I JUST HAD A LONG NIGHT...
MUST... FIGHT CRIME...
SAVE... COW!
...A VERY LONG NIGHT DOING NORMAL TEENAGE EARTH GIRL THINGS. YES!
OH YOU POOR, SLEEPY DARLING. I KNOW JUST THE THING TO HELP YOU RELAX...

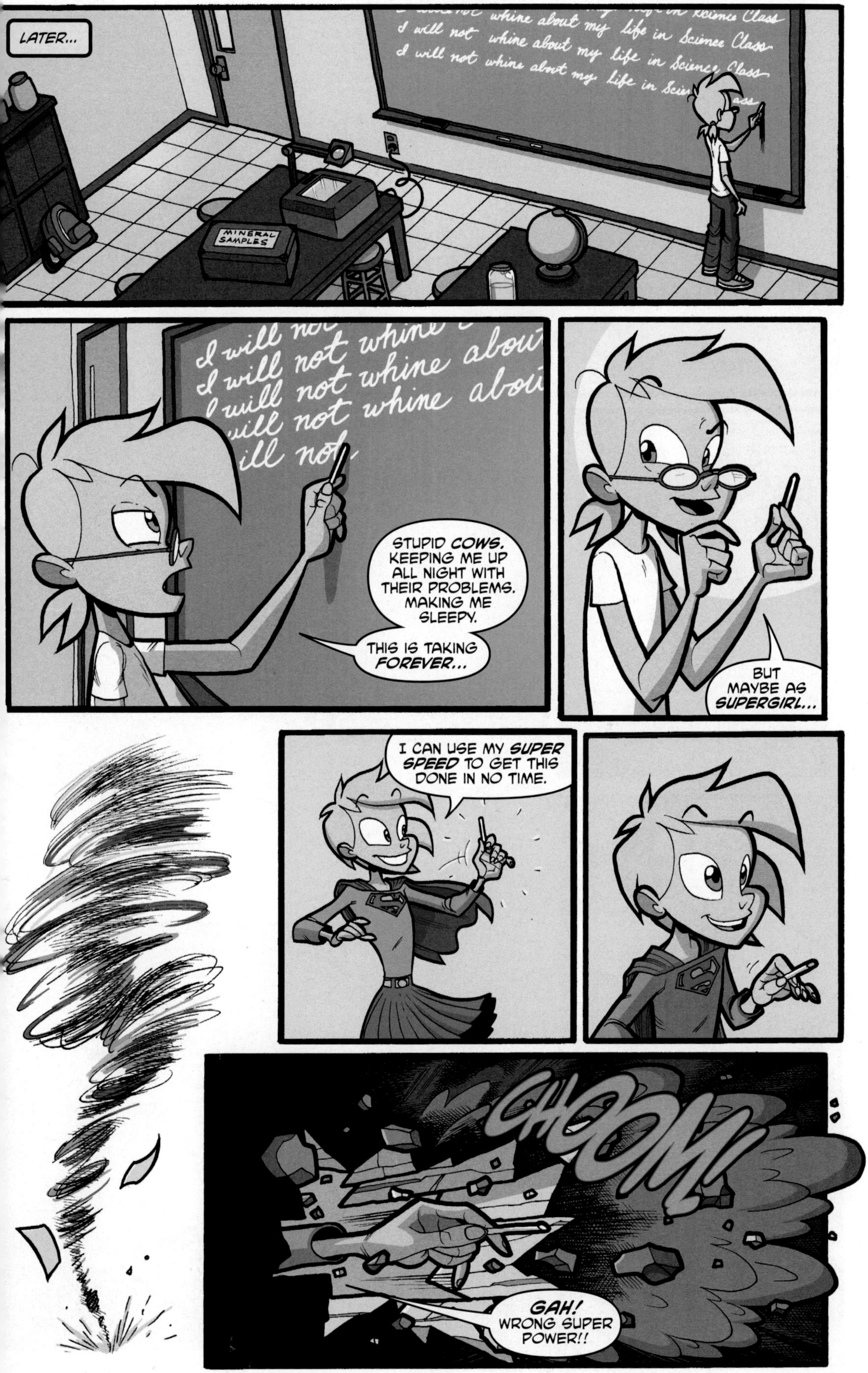
LATER...
I will not whine about my life in Science Class
I will not whine about my life in Science Class
I will not whine about my life in Science Class
MINERAL SAMPLES
STUPID COWS. KEEPING ME UP ALL NIGHT WITH THEIR PROBLEMS. MAKING ME SLEEPY.
THIS IS TAKING FOREVER...
BUT MAYBE AS SUPERGIRL...
I CAN USE MY SUPER SPEED TO GET THIS DONE IN NO TIME.
CHOOM!
GAH! WRONG SUPER POWER!!

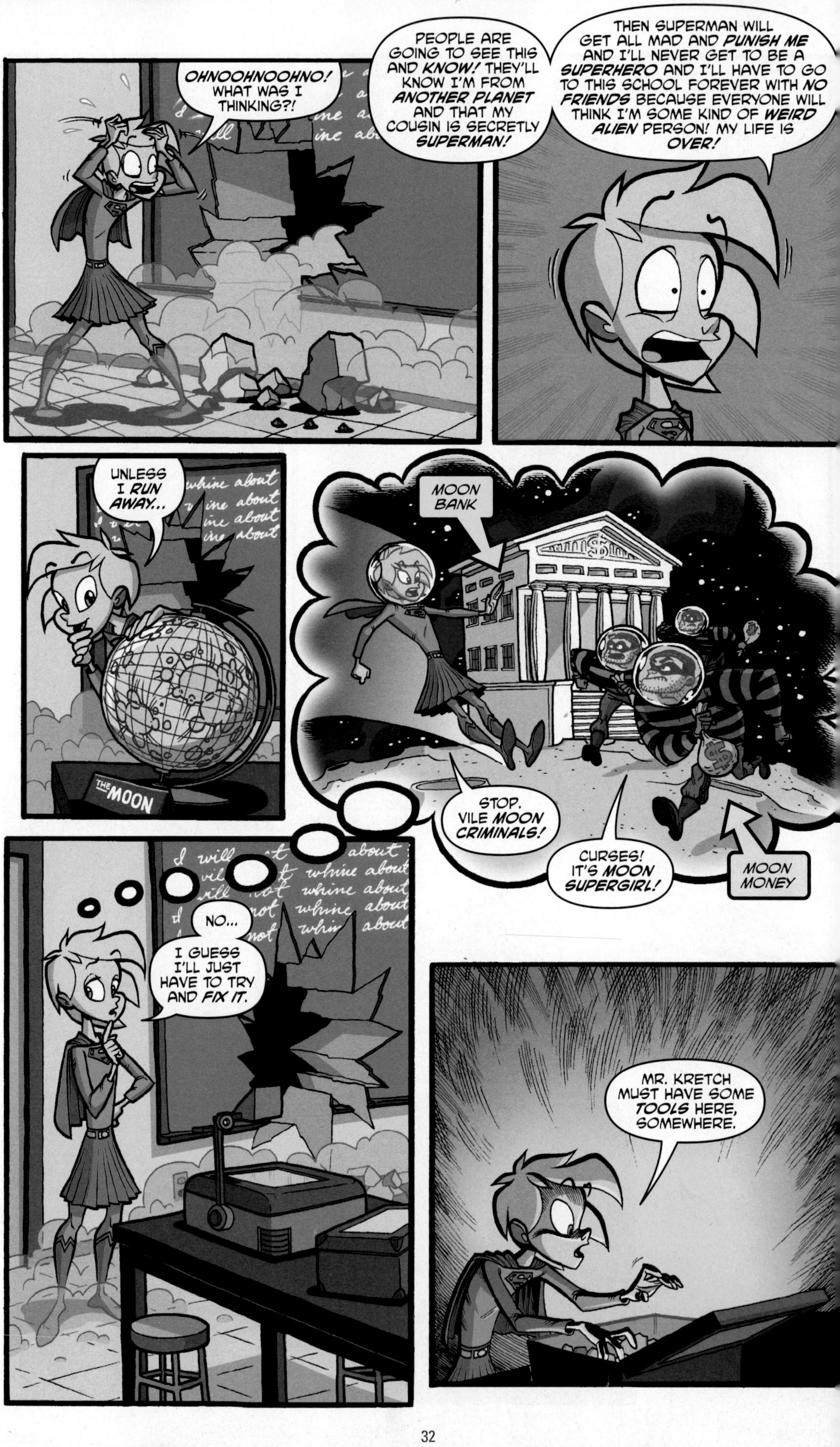
OHNOOHNOOHNO! WHAT WAS I THINKING?!
PEOPLE ARE GOING TO SEE THIS AND KNOW! THEY'LL KNOW I'M FROM ANOTHER PLANET AND THAT MY COUSIN IS SECRETLY SUPERMAN!
THEN SUPERMAN WILL GET ALL MAD AND PUNISH ME AND I'LL NEVER GET TO BE A SUPERHERO AND I'LL HAVE TO GO TO THIS SCHOOL FOREVER WITH NO FRIENDS BECAUSE EVERYONE WILL THINK I'M SOME KIND OF WEIRD ALIEN PERSON! MY LIFE IS OVER!
UNLESS I RUN AWAY...
THE MOON
MOON BANK
STOP. VILE MOON CRIMINALS!
CURSES! IT'S MOON SUPERGIRL!
MOON MONEY
NO...
I GUESS I'LL JUST HAVE TO TRY AND FIX IT.
MR. KRETCH MUST HAVE SOME TOOLS HERE, SOMEWHERE.

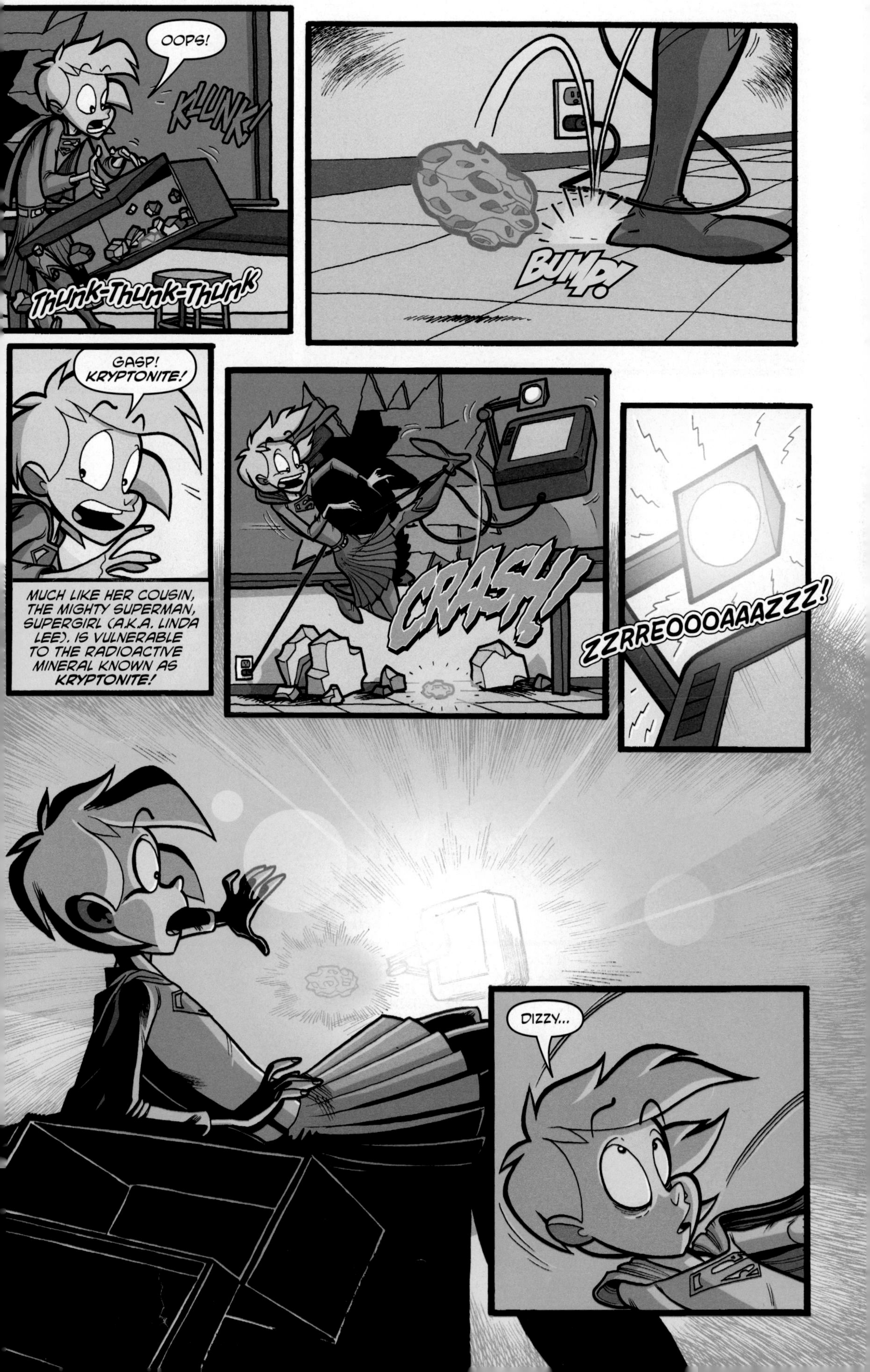
OOPS!
KLUNK!
THUNK-THUNK-THUNK
BUMP!
GASP! KRYPTONITE!
MUCH LIKE HER COUSIN, THE MIGHTY SUPERMAN, SUPERGIRL (A.K.A. LINDA LEE), IS VULNERABLE TO THE RADIOACTIVE MINERAL KNOWN AS KRYPTONITE!
CRASH!
ZZRREOOOAAAZZZ!
DIZZY...

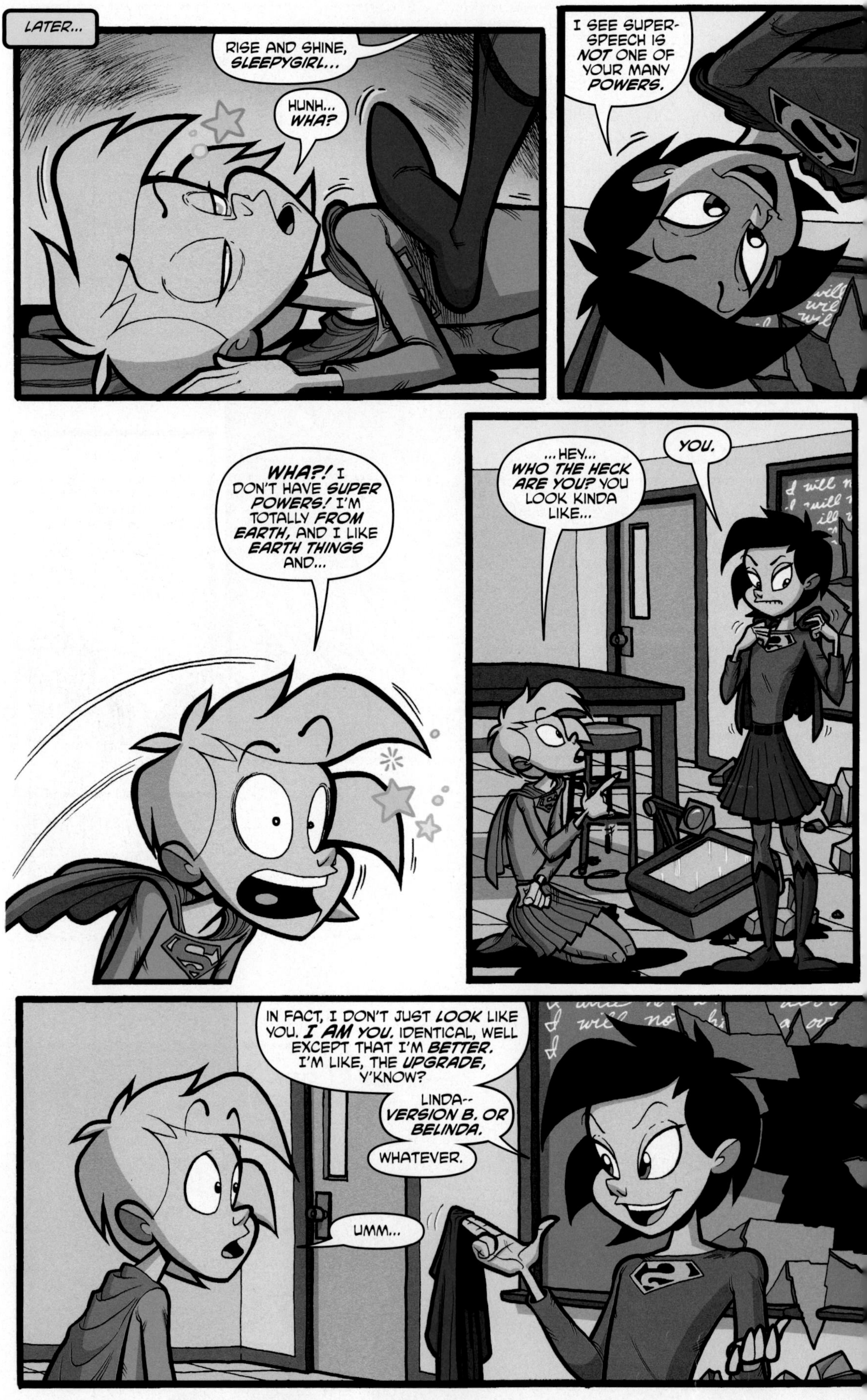
LATER...
RISE AND SHINE, SLEEPYGIRL...
HUNH... WHA?
I SEE SUPER-SPEECH IS NOT ONE OF YOUR MANY POWERS.
WHA?! I DON'T HAVE SUPER POWERS! I'M TOTALLY FROM EARTH, AND I LIKE EARTH THINGS AND...
...HEY... WHO THE HECK ARE YOU? YOU LOOK KINDA LIKE...
YOU.
IN FACT, I DON'T JUST LOOK LIKE YOU. I AM YOU. IDENTICAL, WELL EXCEPT THAT I'M BETTER. I'M LIKE, THE UPGRADE, Y'KNOW?
LINDA--VERSION B. OR BELINDA.
WHATEVER.
UMM...

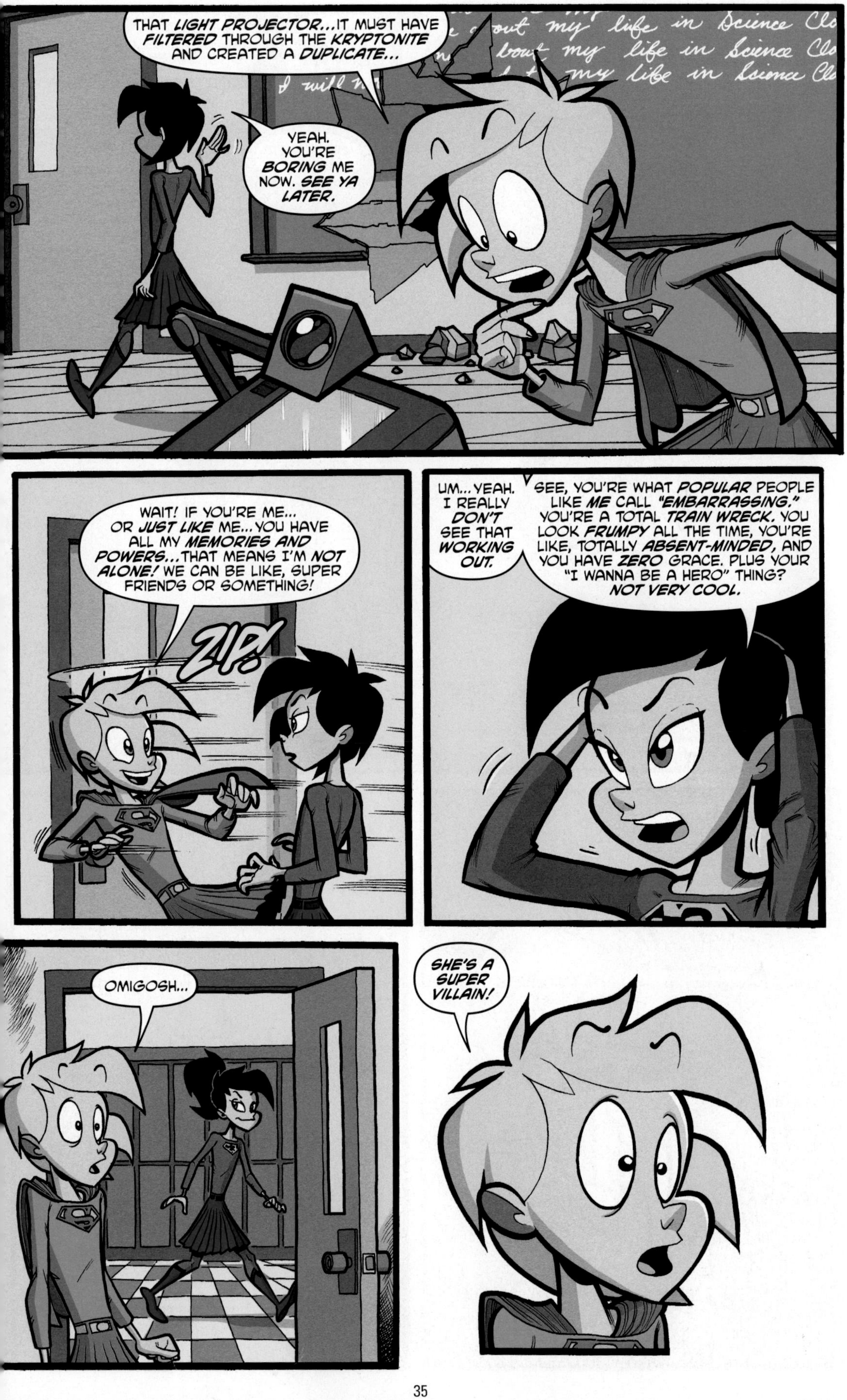

THAT LIGHT PROJECTOR...IT MUST HAVE FILTERED THROUGH THE KRYPTONITE AND CREATED A DUPLICATE...
YEAH. YOU'RE BORING ME NOW. SEE YA LATER.
WAIT! IF YOU'RE ME... OR JUST LIKE ME...YOU HAVE ALL MY MEMORIES AND POWERS...THAT MEANS I'M NOT ALONE! WE CAN BE LIKE, SUPER FRIENDS OR SOMETHING!
ZIP!
UM...YEAH. I REALLY DON'T SEE THAT WORKING OUT.
SEE, YOU'RE WHAT POPULAR PEOPLE LIKE ME CALL "EMBARRASSING." YOU'RE A TOTAL TRAIN WRECK. YOU LOOK FRUMPY ALL THE TIME, YOU'RE LIKE, TOTALLY ABSENT-MINDED, AND YOU HAVE ZERO GRACE. PLUS YOUR "I WANNA BE A HERO" THING? NOT VERY COOL.
OMIGOSH...
SHE'S A SUPER VILLAIN!

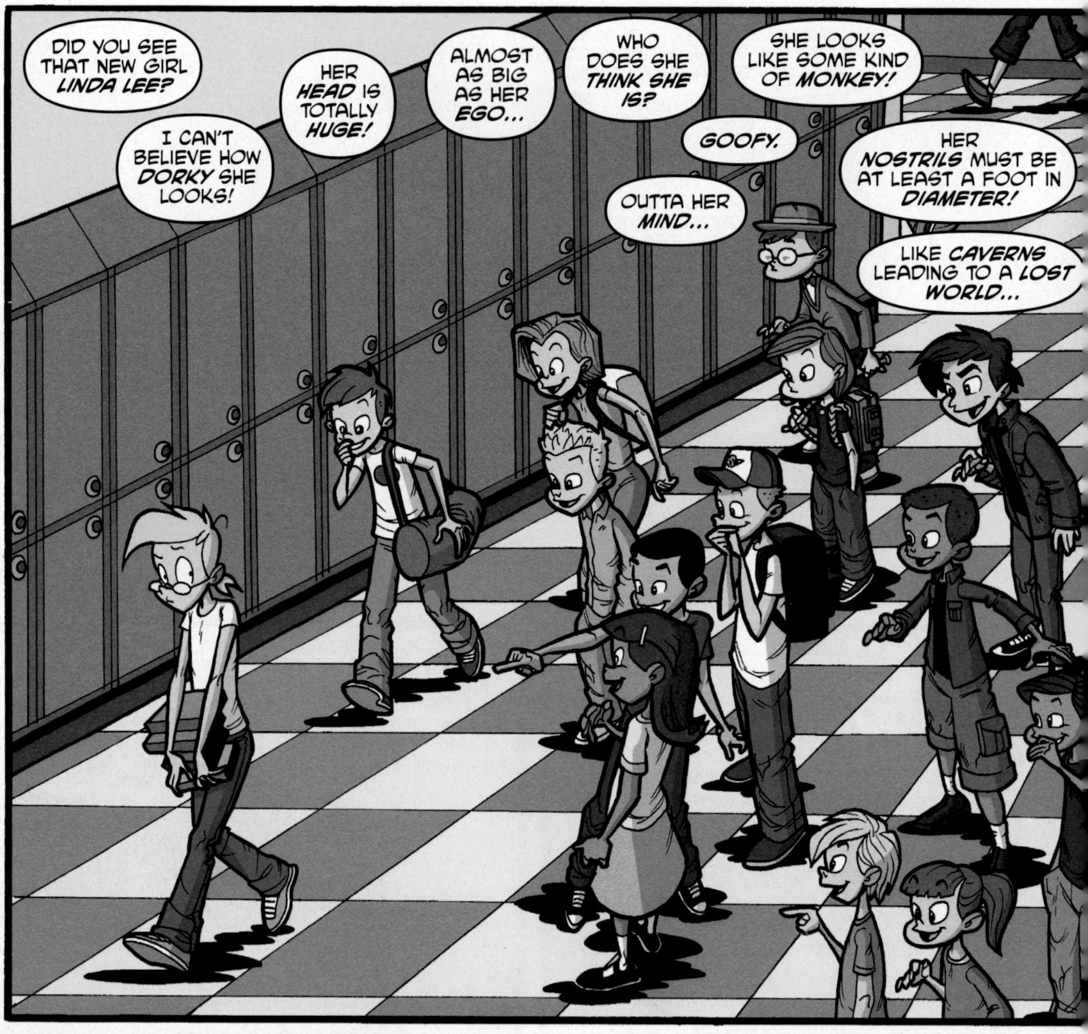
DID YOU SEE THAT NEW GIRL LINDA LEE?
I CAN'T BELIEVE HOW DORKY SHE LOOKS!
HER HEAD IS TOTALLY HUGE!
ALMOST AS BIG AS HER EGO...
WHO DOES SHE THINK SHE IS?
OUTTA HER MIND...
GOOFY.
SHE LOOKS LIKE SOME KIND OF MONKEY!
HER NOSTRILS MUST BE AT LEAST A FOOT IN DIAMETER!
LIKE CAVERNS LEADING TO A LOST WORLD...

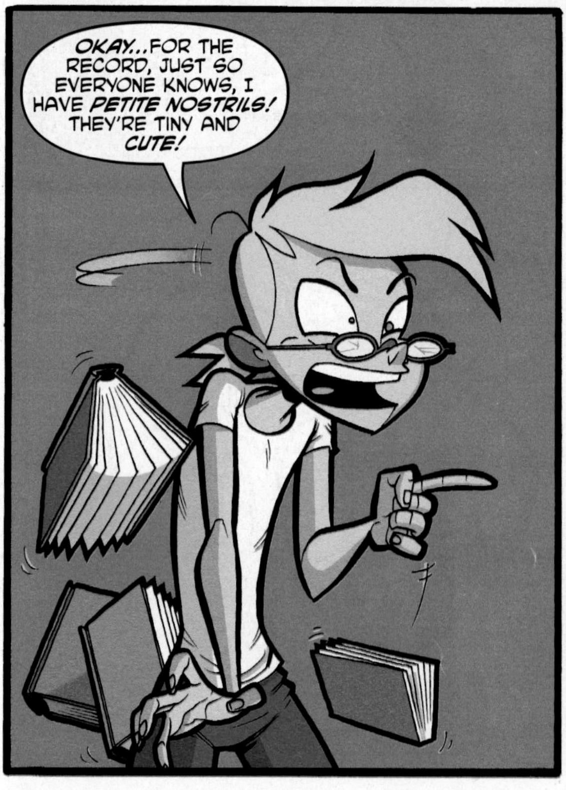
OKAY...FOR THE RECORD, JUST SO EVERYONE KNOWS, I HAVE PETITE NOSTRILS! THEY'RE TINY AND CUTE!

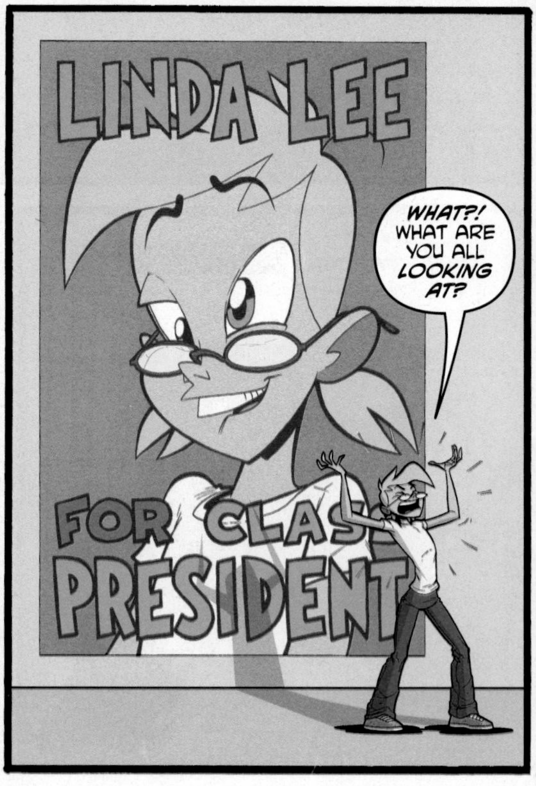
LINDA LEE
FOR CLAS
PRESIDENT
WHAT?! WHAT ARE YOU ALL LOOKING AT?

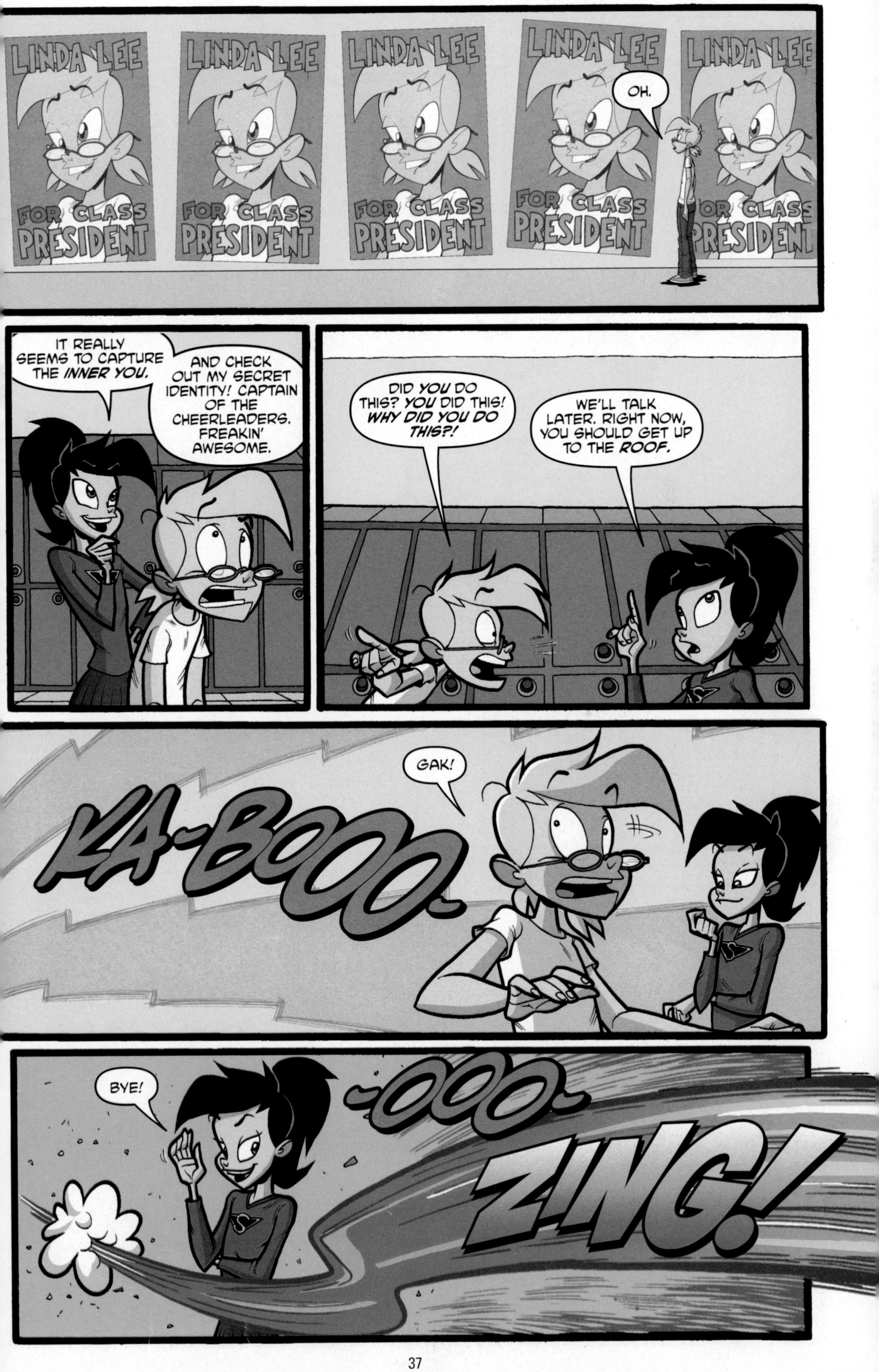
LINDA LEE FOR CLASS PRESIDENT
OH.
IT REALLY SEEMS TO CAPTURE THE *INNER YOU.*
AND CHECK OUT MY SECRET IDENTITY! CAPTAIN OF THE CHEERLEADERS. FREAKIN' AWESOME.
DID *YOU* DO THIS? *YOU* DID THIS! ***WHY DID YOU DO THIS?!***
WE'LL TALK LATER. RIGHT NOW, YOU SHOULD GET UP TO THE *ROOF.*
KA-BOOO-
GAK!
BYE!
-OOO-
ZING!

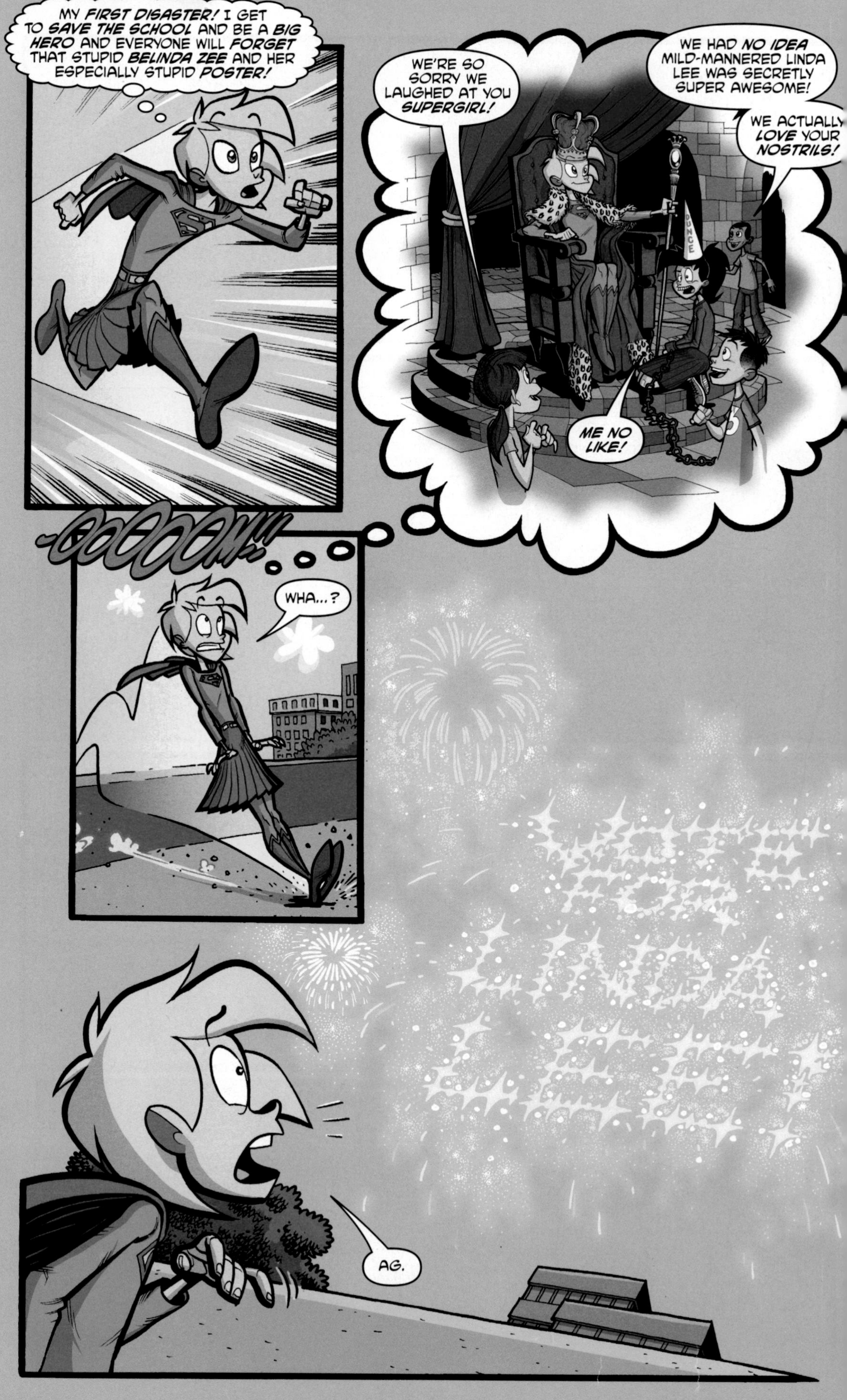

MY FIRST DISASTER! I GET TO SAVE THE SCHOOL AND BE A BIG HERO AND EVERYONE WILL FORGET THAT STUPID BELINDA ZEE AND HER ESPECIALLY STUPID POSTER!
WE'RE SO SORRY WE LAUGHED AT YOU SUPERGIRL!
WE HAD NO IDEA MILD-MANNERED LINDA LEE WAS SECRETLY SUPER AWESOME!
WE ACTUALLY LOVE YOUR NOSTRILS!
DUNCE
ME NO LIKE!
-OOOOOM!!
WHA...?
AG.

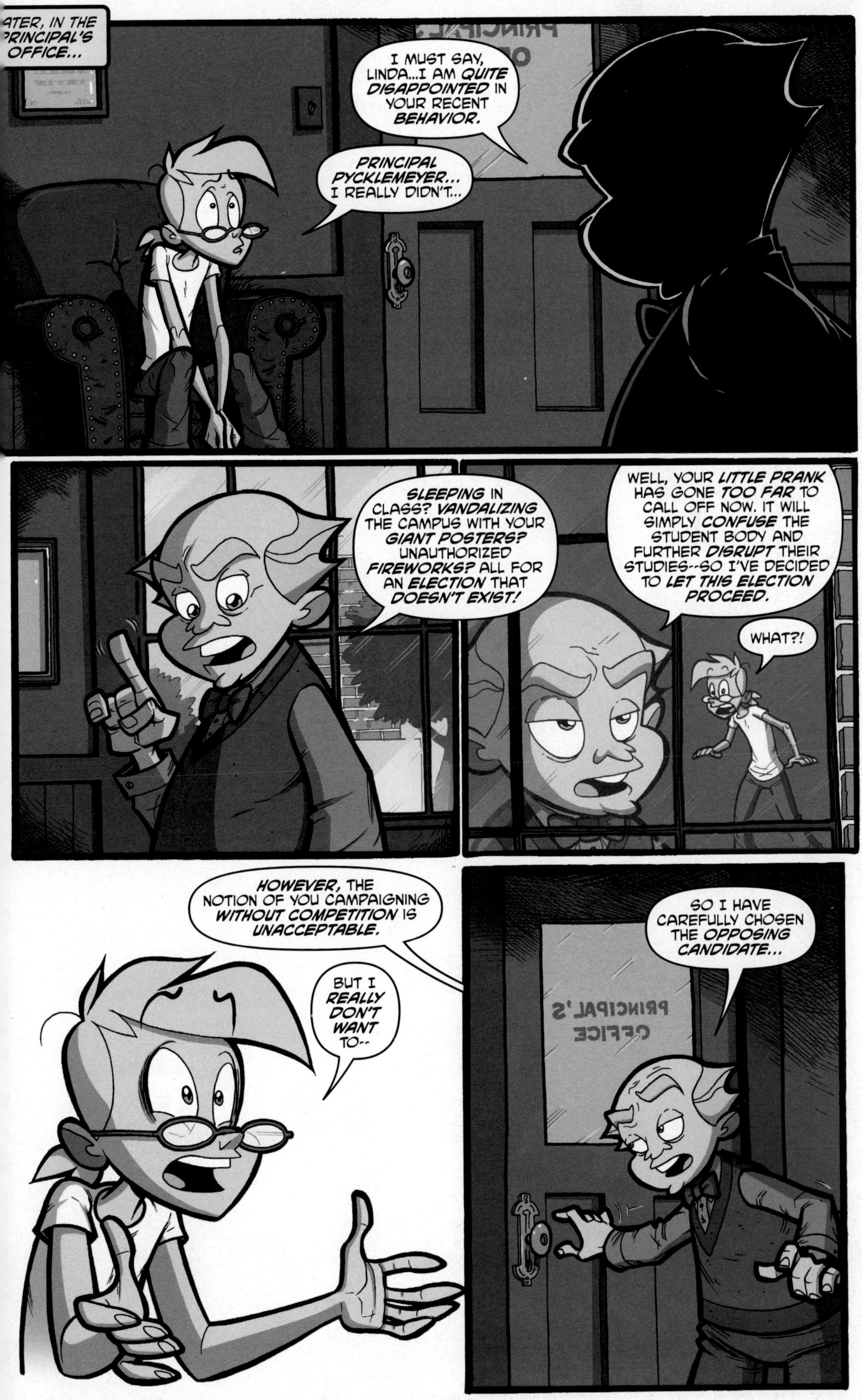

ATER, IN THE PRINCIPAL'S OFFICE...
I MUST SAY, LINDA...I AM QUITE DISAPPOINTED IN YOUR RECENT BEHAVIOR.
PRINCIPAL PYCKLEMEYER... I REALLY DIDN'T...
SLEEPING IN CLASS? VANDALIZING THE CAMPUS WITH YOUR GIANT POSTERS? UNAUTHORIZED FIREWORKS? ALL FOR AN ELECTION THAT DOESN'T EXIST!
WELL, YOUR LITTLE PRANK HAS GONE TOO FAR TO CALL OFF NOW. IT WILL SIMPLY CONFUSE THE STUDENT BODY AND FURTHER DISRUPT THEIR STUDIES--SO I'VE DECIDED TO LET THIS ELECTION PROCEED.
WHAT?!
HOWEVER, THE NOTION OF YOU CAMPAIGNING WITHOUT COMPETITION IS UNACCEPTABLE.
BUT I REALLY DON'T WANT TO--
SO I HAVE CAREFULLY CHOSEN THE OPPOSING CANDIDATE...

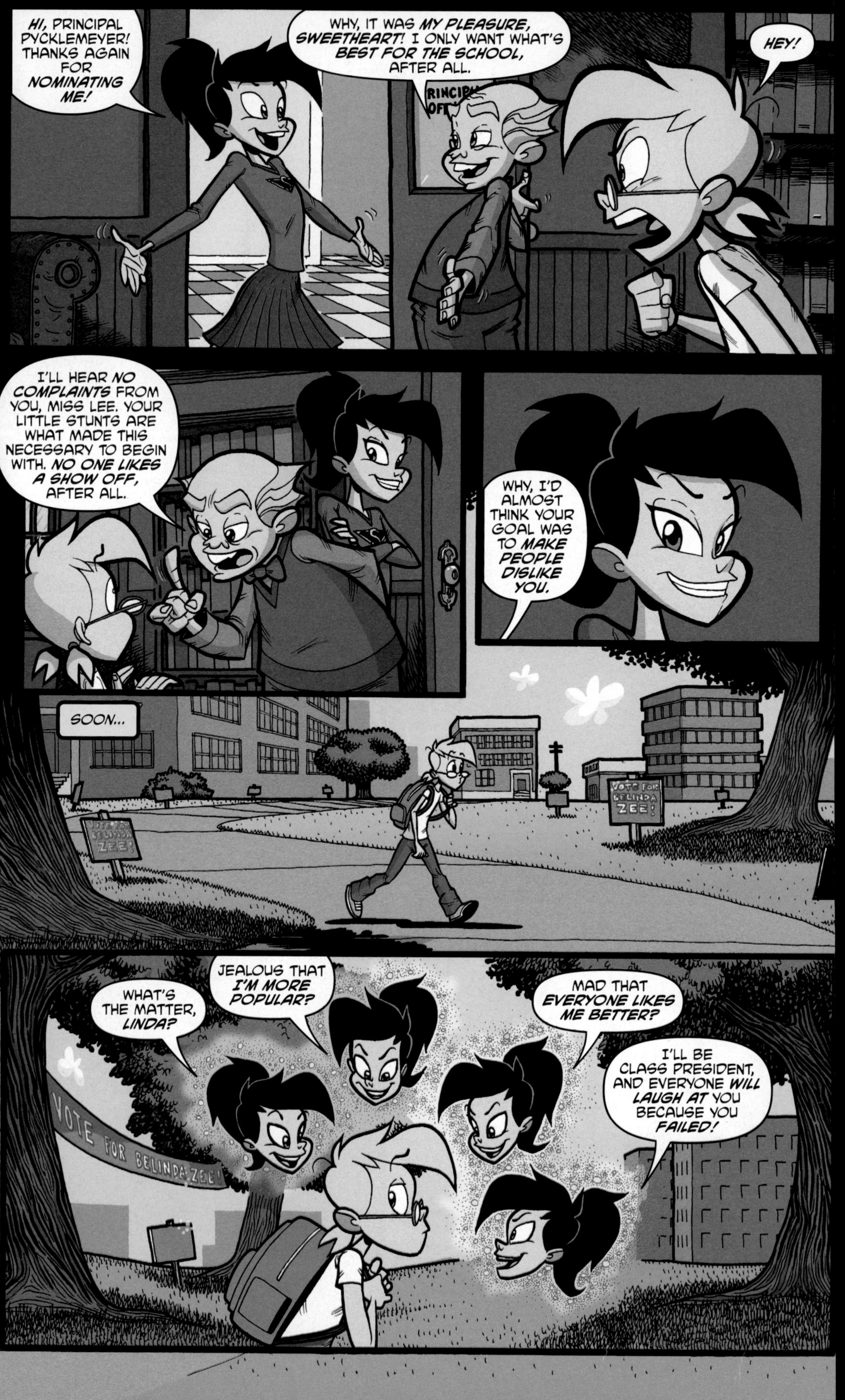
HI, PRINCIPAL PYCKLEMEYER! THANKS AGAIN FOR NOMINATING ME!
WHY, IT WAS MY PLEASURE, SWEETHEART! I ONLY WANT WHAT'S BEST FOR THE SCHOOL, AFTER ALL.
HEY!
I'LL HEAR NO COMPLAINTS FROM YOU, MISS LEE. YOUR LITTLE STUNTS ARE WHAT MADE THIS NECESSARY TO BEGIN WITH. NO ONE LIKES A SHOW OFF, AFTER ALL.
WHY, I'D ALMOST THINK YOUR GOAL WAS TO MAKE PEOPLE DISLIKE YOU.
SOON...
VOTE FOR BELINDA ZEE!
WHAT'S THE MATTER, LINDA?
JEALOUS THAT I'M MORE POPULAR?
MAD THAT EVERYONE LIKES ME BETTER?
I'LL BE CLASS PRESIDENT, AND EVERYONE WILL LAUGH AT YOU BECAUSE YOU FAILED!
VOTE FOR BELINDA ZEE!

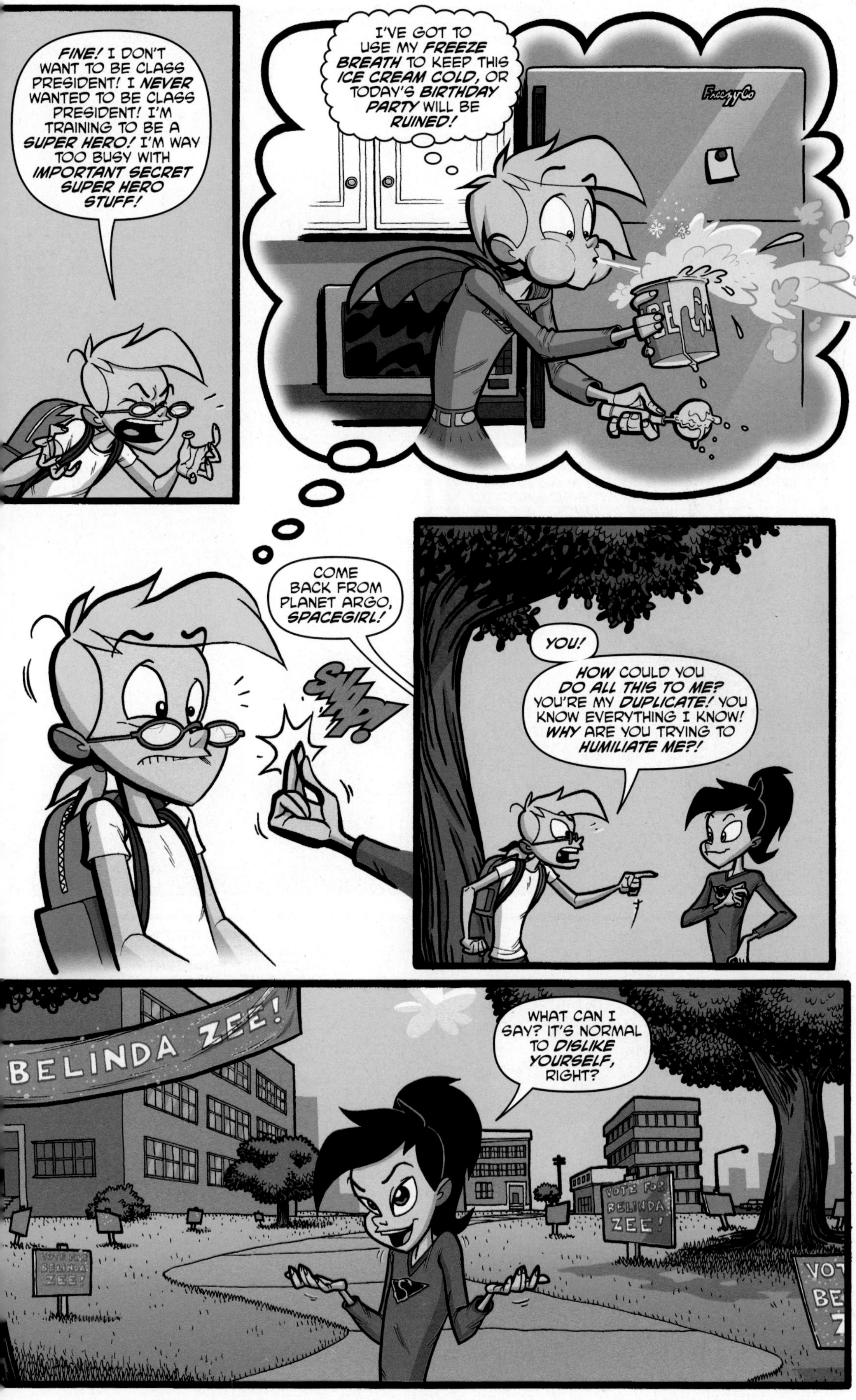
FINE! I DON'T WANT TO BE CLASS PRESIDENT! I NEVER WANTED TO BE CLASS PRESIDENT! I'M TRAINING TO BE A SUPER HERO! I'M WAY TOO BUSY WITH IMPORTANT SECRET SUPER HERO STUFF!
I'VE GOT TO USE MY FREEZE BREATH TO KEEP THIS ICE CREAM COLD, OR TODAY'S BIRTHDAY PARTY WILL BE RUINED!
COME BACK FROM PLANET ARGO, SPACEGIRL!
SNAP!
YOU!
HOW COULD YOU DO ALL THIS TO ME? YOU'RE MY DUPLICATE! YOU KNOW EVERYTHING I KNOW! WHY ARE YOU TRYING TO HUMILIATE ME?!
BELINDA ZEE!
WHAT CAN I SAY? IT'S NORMAL TO DISLIKE YOURSELF, RIGHT?
VOTE FOR BELINDA ZEE!
VOTE FOR BELINDA ZEE!

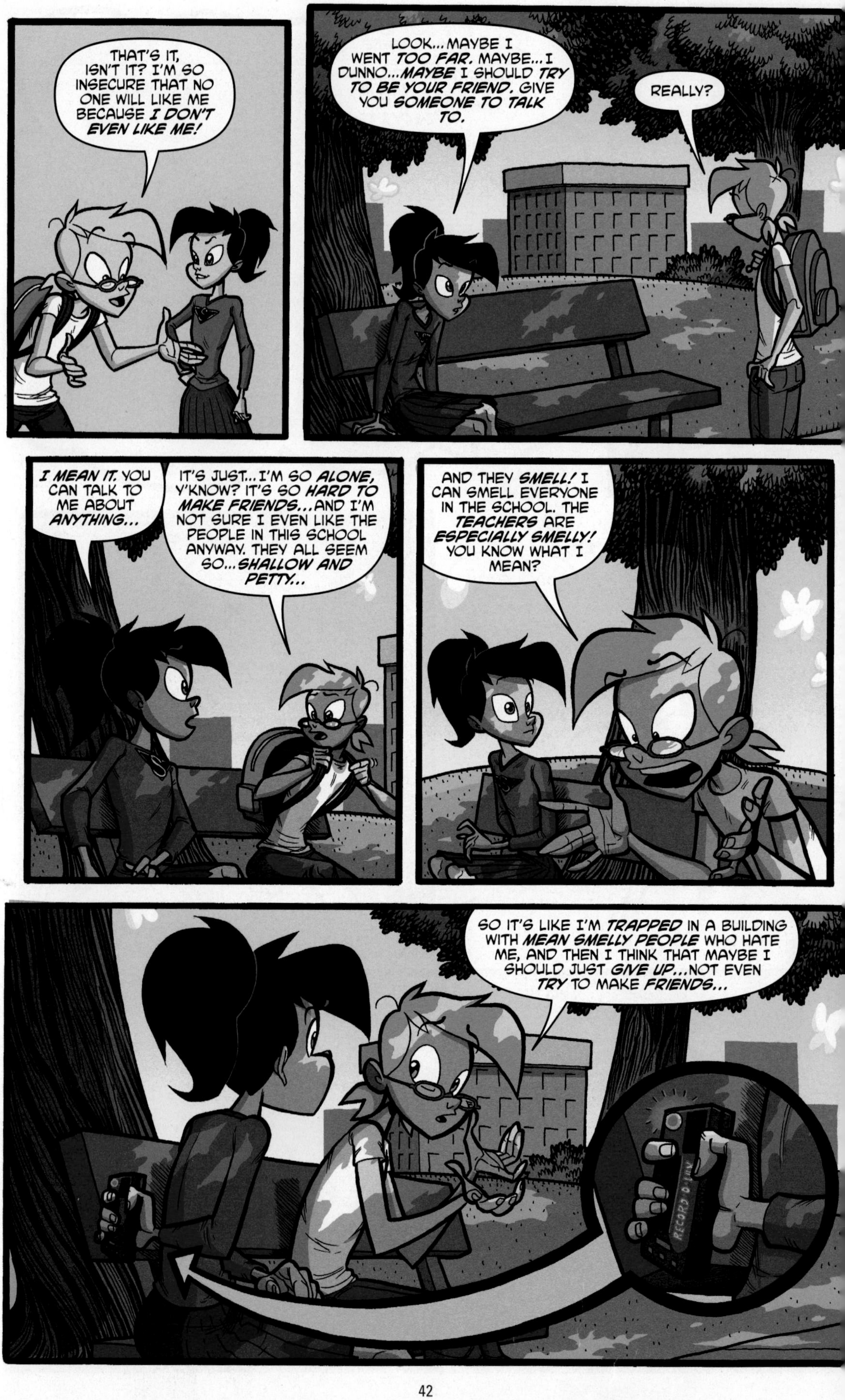
THAT'S IT, ISN'T IT? I'M SO INSECURE THAT NO ONE WILL LIKE ME BECAUSE I DON'T EVEN LIKE ME!
LOOK... MAYBE I WENT TOO FAR. MAYBE... I DUNNO... MAYBE I SHOULD TRY TO BE YOUR FRIEND. GIVE YOU SOMEONE TO TALK TO.
REALLY?
I MEAN IT. YOU CAN TALK TO ME ABOUT ANYTHING...
IT'S JUST... I'M SO ALONE, Y'KNOW? IT'S SO HARD TO MAKE FRIENDS... AND I'M NOT SURE I EVEN LIKE THE PEOPLE IN THIS SCHOOL ANYWAY. THEY ALL SEEM SO... SHALLOW AND PETTY...
AND THEY SMELL! I CAN SMELL EVERYONE IN THE SCHOOL. THE TEACHERS ARE ESPECIALLY SMELLY! YOU KNOW WHAT I MEAN?
SO IT'S LIKE I'M TRAPPED IN A BUILDING WITH MEAN SMELLY PEOPLE WHO HATE ME, AND THEN I THINK THAT MAYBE I SHOULD JUST GIVE UP... NOT EVEN TRY TO MAKE FRIENDS...

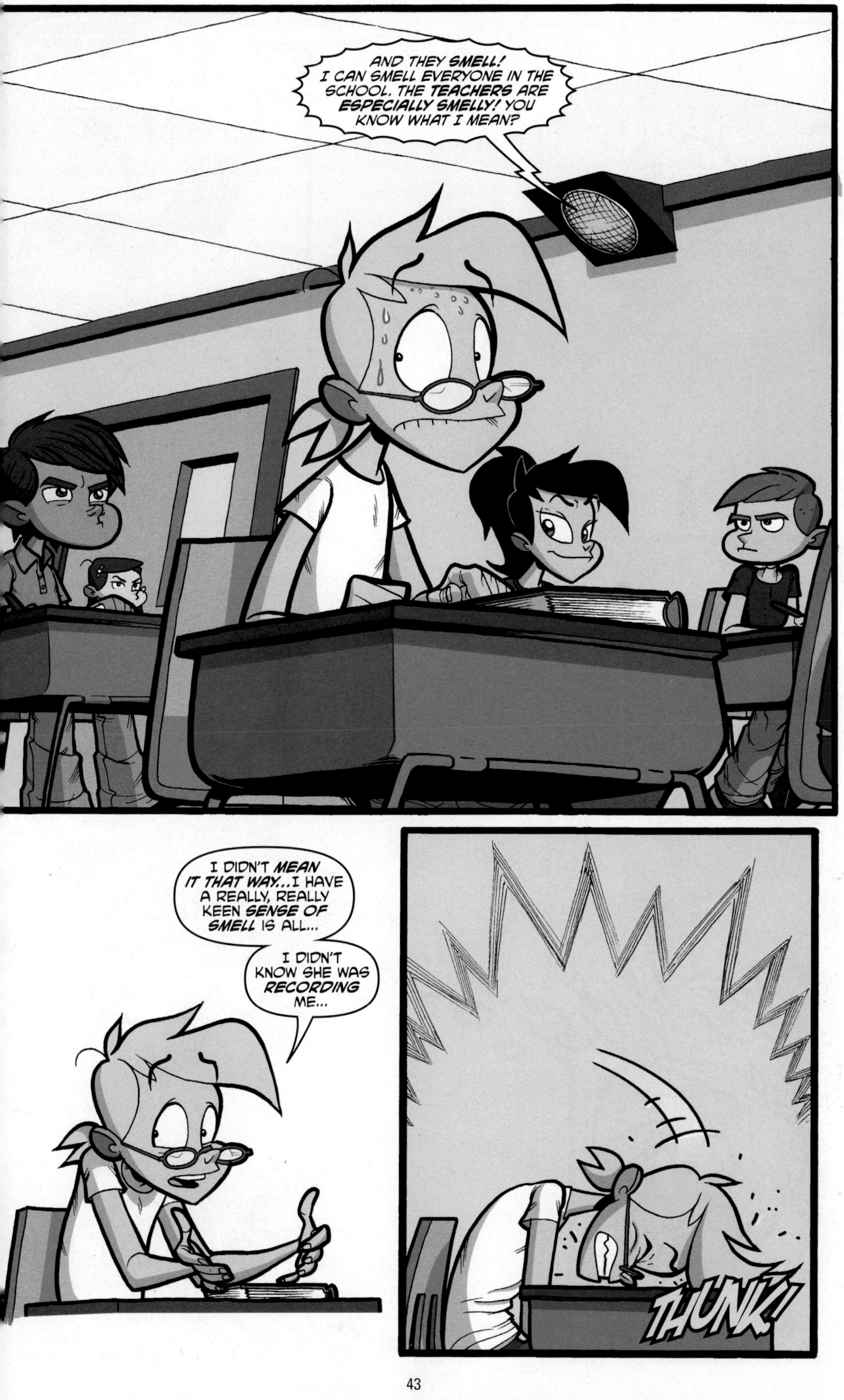
AND THEY SMELL! I CAN SMELL EVERYONE IN THE SCHOOL. THE TEACHERS ARE ESPECIALLY SMELLY! YOU KNOW WHAT I MEAN?
I DIDN'T MEAN IT THAT WAY...I HAVE A REALLY, REALLY KEEN SENSE OF SMELL IS ALL...
I DIDN'T KNOW SHE WAS RECORDING ME...
THUNK!

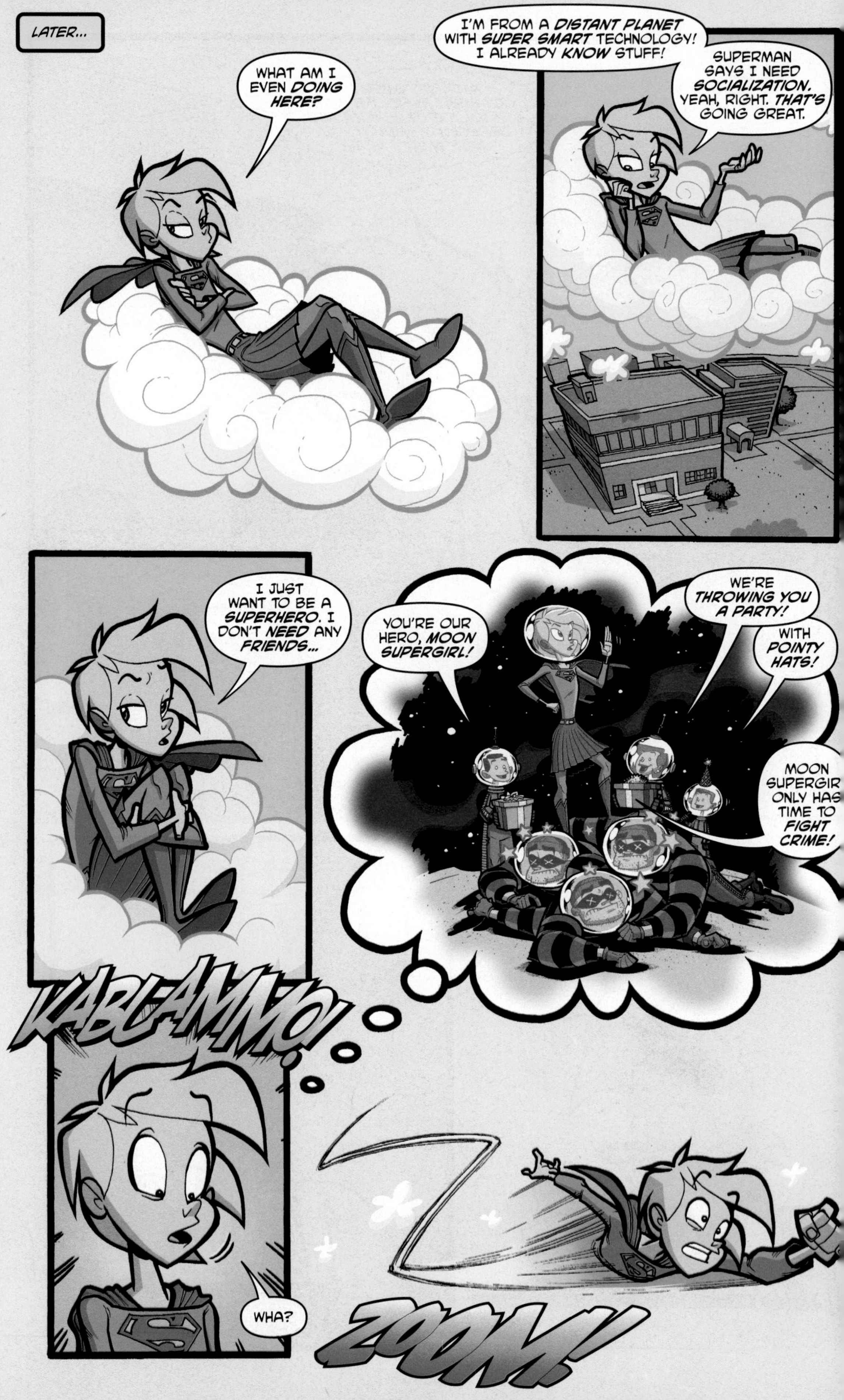
LATER...
WHAT AM I EVEN DOING HERE?
I'M FROM A DISTANT PLANET WITH SUPER SMART TECHNOLOGY! I ALREADY KNOW STUFF!
SUPERMAN SAYS I NEED SOCIALIZATION. YEAH, RIGHT. THAT'S GOING GREAT.
I JUST WANT TO BE A SUPERHERO. I DON'T NEED ANY FRIENDS...
YOU'RE OUR HERO, MOON SUPERGIRL!
WE'RE THROWING YOU A PARTY!
WITH POINTY HATS!
MOON SUPERGIR ONLY HAS TIME TO FIGHT CRIME!
KABLAMMO!
WHA?
ZOOM!

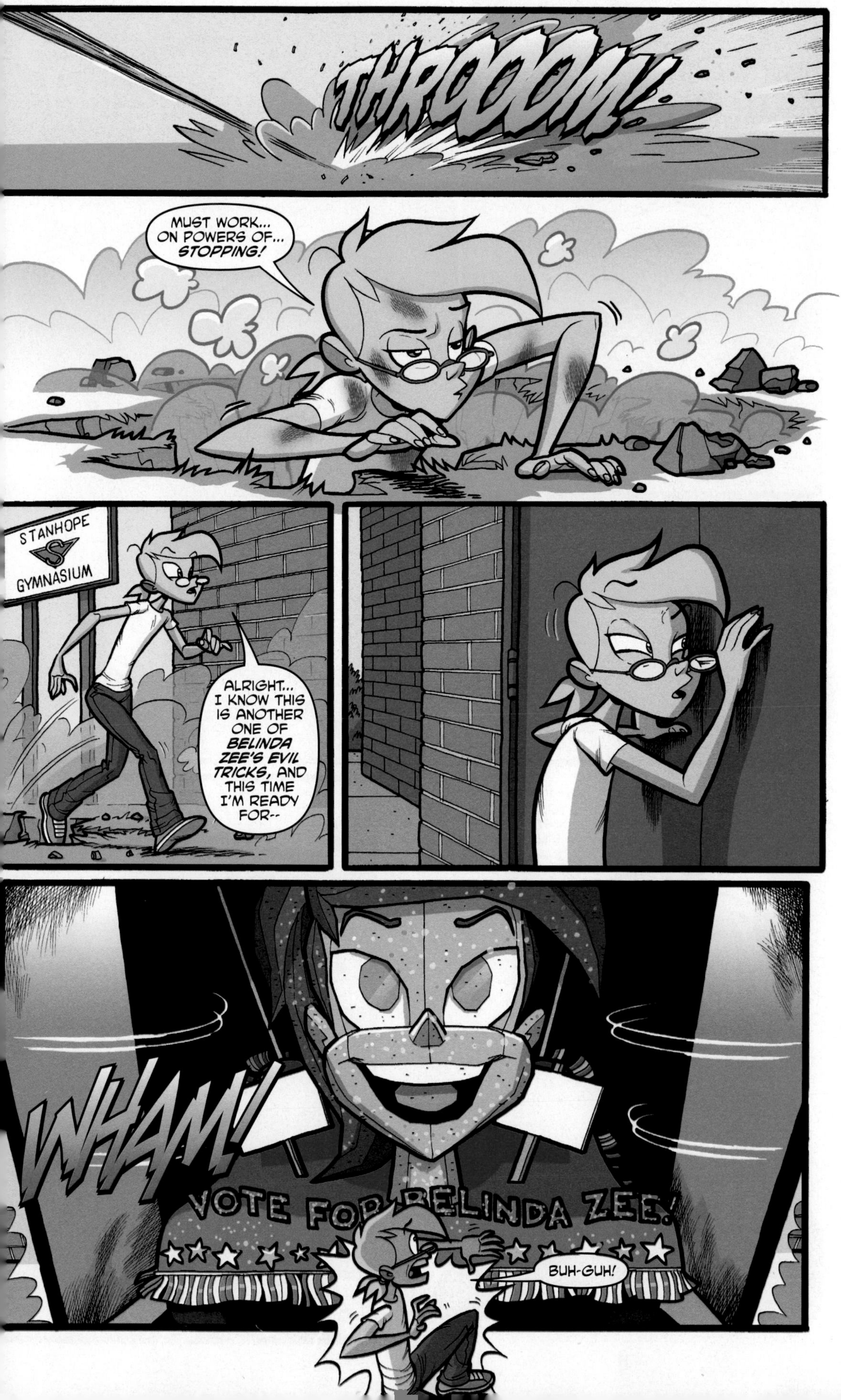
THROOOM!
MUST WORK... ON POWERS OF... STOPPING!
STANHOPE GYMNASIUM
ALRIGHT... I KNOW THIS IS ANOTHER ONE OF BELINDA ZEE'S EVIL TRICKS, AND THIS TIME I'M READY FOR--
WHAM!
VOTE FOR BELINDA ZEE!
BUH-GUH!

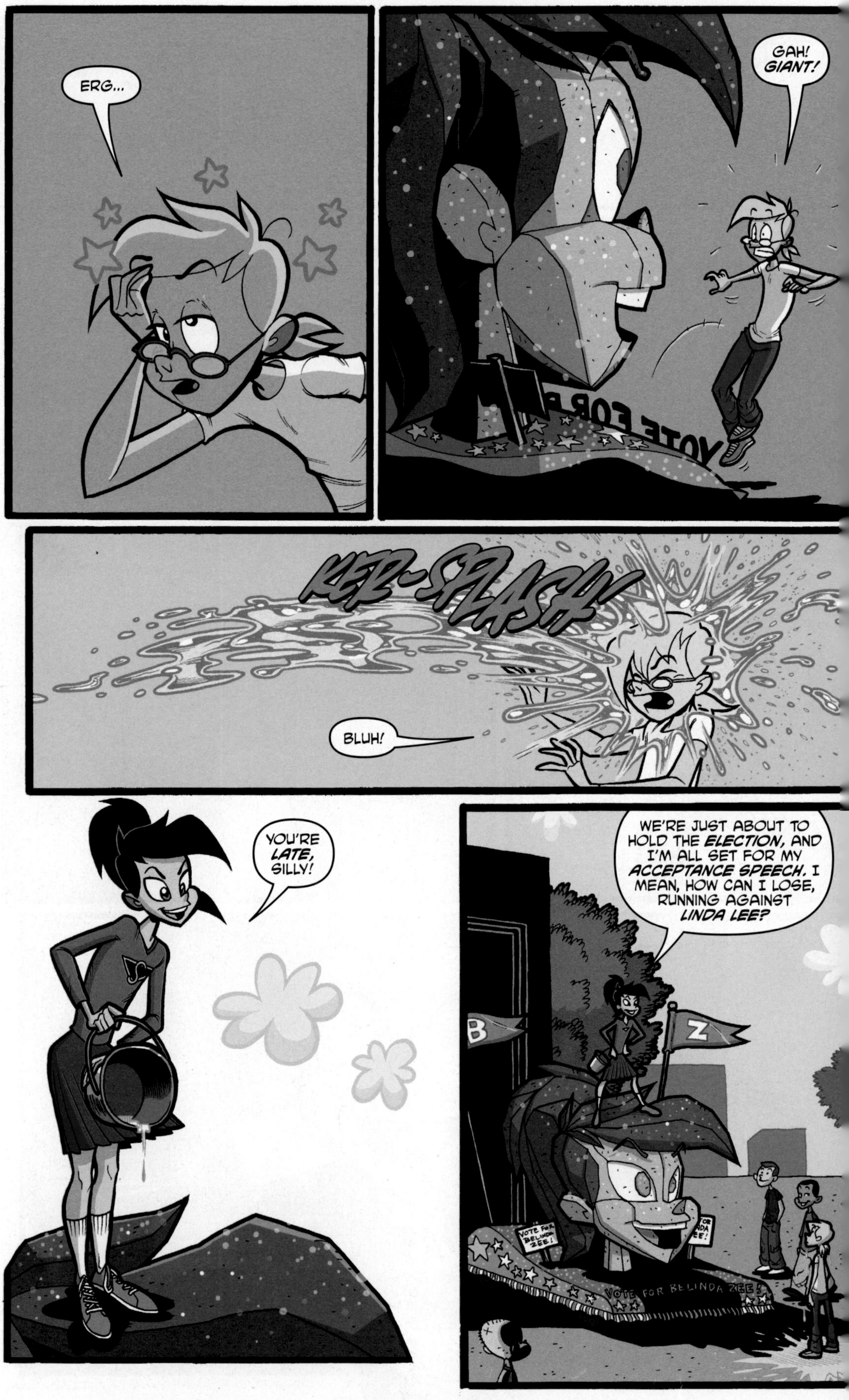
ERG...
GAH! GIANT!
KER-SPLASH!
BLUH!
YOU'RE LATE, SILLY!
WE'RE JUST ABOUT TO HOLD THE ELECTION, AND I'M ALL SET FOR MY ACCEPTANCE SPEECH. I MEAN, HOW CAN I LOSE, RUNNING AGAINST LINDA LEE?
B
Z
VOTE FOR BELINDA ZEE!
VOTE FOR BELINDA ZEE!

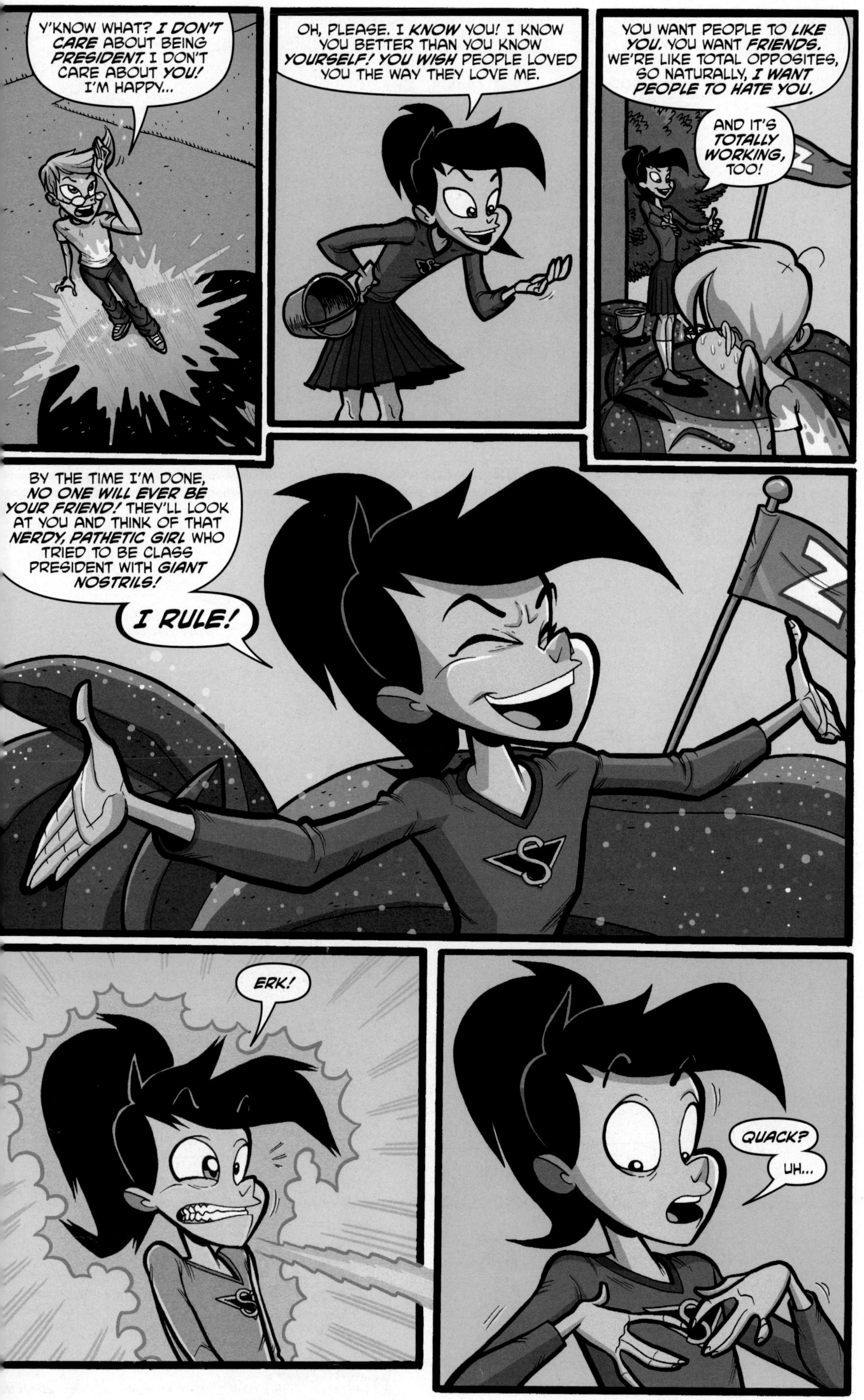
Y'KNOW WHAT? I DON'T CARE ABOUT BEING PRESIDENT. I DON'T CARE ABOUT YOU! I'M HAPPY...
OH, PLEASE. I KNOW YOU! I KNOW YOU BETTER THAN YOU KNOW YOURSELF! YOU WISH PEOPLE LOVED YOU THE WAY THEY LOVE ME.
YOU WANT PEOPLE TO LIKE YOU. YOU WANT FRIENDS. WE'RE LIKE TOTAL OPPOSITES, SO NATURALLY, I WANT PEOPLE TO HATE YOU.
AND IT'S TOTALLY WORKING, TOO!
BY THE TIME I'M DONE, NO ONE WILL EVER BE YOUR FRIEND! THEY'LL LOOK AT YOU AND THINK OF THAT NERDY, PATHETIC GIRL WHO TRIED TO BE CLASS PRESIDENT WITH GIANT NOSTRILS!
I RULE!
ERK!
QUACK?
UH...

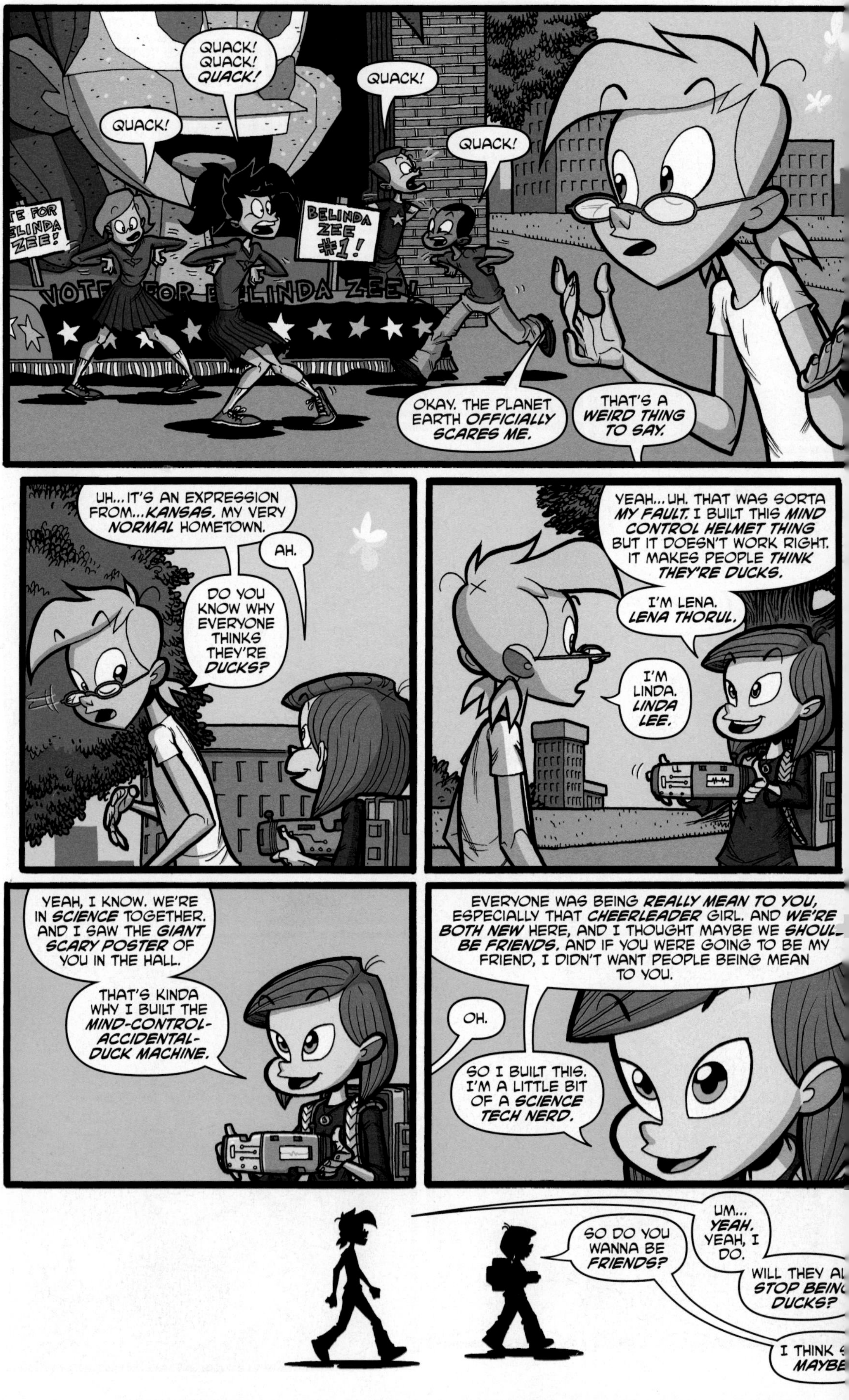

BELINDA ZEE #1!
QUACK!
QUACK! QUACK! QUACK!
QUACK!
QUACK!
OKAY. THE PLANET EARTH OFFICIALLY SCARES ME.
THAT'S A WEIRD THING TO SAY.
UH... IT'S AN EXPRESSION FROM... KANSAS. MY VERY NORMAL HOMETOWN.
AH.
DO YOU KNOW WHY EVERYONE THINKS THEY'RE DUCKS?
YEAH... UH. THAT WAS SORTA MY FAULT. I BUILT THIS MIND CONTROL HELMET THING BUT IT DOESN'T WORK RIGHT. IT MAKES PEOPLE THINK THEY'RE DUCKS.
I'M LENA. LENA THORUL.
I'M LINDA. LINDA LEE.
YEAH, I KNOW. WE'RE IN SCIENCE TOGETHER. AND I SAW THE GIANT SCARY POSTER OF YOU IN THE HALL.
THAT'S KINDA WHY I BUILT THE MIND-CONTROL-ACCIDENTAL-DUCK MACHINE.
EVERYONE WAS BEING REALLY MEAN TO YOU, ESPECIALLY THAT CHEERLEADER GIRL. AND WE'RE BOTH NEW HERE, AND I THOUGHT MAYBE WE SHOUL BE FRIENDS. AND IF YOU WERE GOING TO BE MY FRIEND, I DIDN'T WANT PEOPLE BEING MEAN TO YOU.
OH.
SO I BUILT THIS. I'M A LITTLE BIT OF A SCIENCE TECH NERD.
SO DO YOU WANNA BE FRIENDS?
UM... YEAH. YEAH, I DO.
WILL THEY AL STOP BEIN DUCKS?
I THINK MAYBE

ATER...

This has been the craziest week.

I'm not really popular. It's hard to fit in to this culture. No one really liked me much at first.

made my first per enemy. An il doppelganger me. She's a eerleader, and ally popular, d a jerk.

But now I have a new best friend. She's kinda nerdy (in a good way) and she likes helping people like me, and we even managed to get into the same dorm room.

✉ Send

From: LINDA LEE

To: SUPERMAN

Subject: The usual ramblings...

This has been the craziest week. I'... really popular. It's hard to fit in to thi... No one really liked me much ...enemy. An evil ...She's a cheerle ...d a jerk.

For the first time, I feel like I'll be okay on this planet. Anyway, I hope you visit soon.

Love, Linda.

Send

KLICK

This has been the craziest week. I'm not really popular. It's hard to fit in to this culture. No one really liked me much at first. I made my first super enemy. An evil doppelganger of me. She's a cheerleader, and really popular, and a jerk.

I finally feel settled in.

The school is kinda weird. Science class is too easy, and the teachers are dumb.

But I have a best friend now. You'd like her. She's not at all like the regular people of Metropolis.

49

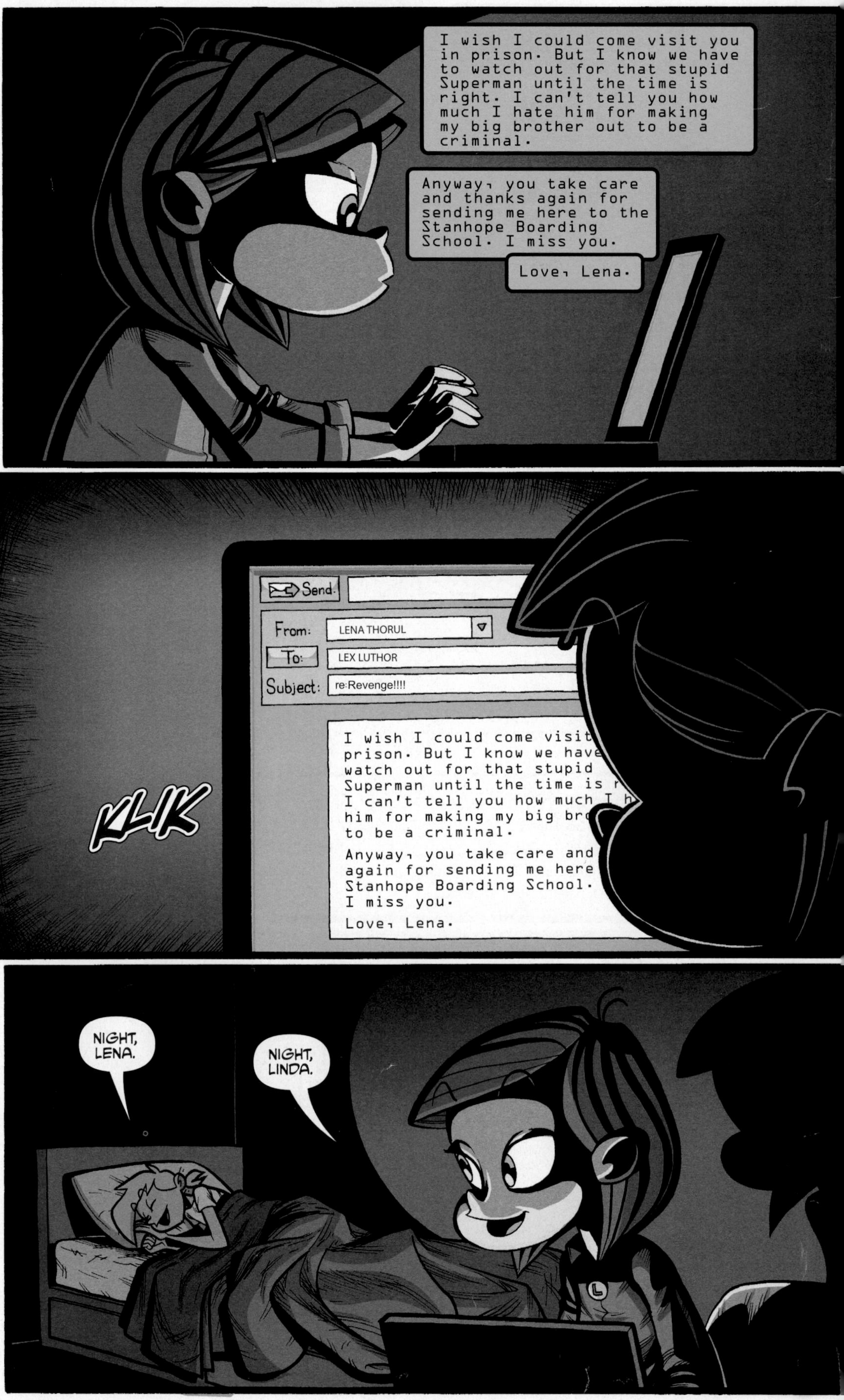
I wish I could come visit you in prison. But I know we have to watch out for that stupid Superman until the time is right. I can't tell you how much I hate him for making my big brother out to be a criminal.
Anyway, you take care and thanks again for sending me here to the Stanhope Boarding School. I miss you.
Love, Lena.
Send
From: LENA THORUL
To: LEX LUTHOR
Subject: re:Revenge!!!!
I wish I could come visit
prison. But I know we have
watch out for that stupid
Superman until the time is
I can't tell you how much I
him for making my big
to be a criminal.
Anyway, you take care and
again for sending me here
Stanhope Boarding School.
I miss you.
Love, Lena.
KLIK
NIGHT, LENA.
NIGHT, LINDA.

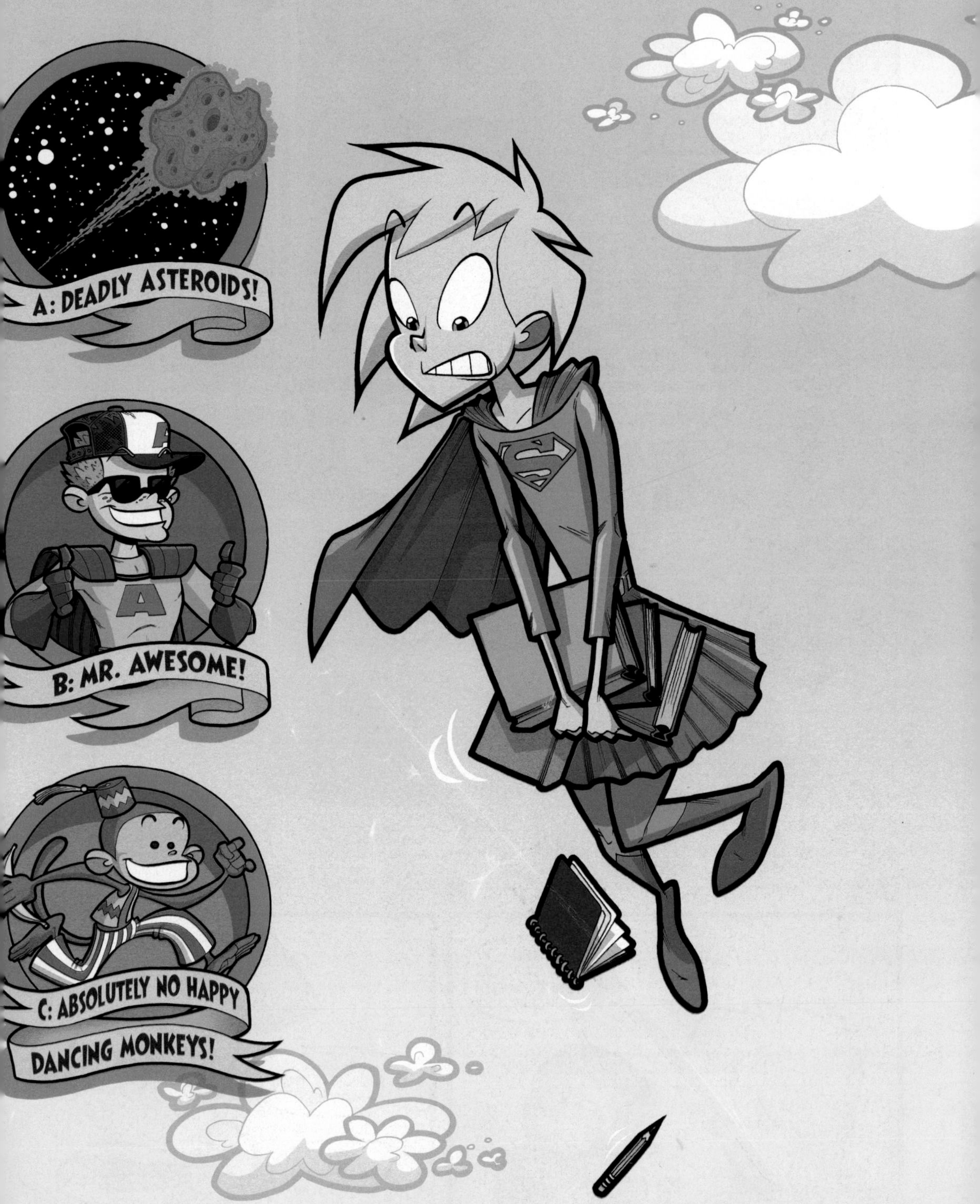
A: DEADLY ASTEROIDS!
B: MR. AWESOME!
C: ABSOLUTELY NO HAPPY DANCING MONKEYS!

PART 1: LOOK! UP IN THE SKY!

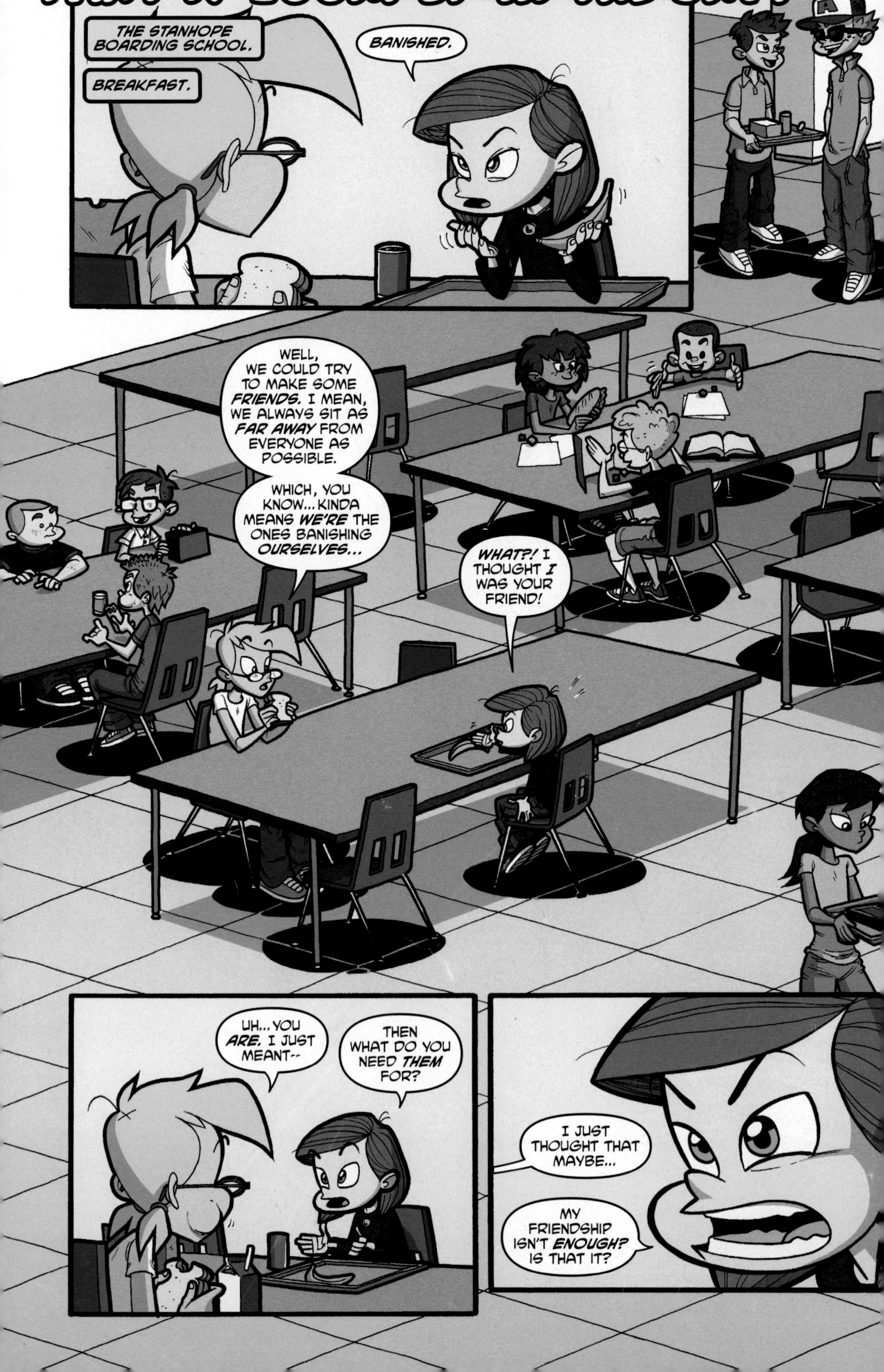
THE STANHOPE BOARDING SCHOOL.
BREAKFAST.
BANISHED.
WELL, WE COULD TRY TO MAKE SOME FRIENDS. I MEAN, WE ALWAYS SIT AS FAR AWAY FROM EVERYONE AS POSSIBLE.
WHICH, YOU KNOW... KINDA MEANS WE'RE THE ONES BANISHING OURSELVES...
WHAT?! I THOUGHT I WAS YOUR FRIEND!
UH... YOU ARE. I JUST MEANT--
THEN WHAT DO YOU NEED THEM FOR?
I JUST THOUGHT THAT MAYBE...
MY FRIENDSHIP ISN'T ENOUGH? IS THAT IT?

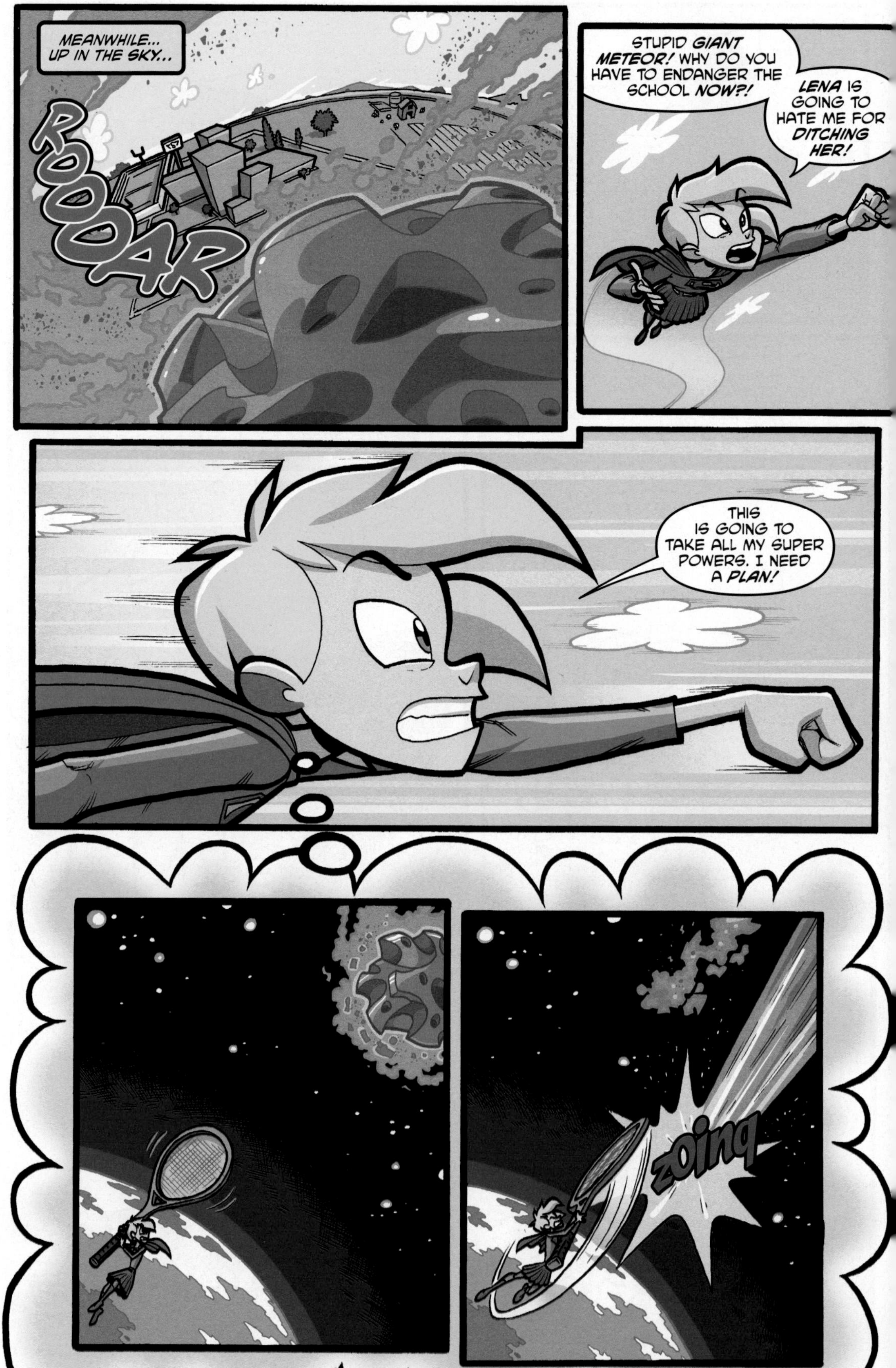
MEANWHILE... UP IN THE SKY...
RDDOAR
STUPID GIANT METEOR! WHY DO YOU HAVE TO ENDANGER THE SCHOOL NOW?!
LENA IS GOING TO HATE ME FOR DITCHING HER!
THIS IS GOING TO TAKE ALL MY SUPER POWERS. I NEED A PLAN!
zoinq

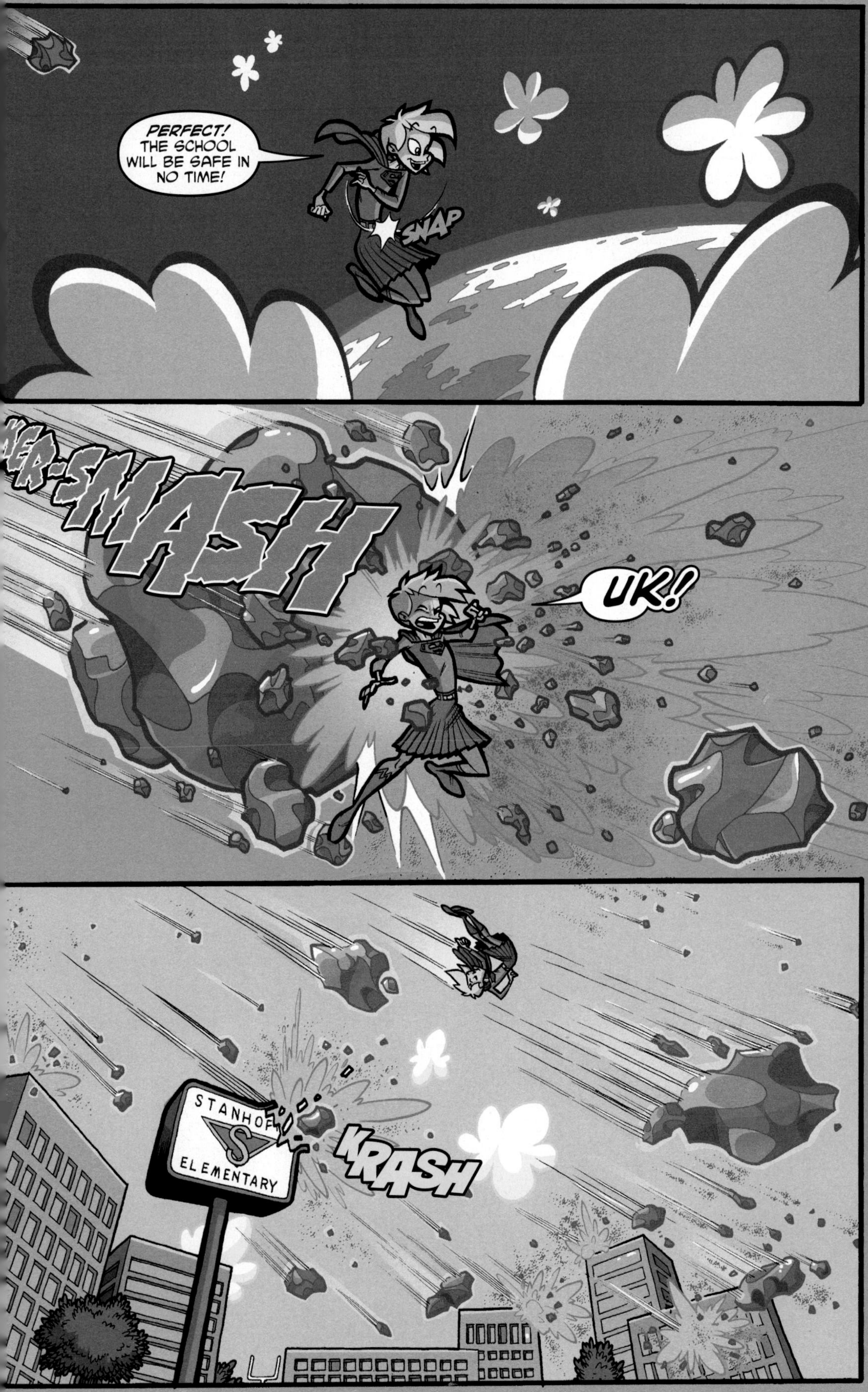
PERFECT! THE SCHOOL WILL BE SAFE IN NO TIME!
SNAP
KER-SMASH
UK!
STANHOPE ELEMENTARY
KRASH

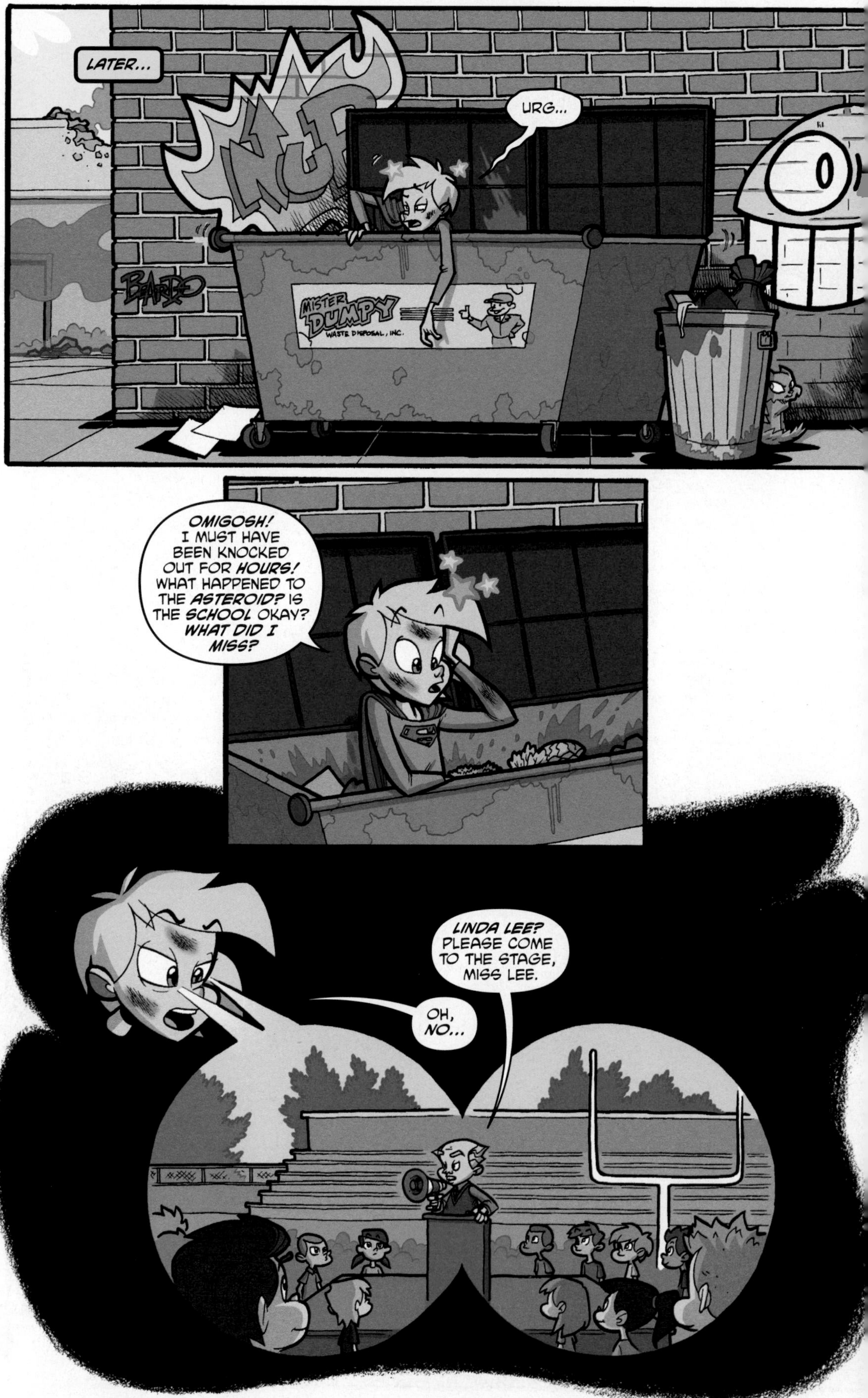
LATER...
URG...
MISTER DUMPY WASTE DISPOSAL, INC.
OMIGOSH! I MUST HAVE BEEN KNOCKED OUT FOR HOURS! WHAT HAPPENED TO THE ASTEROID? IS THE SCHOOL OKAY? WHAT DID I MISS?
LINDA LEE? PLEASE COME TO THE STAGE, MISS LEE.
OH, NO...

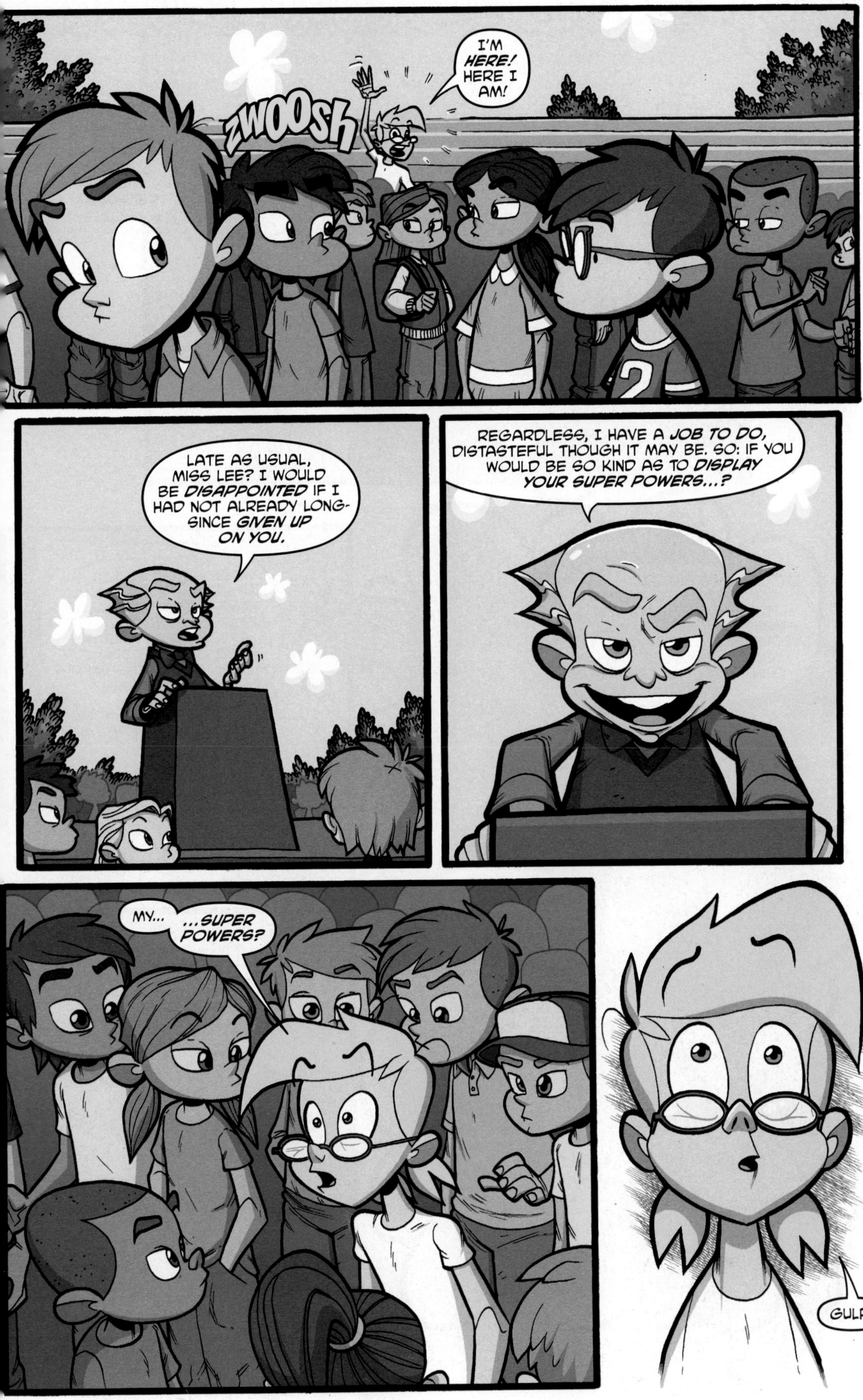

I'M HERE! HERE I AM!
ZWOOSH
LATE AS USUAL, MISS LEE? I WOULD BE DISAPPOINTED IF I HAD NOT ALREADY LONG-SINCE GIVEN UP ON YOU.
REGARDLESS, I HAVE A JOB TO DO, DISTASTEFUL THOUGH IT MAY BE. SO: IF YOU WOULD BE SO KIND AS TO DISPLAY YOUR SUPER POWERS...?
MY...
...SUPER POWERS?
GULP.

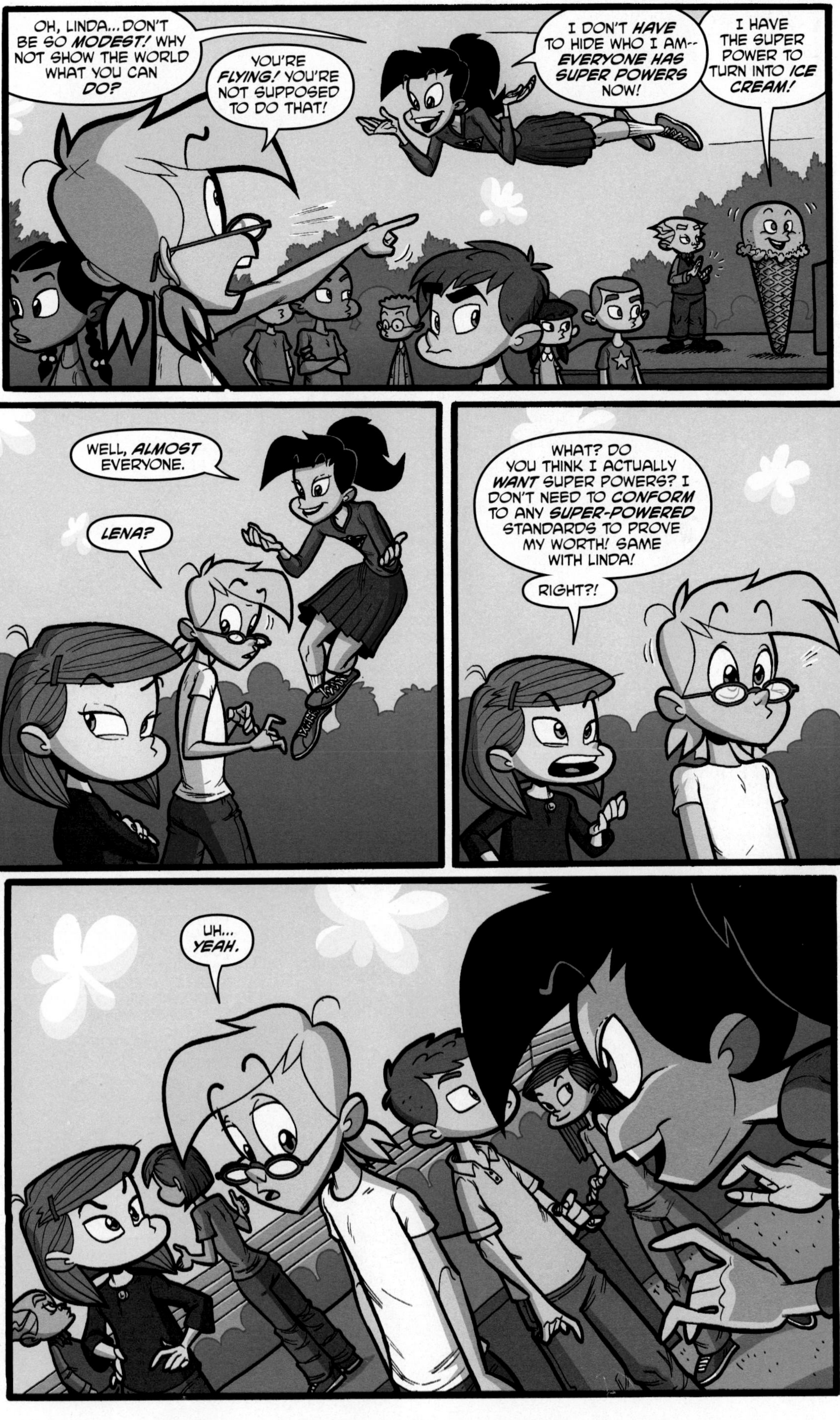
OH, LINDA... DON'T BE SO MODEST! WHY NOT SHOW THE WORLD WHAT YOU CAN DO?
YOU'RE FLYING! YOU'RE NOT SUPPOSED TO DO THAT!
I DON'T HAVE TO HIDE WHO I AM-- EVERYONE HAS SUPER POWERS NOW!
I HAVE THE SUPER POWER TO TURN INTO ICE CREAM!
WELL, ALMOST EVERYONE.
LENA?
WHAT? DO YOU THINK I ACTUALLY WANT SUPER POWERS? I DON'T NEED TO CONFORM TO ANY SUPER-POWERED STANDARDS TO PROVE MY WORTH! SAME WITH LINDA!
RIGHT?!
UH... YEAH.

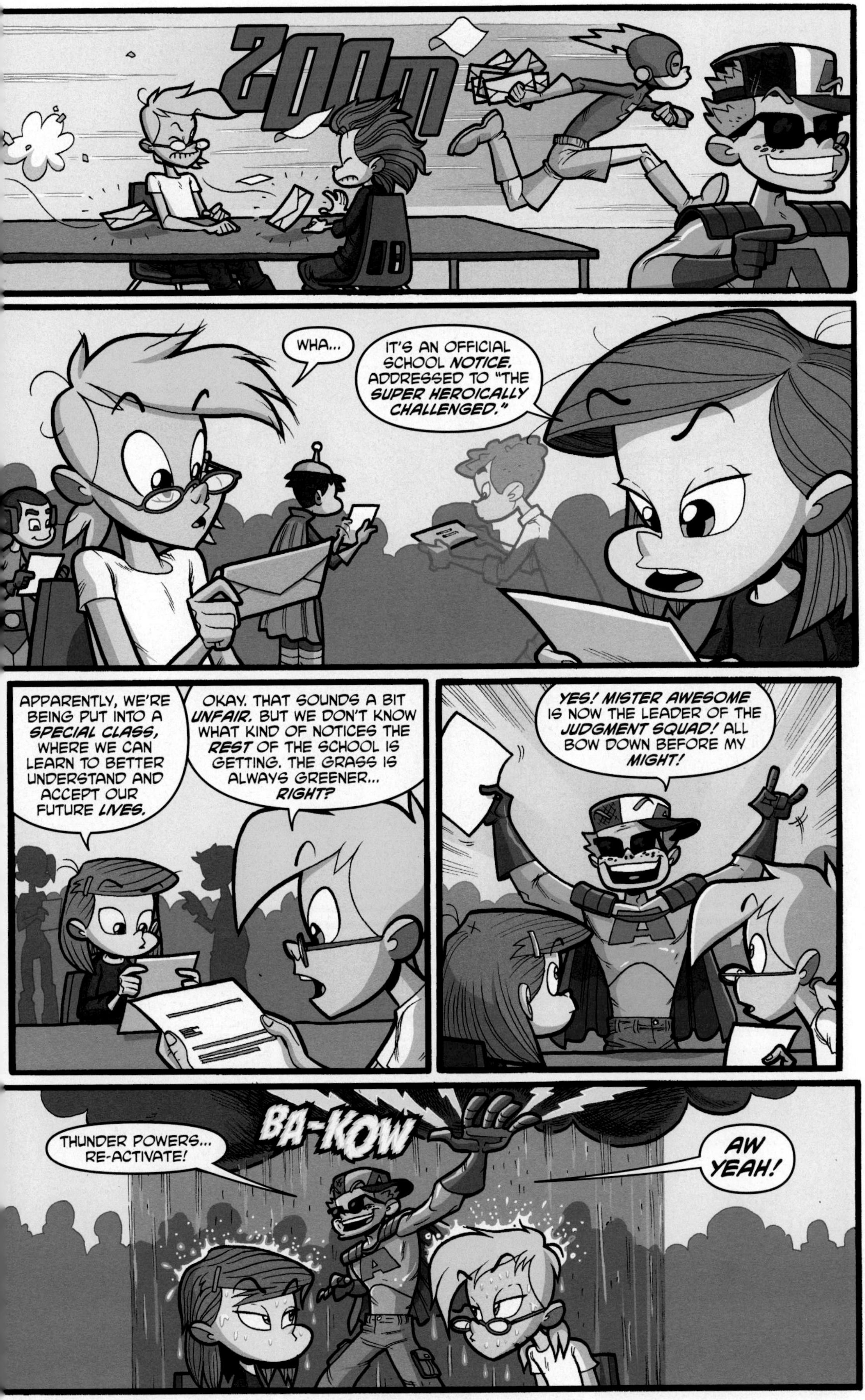
ZOOM
WHA...
IT'S AN OFFICIAL SCHOOL NOTICE. ADDRESSED TO "THE SUPER HEROICALLY CHALLENGED."
APPARENTLY, WE'RE BEING PUT INTO A SPECIAL CLASS, WHERE WE CAN LEARN TO BETTER UNDERSTAND AND ACCEPT OUR FUTURE LIVES.
OKAY. THAT SOUNDS A BIT UNFAIR. BUT WE DON'T KNOW WHAT KIND OF NOTICES THE REST OF THE SCHOOL IS GETTING. THE GRASS IS ALWAYS GREENER... RIGHT?
YES! MISTER AWESOME IS NOW THE LEADER OF THE JUDGMENT SQUAD! ALL BOW DOWN BEFORE MY MIGHT!
BA-KOW
THUNDER POWERS... RE-ACTIVATE!
AW YEAH!

SUPER-
HEROICALLY
CHALLENGED

HELLO, CLASS. I WOULD *LIKE* TO *WELCOME* YOU TO THE FIRST DAY OF AN *EXCITING NEW CURRICULUM.* TRAGICALLY FOR US ALL, I *CANNOT DO SO.* THE INTERESTING CLASSES HAVE ALL BEEN *RESERVED* FOR STUDENTS WITH *SUPER POWERS.*

UM....*MS. BIGGLESTONE?* AREN'T WE ALL *EQUAL* AND STUFF? I MEAN, JUST BECAUSE WE'RE NOT SUPER-POWERED DOESN'T MEAN WE SHOULD BE TREATED ANY *DIFFERENTLY...*

I'M SORRY, BUT *NO.* THAT IS *INCORRECT.*

YOUR *FATE,* WHICH I AM HERE TO ENSURE YOU *EMBRACE,* IS ONE OF *MEDIOCRITY AND FEAR.* AS NON-SUPER-POWERED CITIZENS, YOU MAY STAND BACK AND WITNESS THE *MAJESTY* OF YOUR *BETTERS.*

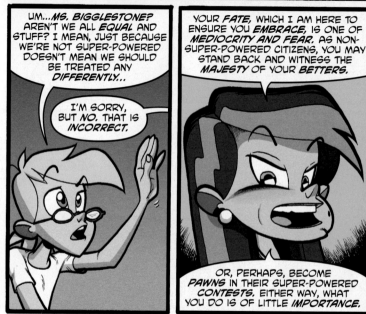

OR, PERHAPS, BECOME *PAWNS* IN THEIR SUPER-POWERED *CONTESTS.* EITHER WAY, WHAT YOU DO IS OF LITTLE *IMPORTANCE.*

NOW PLEASE, STUDENTS... DO NOT *TROUBLE* ME WITH ANY MORE BOTHERSOME QUESTIONS. I EXPECT YOU TO SPEND THE NEXT FEW HOURS CONTEMPLATING THE *BLEAKNESS* OF YOUR FUTURE.

HELP!

EH?

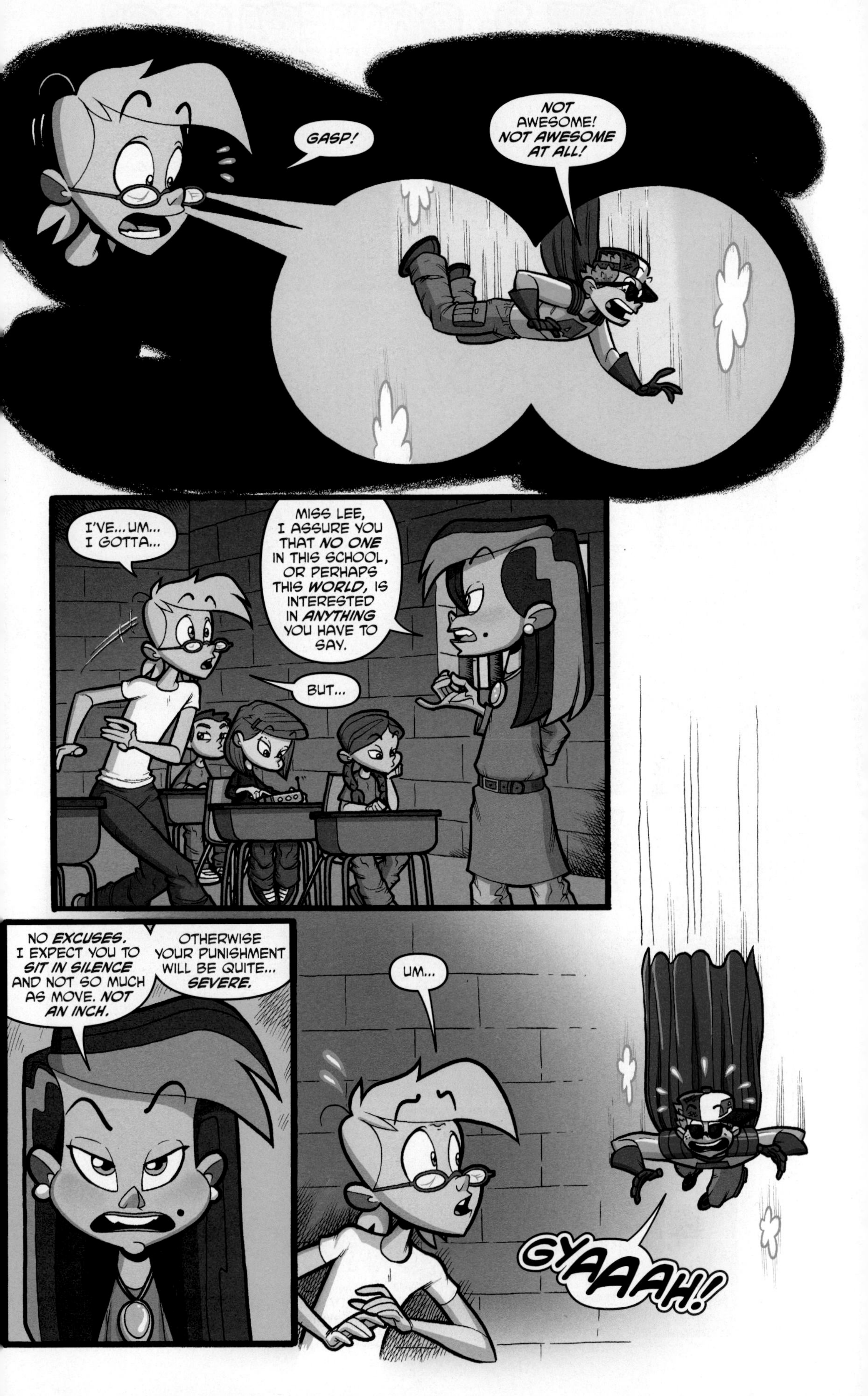
GASP!
NOT AWESOME! NOT AWESOME AT ALL!
I'VE...UM... I GOTTA...
MISS LEE, I ASSURE YOU THAT NO ONE IN THIS SCHOOL, OR PERHAPS THIS WORLD, IS INTERESTED IN ANYTHING YOU HAVE TO SAY.
BUT...
NO EXCUSES. I EXPECT YOU TO SIT IN SILENCE AND NOT SO MUCH AS MOVE. NOT AN INCH.
OTHERWISE YOUR PUNISHMENT WILL BE QUITE... SEVERE.
UM...
GYAAAH!

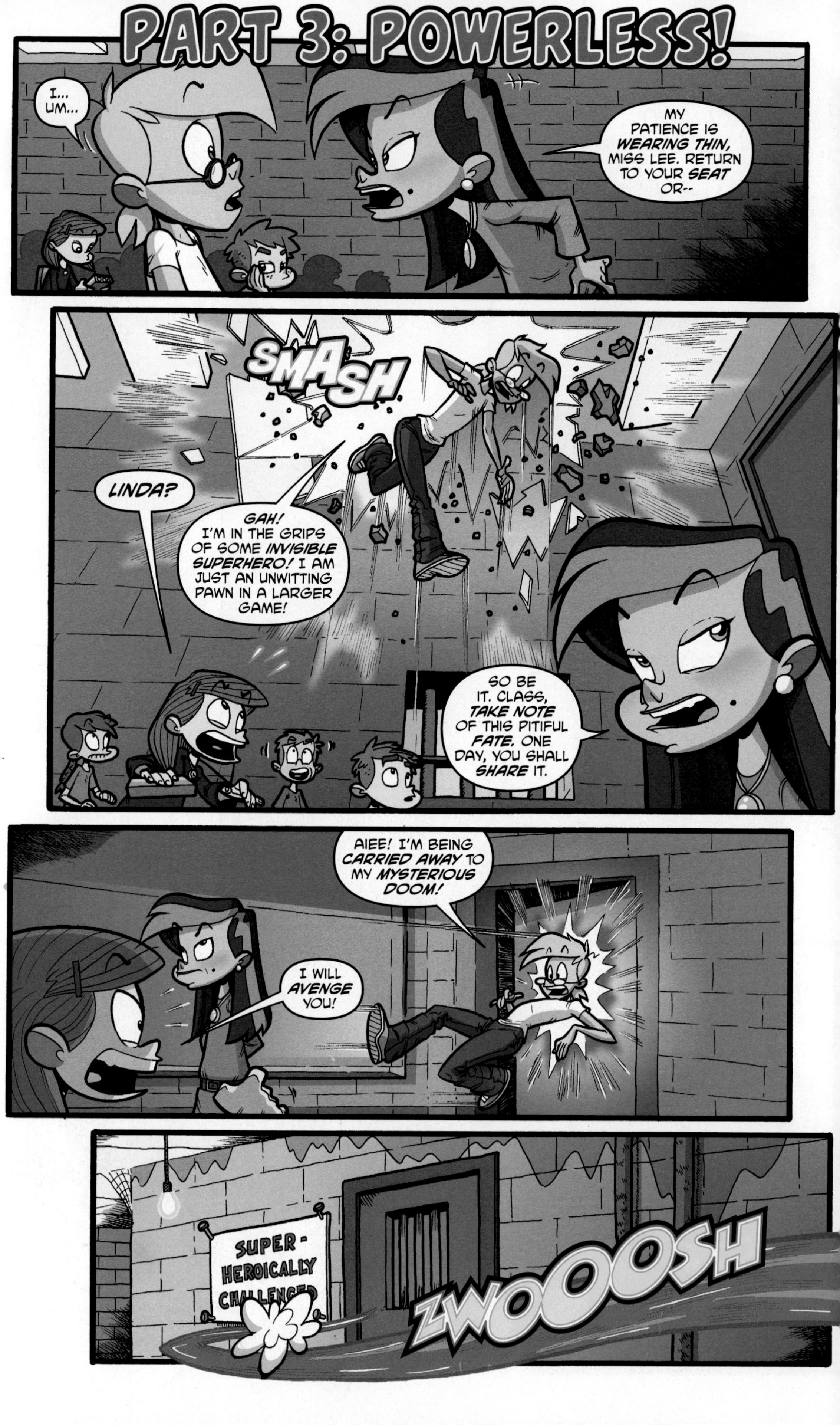
PART 3: POWERLESS!
I... UM...
MY PATIENCE IS WEARING THIN, MISS LEE. RETURN TO YOUR SEAT OR--
SMASH
LINDA?
GAH! I'M IN THE GRIPS OF SOME INVISIBLE SUPERHERO! I AM JUST AN UNWITTING PAWN IN A LARGER GAME!
SO BE IT. CLASS, TAKE NOTE OF THIS PITIFUL FATE. ONE DAY, YOU SHALL SHARE IT.
AIEE! I'M BEING CARRIED AWAY TO MY MYSTERIOUS DOOM!
I WILL AVENGE YOU!
SUPER-HEROICALLY CHALLENGED
ZWOOOOSH

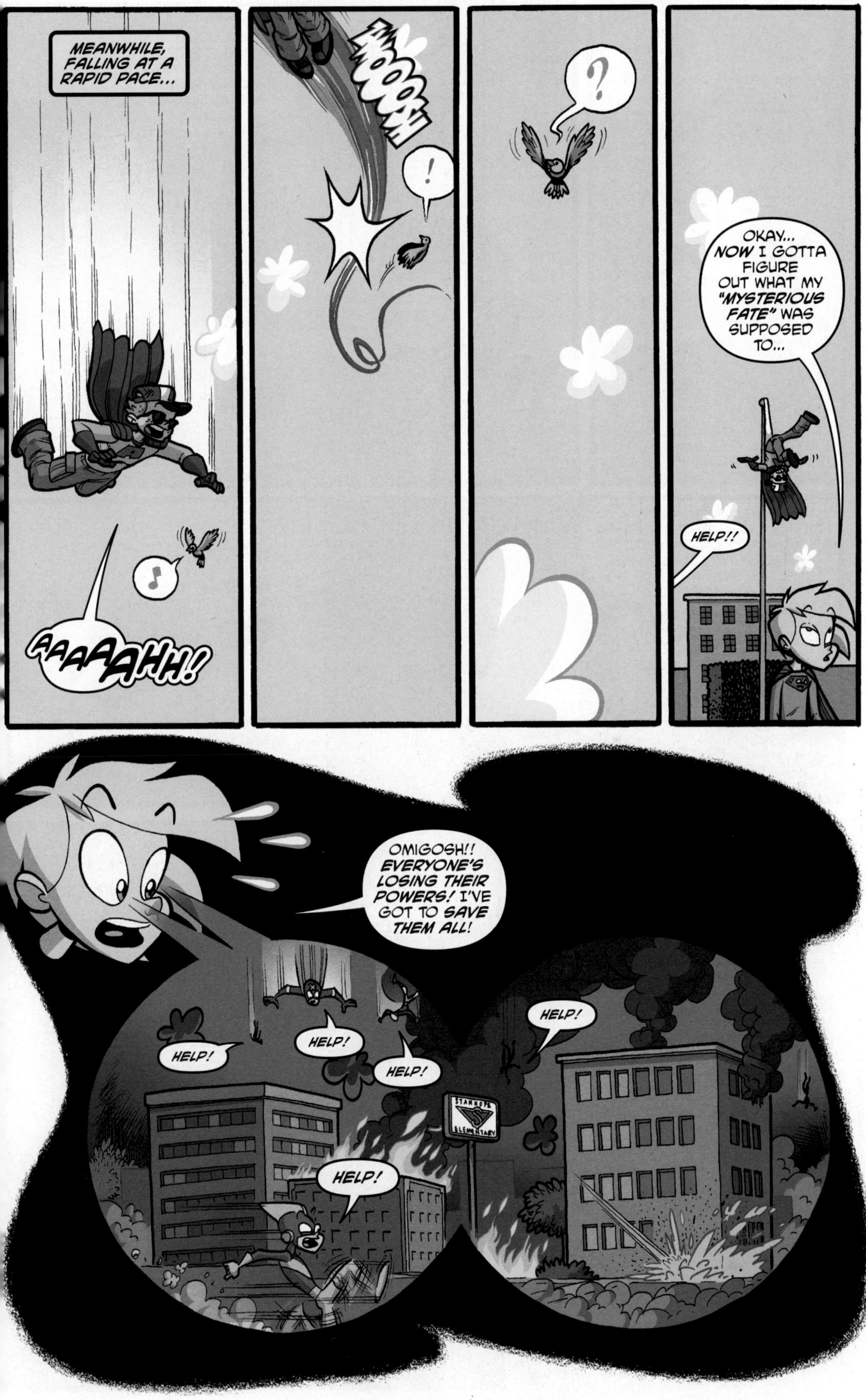
MEANWHILE, FALLING AT A RAPID PACE...
AAAAAHH!
WHOOOOOM!
!
?
OKAY... NOW I GOTTA FIGURE OUT WHAT MY "MYSTERIOUS FATE" WAS SUPPOSED TO...
HELP!!
OMIGOSH!! EVERYONE'S LOSING THEIR POWERS! I'VE GOT TO SAVE THEM ALL!
HELP!
HELP!
HELP!
HELP!
HELP!
STANHOPE ELEMENTARY

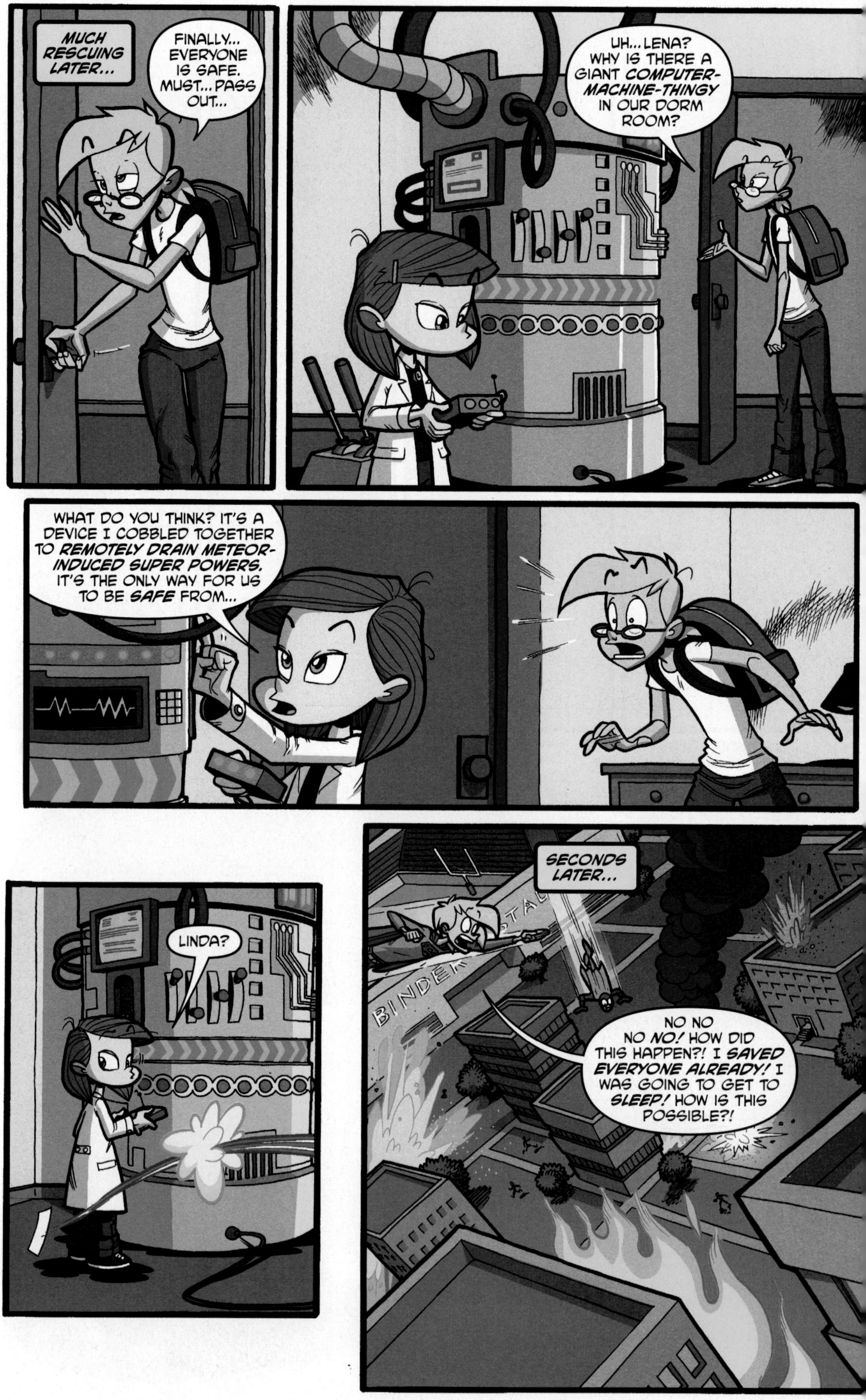
MUCH RESCUING LATER...
FINALLY... EVERYONE IS SAFE. MUST... PASS OUT...
UH... LENA? WHY IS THERE A GIANT COMPUTER-MACHINE-THINGY IN OUR DORM ROOM?
WHAT DO YOU THINK? IT'S A DEVICE I COBBLED TOGETHER TO REMOTELY DRAIN METEOR-INDUCED SUPER POWERS. IT'S THE ONLY WAY FOR US TO BE SAFE FROM...
LINDA?
SECONDS LATER...
NO NO NO NO! HOW DID THIS HAPPEN?! I SAVED EVERYONE ALREADY! I WAS GOING TO GET TO SLEEP! HOW IS THIS POSSIBLE?!

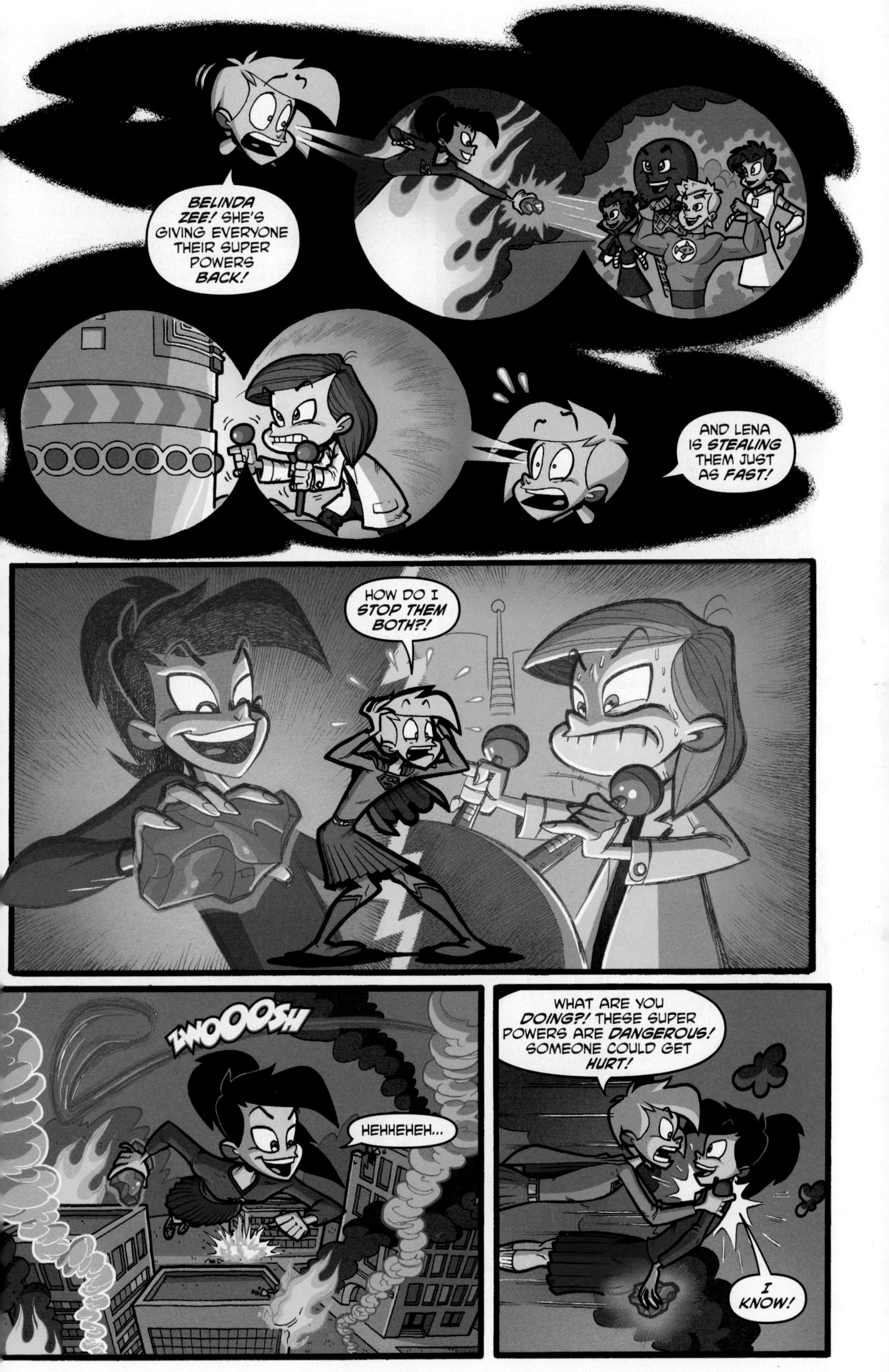

BELINDA ZEE! SHE'S GIVING EVERYONE THEIR SUPER POWERS BACK!
AND LENA IS STEALING THEM JUST AS FAST!
HOW DO I STOP THEM BOTH?!
ZWOOOSH
HEHHEHEH...
WHAT ARE YOU DOING?! THESE SUPER POWERS ARE DANGEROUS! SOMEONE COULD GET HURT!
I KNOW!

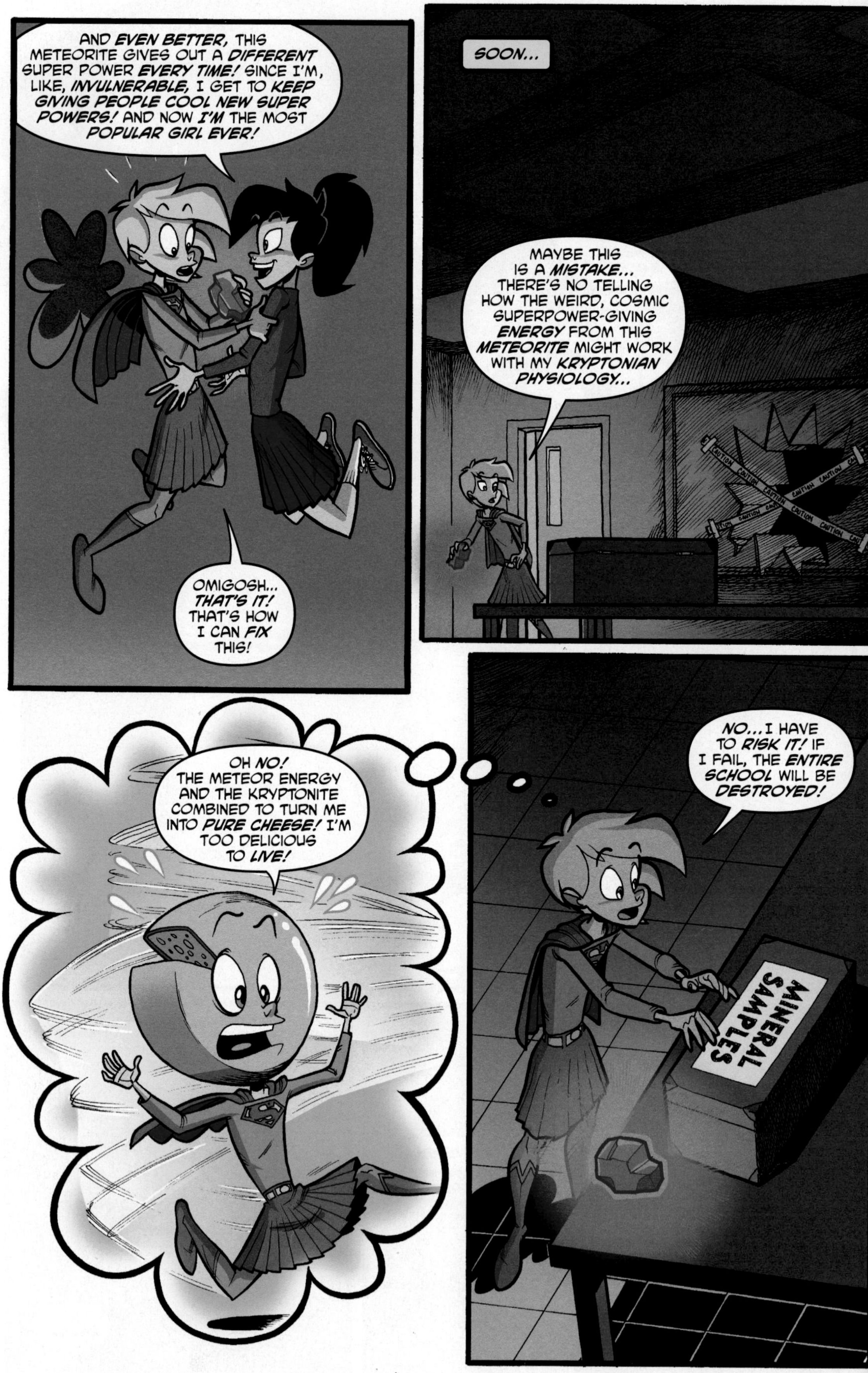
AND EVEN BETTER, THIS METEORITE GIVES OUT A DIFFERENT SUPER POWER EVERY TIME! SINCE I'M, LIKE, INVULNERABLE, I GET TO KEEP GIVING PEOPLE COOL NEW SUPER POWERS! AND NOW I'M THE MOST POPULAR GIRL EVER!
OMIGOSH... THAT'S IT! THAT'S HOW I CAN FIX THIS!
SOON...
MAYBE THIS IS A MISTAKE... THERE'S NO TELLING HOW THE WEIRD, COSMIC SUPERPOWER-GIVING ENERGY FROM THIS METEORITE MIGHT WORK WITH MY KRYPTONIAN PHYSIOLOGY...
CAUTION
OH NO! THE METEOR ENERGY AND THE KRYPTONITE COMBINED TO TURN ME INTO PURE CHEESE! I'M TOO DELICIOUS TO LIVE!
NO...I HAVE TO RISK IT! IF I FAIL, THE ENTIRE SCHOOL WILL BE DESTROYED!
MINERAL SAMPLES

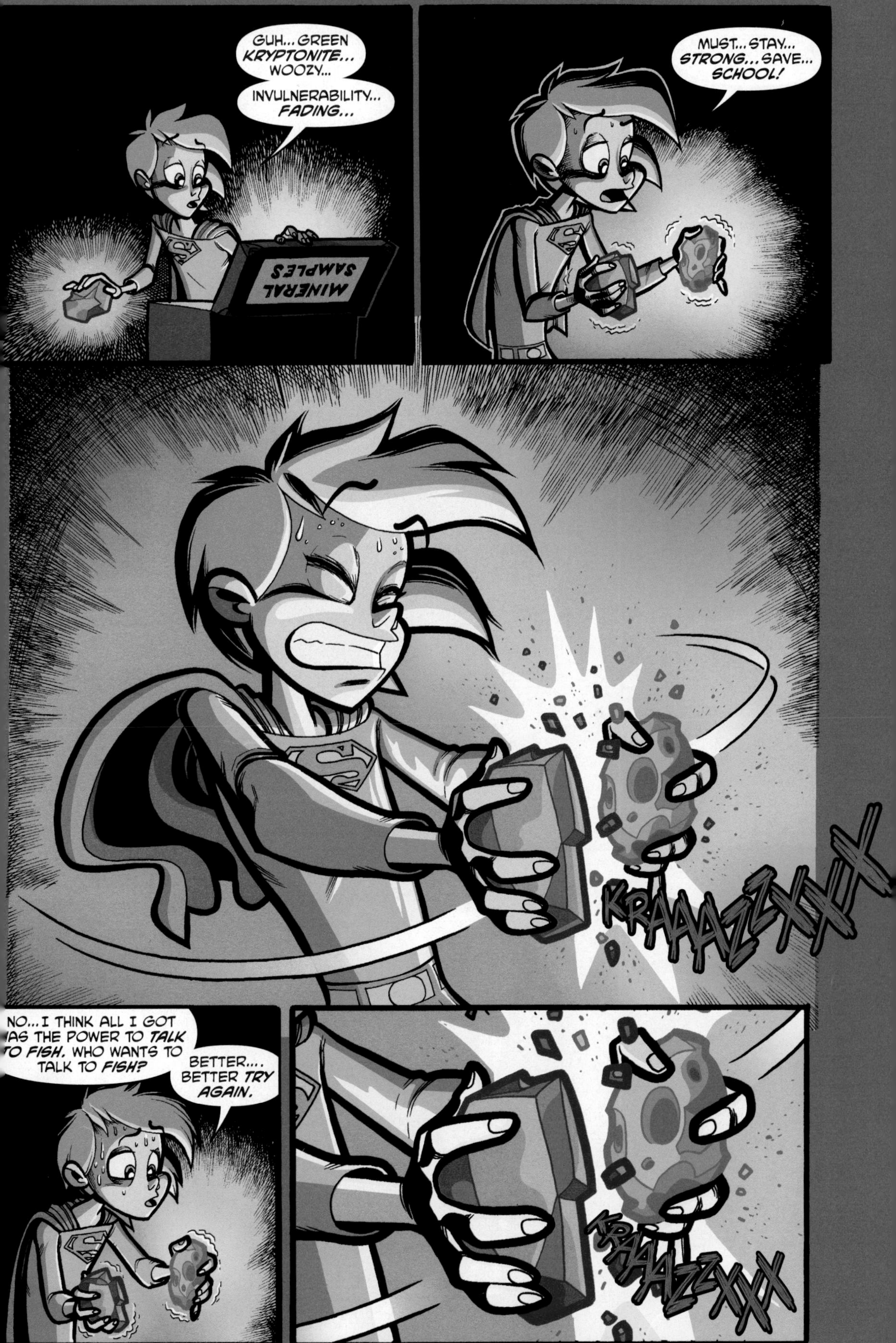
GUH... GREEN KRYPTONITE... WOOZY...
INVULNERABILITY... FADING...
MINERAL SAMPLES
MUST... STAY... STRONG... SAVE... SCHOOL!
KRAAAAZZXXXX
NO... I THINK ALL I GOT AS THE POWER TO TALK TO FISH. WHO WANTS TO TALK TO FISH?
BETTER.... BETTER TRY AGAIN.
KRAAAZZXXX

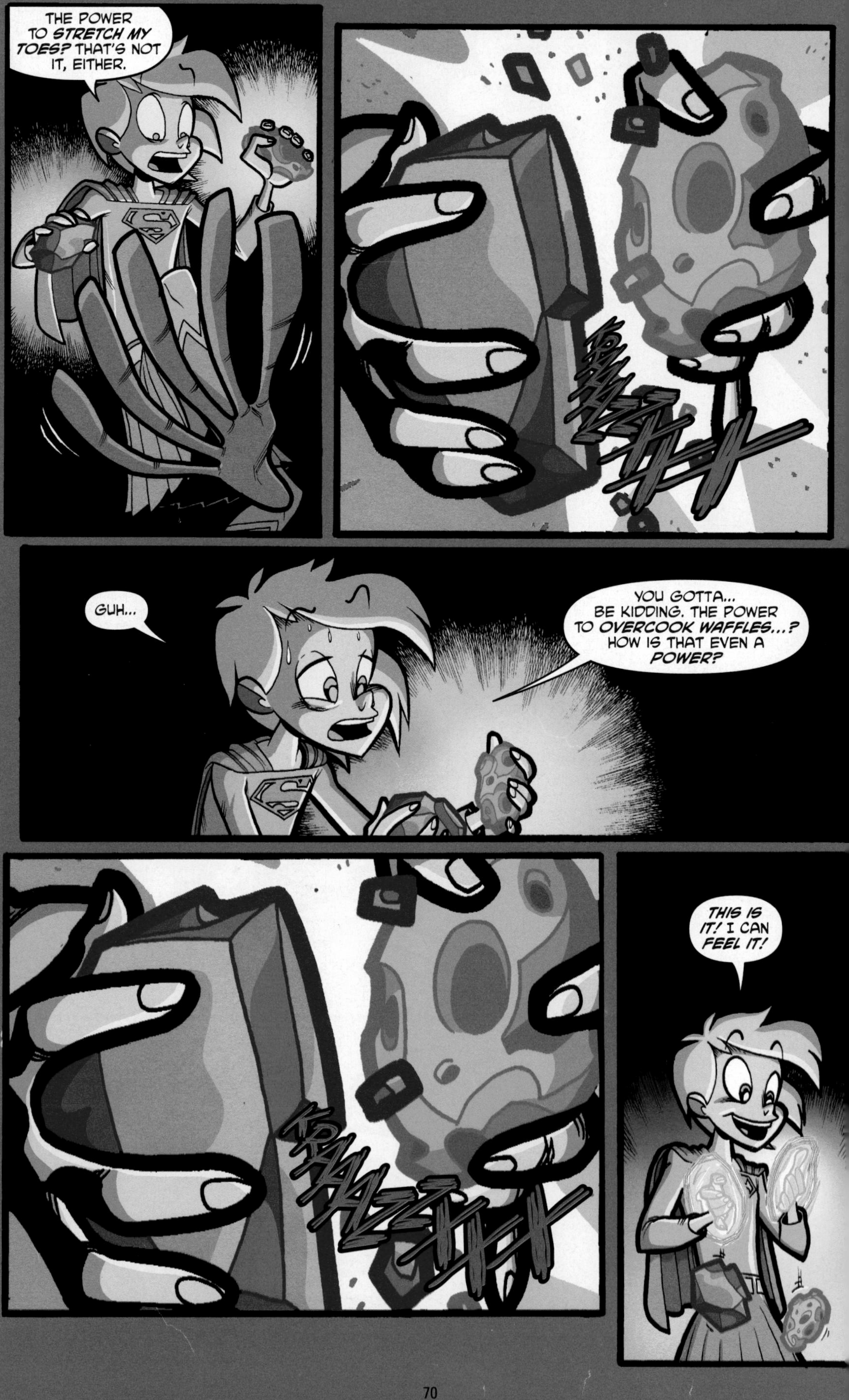
THE POWER TO STRETCH MY TOES? THAT'S NOT IT, EITHER.
GUH...
YOU GOTTA... BE KIDDING. THE POWER TO OVERCOOK WAFFLES...? HOW IS THAT EVEN A POWER?
THIS IS IT! I CAN FEEL IT!

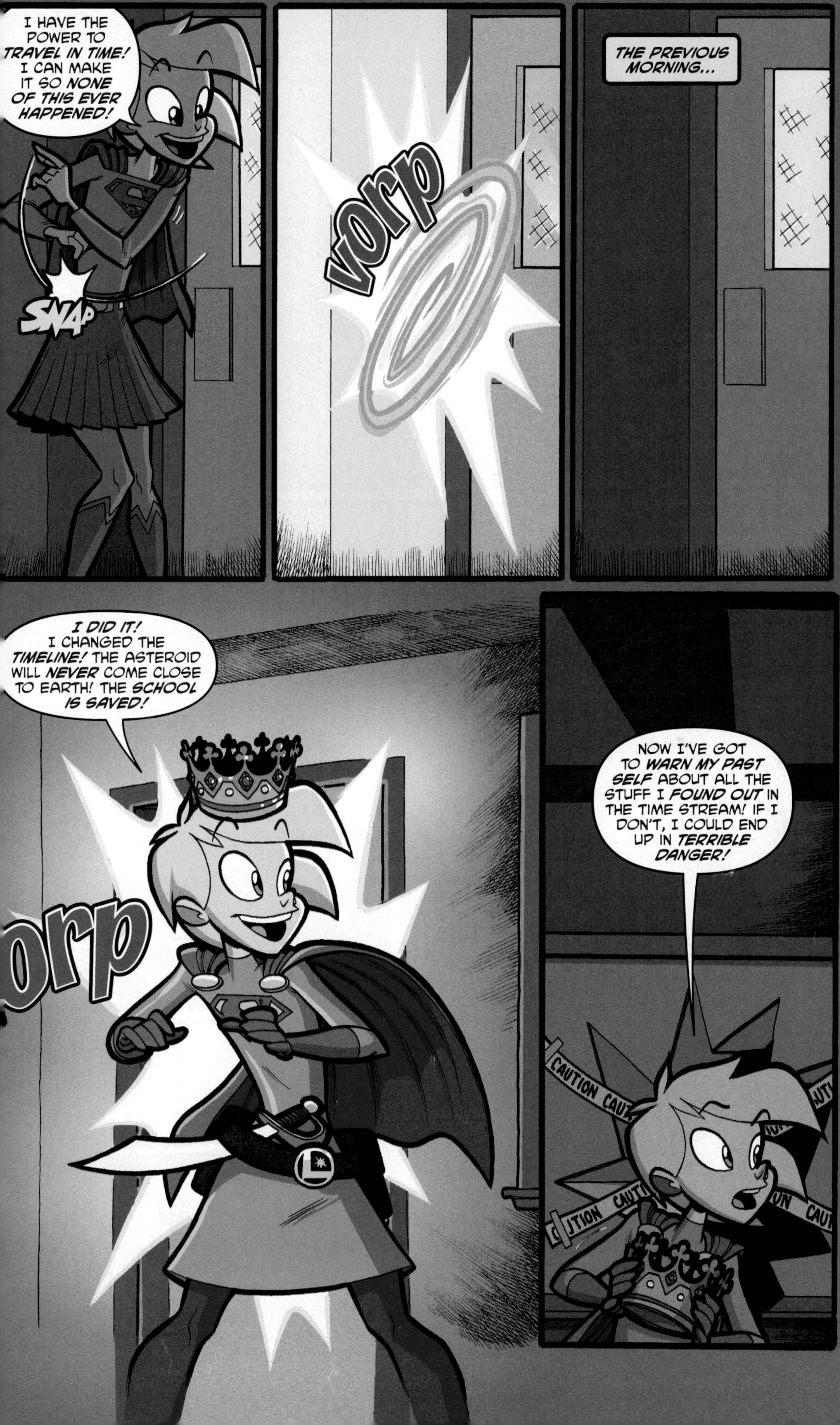
I HAVE THE POWER TO TRAVEL IN TIME! I CAN MAKE IT SO NONE OF THIS EVER HAPPENED!
SNAP
VORP
THE PREVIOUS MORNING...
I DID IT! I CHANGED THE TIMELINE! THE ASTEROID WILL NEVER COME CLOSE TO EARTH! THE SCHOOL IS SAVED!
VORP
NOW I'VE GOT TO WARN MY PAST SELF ABOUT ALL THE STUFF I FOUND OUT IN THE TIME STREAM! IF I DON'T, I COULD END UP IN TERRIBLE DANGER!
CAUTION

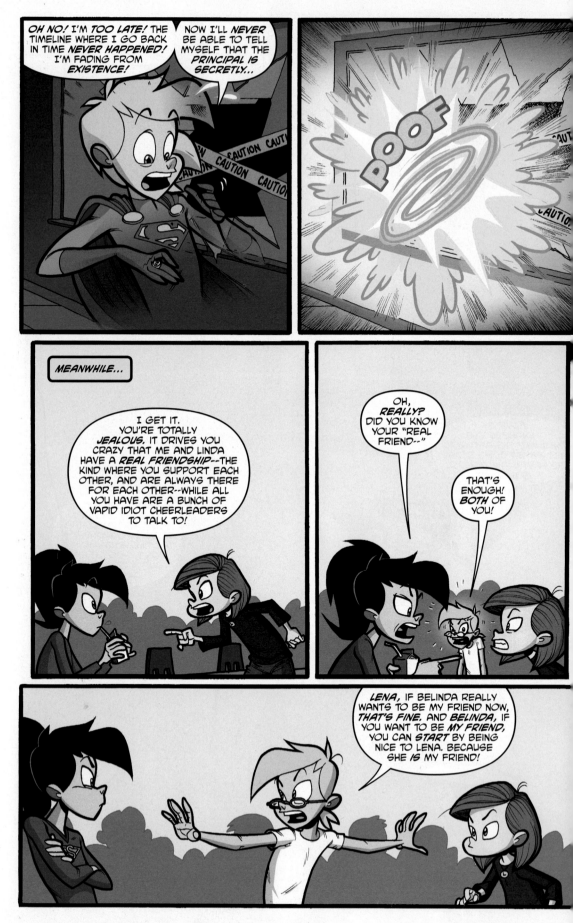

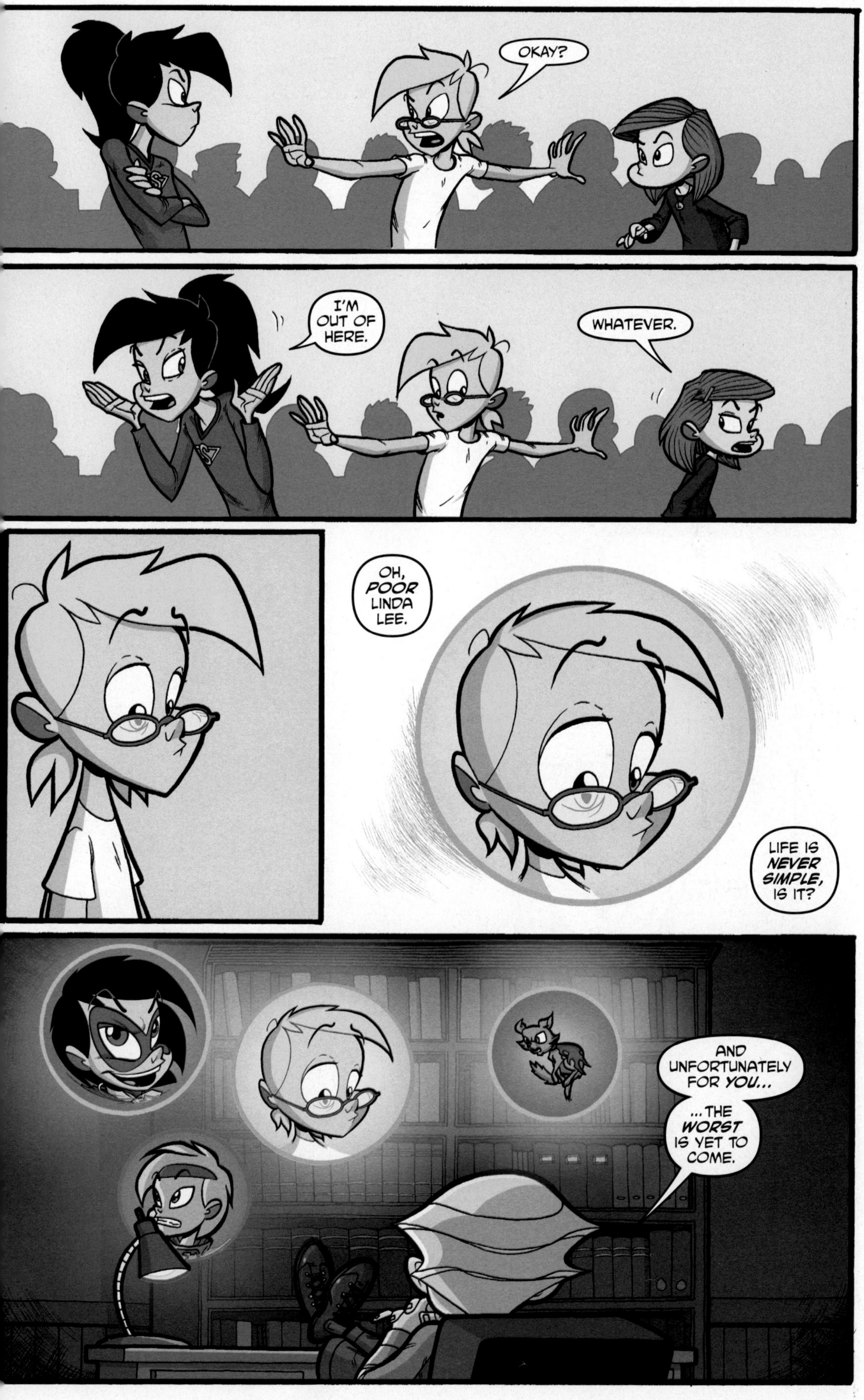
OKAY?
I'M OUT OF HERE.
WHATEVER.
OH, *POOR* LINDA LEE.
LIFE IS *NEVER SIMPLE,* IS IT?
AND UNFORTUNATELY FOR *YOU...*
...THE *WORST* IS YET TO COME.

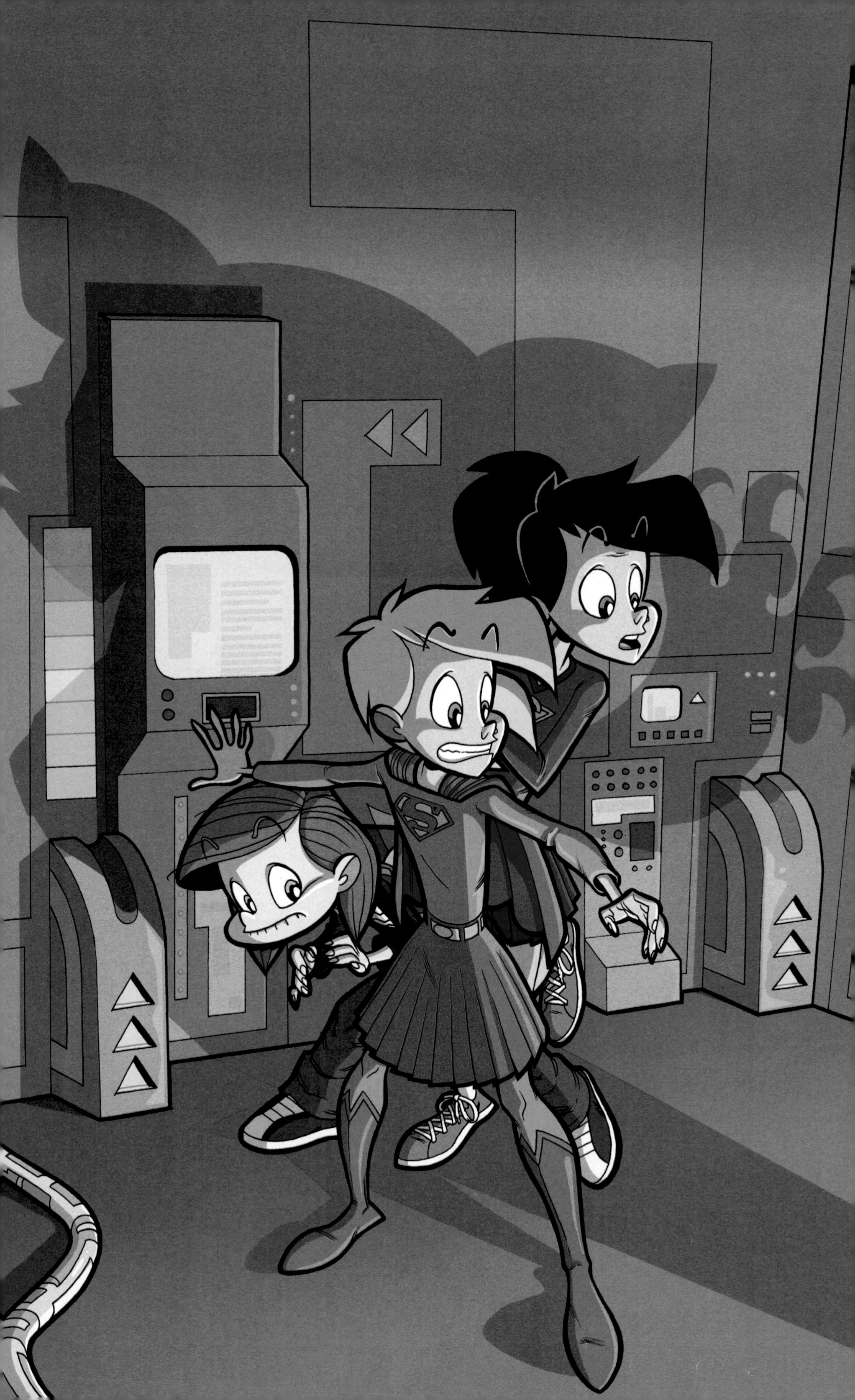

PART 1: "SECRET ENTITY!"

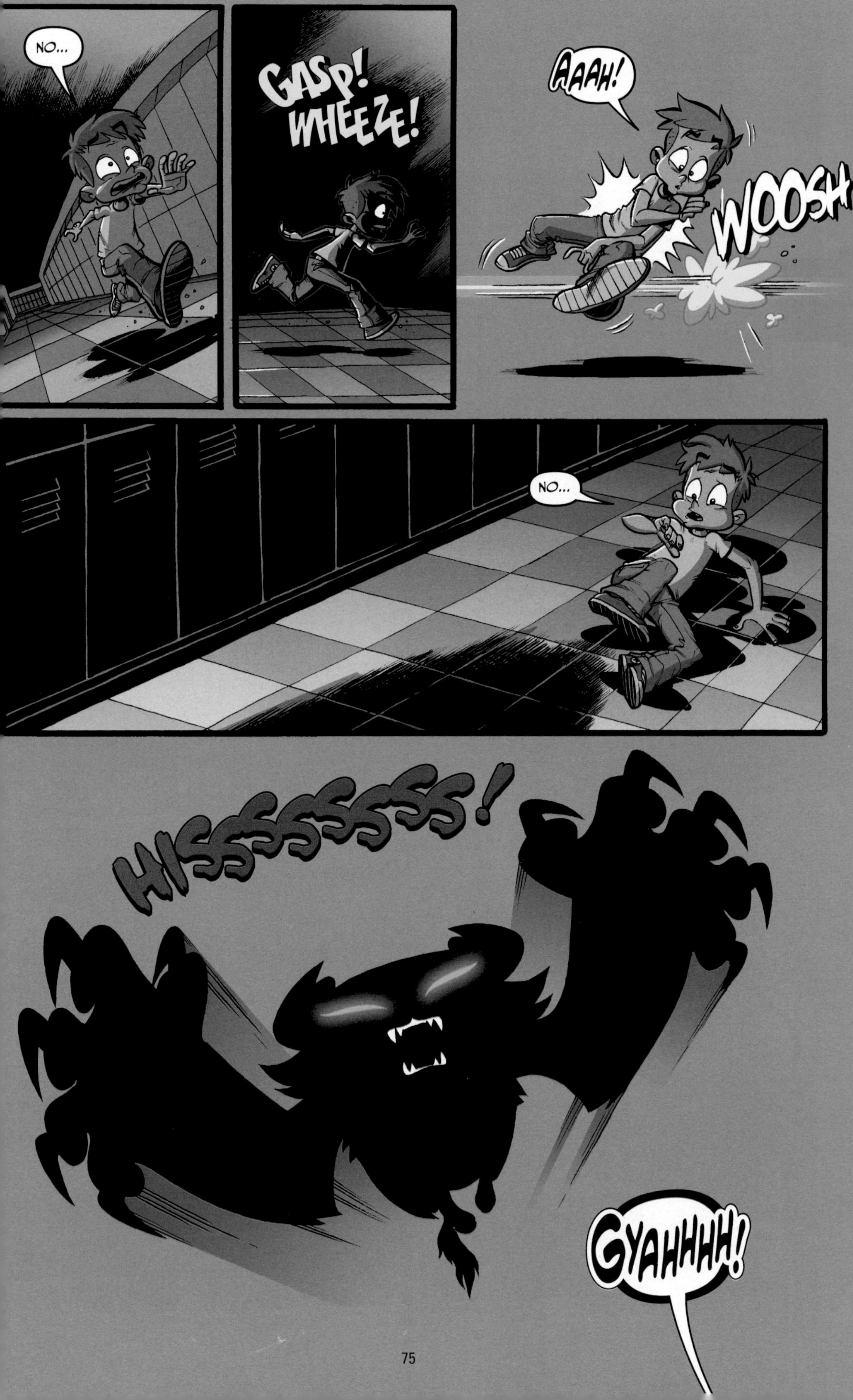

NO...
GASP! WHEEZE!
AAAH!
WOOSH
NO...
HISSSSSSSS!
GYAHHHH!

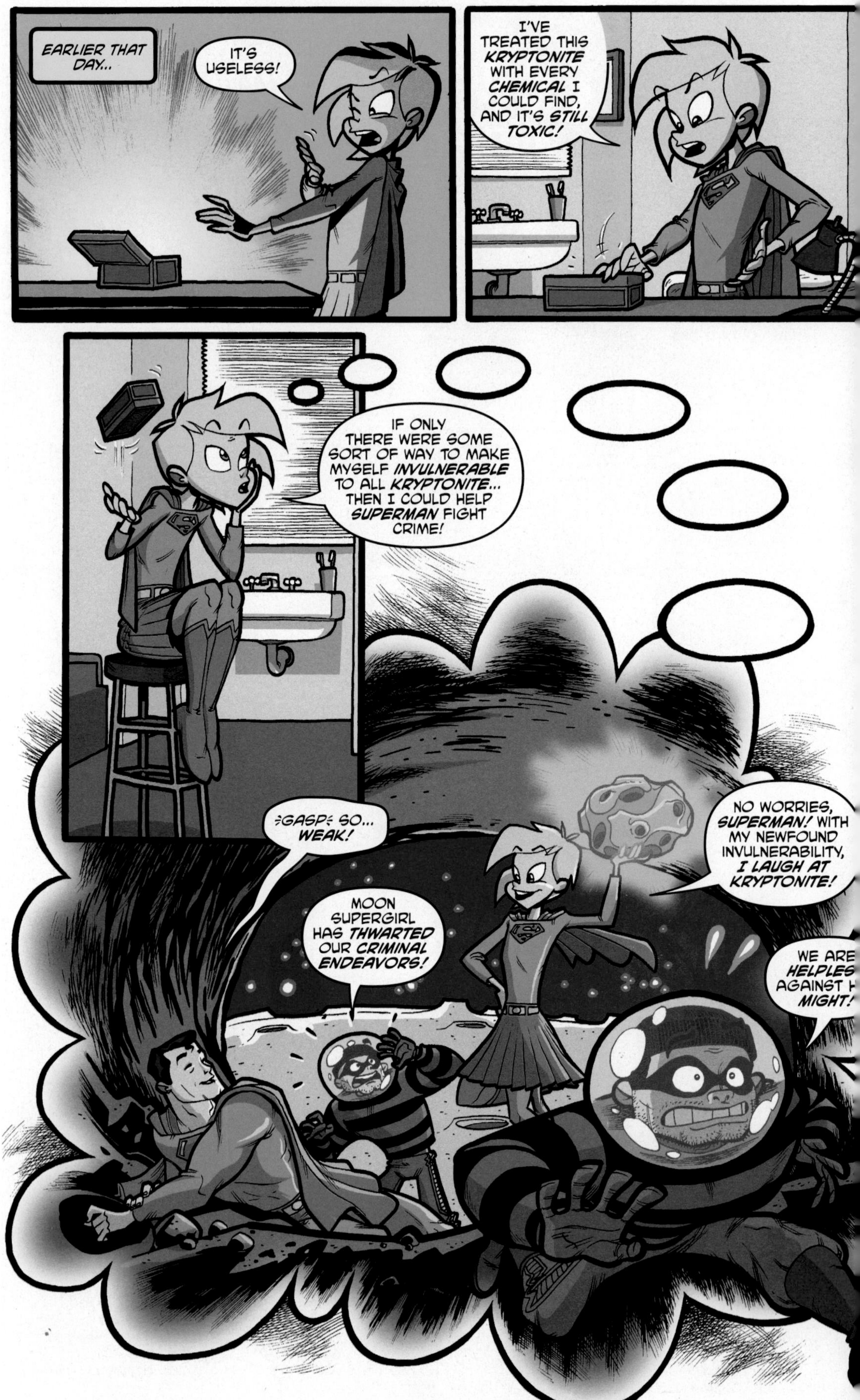

EARLIER THAT DAY...
IT'S USELESS!
I'VE TREATED THIS KRYPTONITE WITH EVERY CHEMICAL I COULD FIND, AND IT'S STILL TOXIC!
IF ONLY THERE WERE SOME SORT OF WAY TO MAKE MYSELF INVULNERABLE TO ALL KRYPTONITE... THEN I COULD HELP SUPERMAN FIGHT CRIME!
GASP SO... WEAK!
NO WORRIES, SUPERMAN! WITH MY NEWFOUND INVULNERABILITY, I LAUGH AT KRYPTONITE!
MOON SUPERGIRL HAS THWARTED OUR CRIMINAL ENDEAVORS!
WE ARE HELPLES AGAINST H MIGHT!

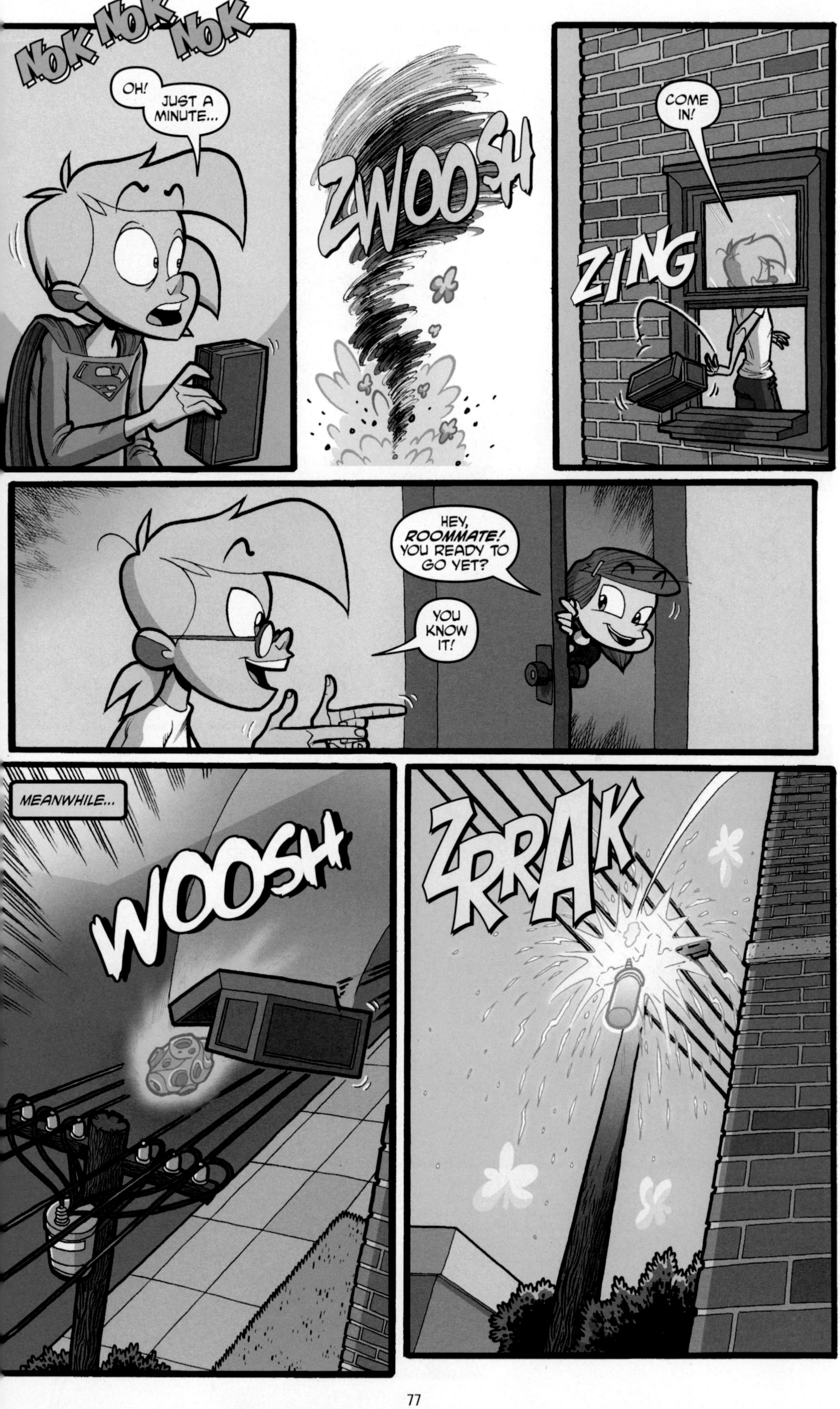
NOK NOK NOK
OH!
JUST A MINUTE...
ZWOOSH
COME IN!
ZING
HEY, ROOMMATE! YOU READY TO GO YET?
YOU KNOW IT!
MEANWHILE...
WOOSH
ZRRAK

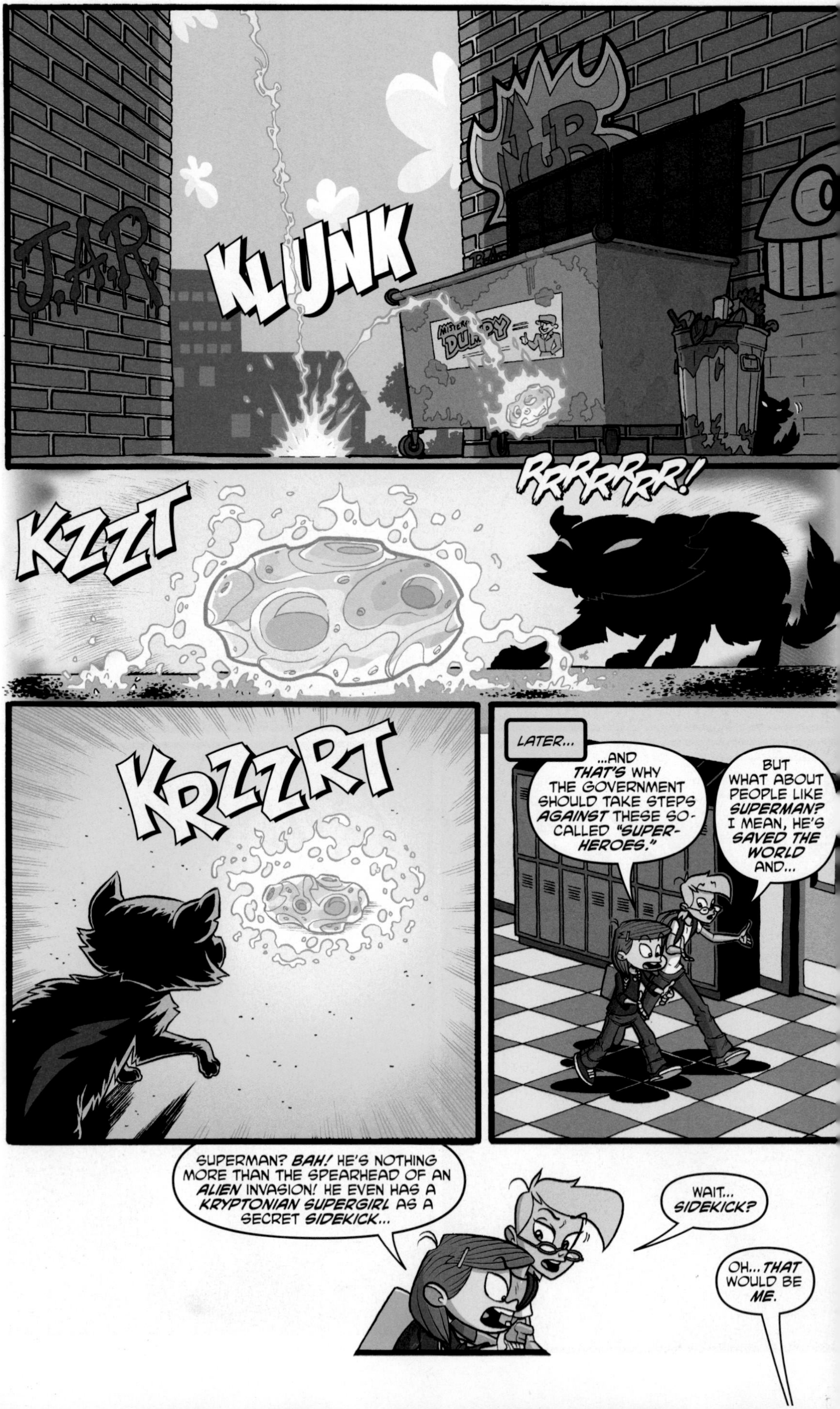
J.A.R.
KLUNK
KZZZT
RRRRRRR!
KRZZZRT
LATER...
...AND THAT'S WHY THE GOVERNMENT SHOULD TAKE STEPS AGAINST THESE SO-CALLED "SUPER-HEROES."
BUT WHAT ABOUT PEOPLE LIKE SUPERMAN? I MEAN, HE'S SAVED THE WORLD AND...
SUPERMAN? BAH! HE'S NOTHING MORE THAN THE SPEARHEAD OF AN ALIEN INVASION! HE EVEN HAS A KRYPTONIAN SUPERGIRL AS A SECRET SIDEKICK...
WAIT... SIDEKICK?
OH... THAT WOULD BE ME.

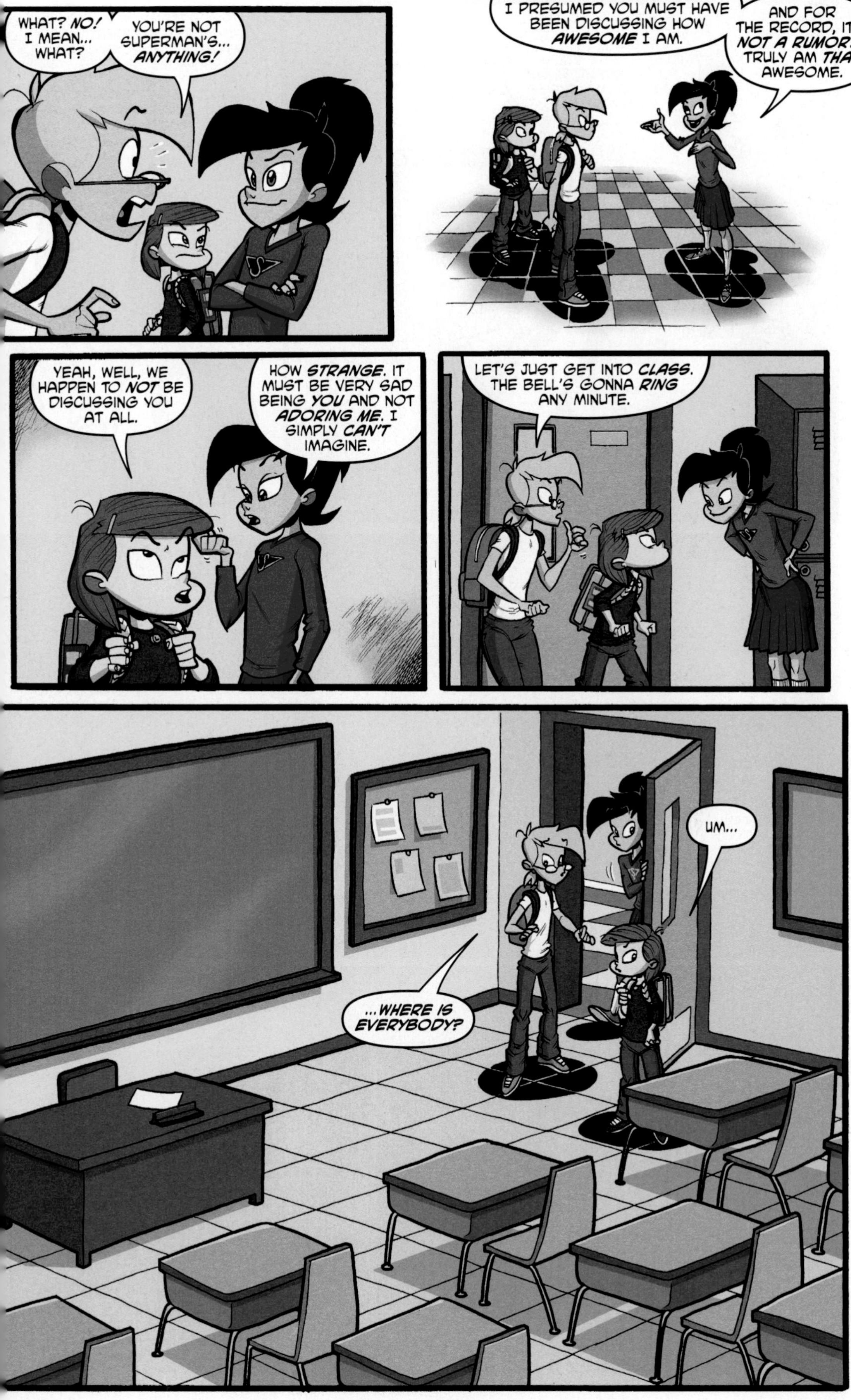
WHAT? NO! I MEAN... WHAT?
YOU'RE NOT SUPERMAN'S... ANYTHING!
OH... IS THAT WHAT YOU'RE TALKING ABOUT? I PRESUMED YOU MUST HAVE BEEN DISCUSSING HOW AWESOME I AM.
AND FOR THE RECORD, IT'S NOT A RUMOR. I TRULY AM THAT AWESOME.
YEAH, WELL, WE HAPPEN TO NOT BE DISCUSSING YOU AT ALL.
HOW STRANGE. IT MUST BE VERY SAD BEING YOU AND NOT ADORING ME. I SIMPLY CAN'T IMAGINE.
LET'S JUST GET INTO CLASS. THE BELL'S GONNA RING ANY MINUTE.
UM...
...WHERE IS EVERYBODY?

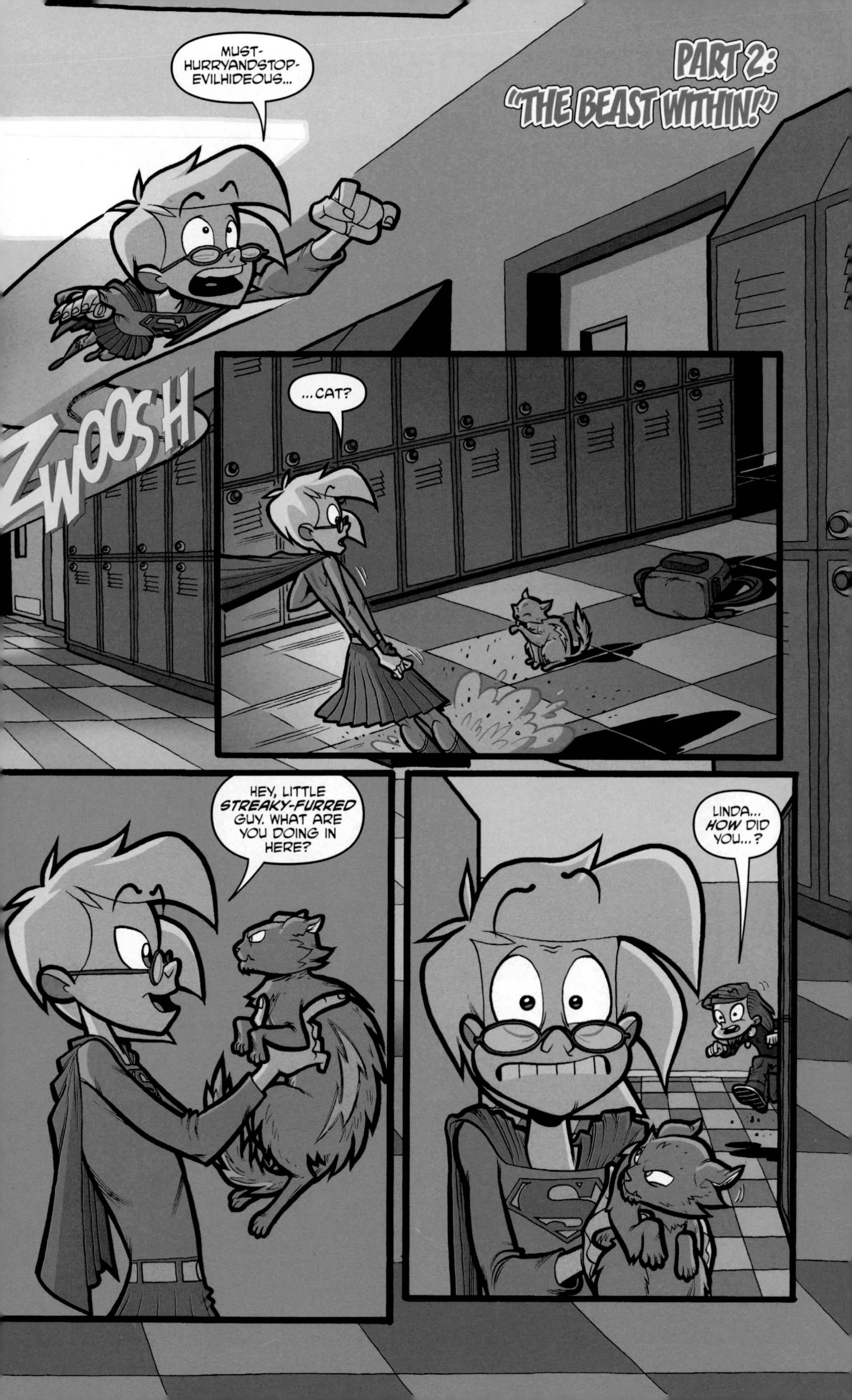
MUST-HURRYANDSTOP-EVILHIDEOUS...
PART 2: "THE BEAST WITHIN!"
ZWOOSH
...CAT?
HEY, LITTLE STREAKY-FURRED GUY. WHAT ARE YOU DOING IN HERE?
LINDA... HOW DID YOU...?

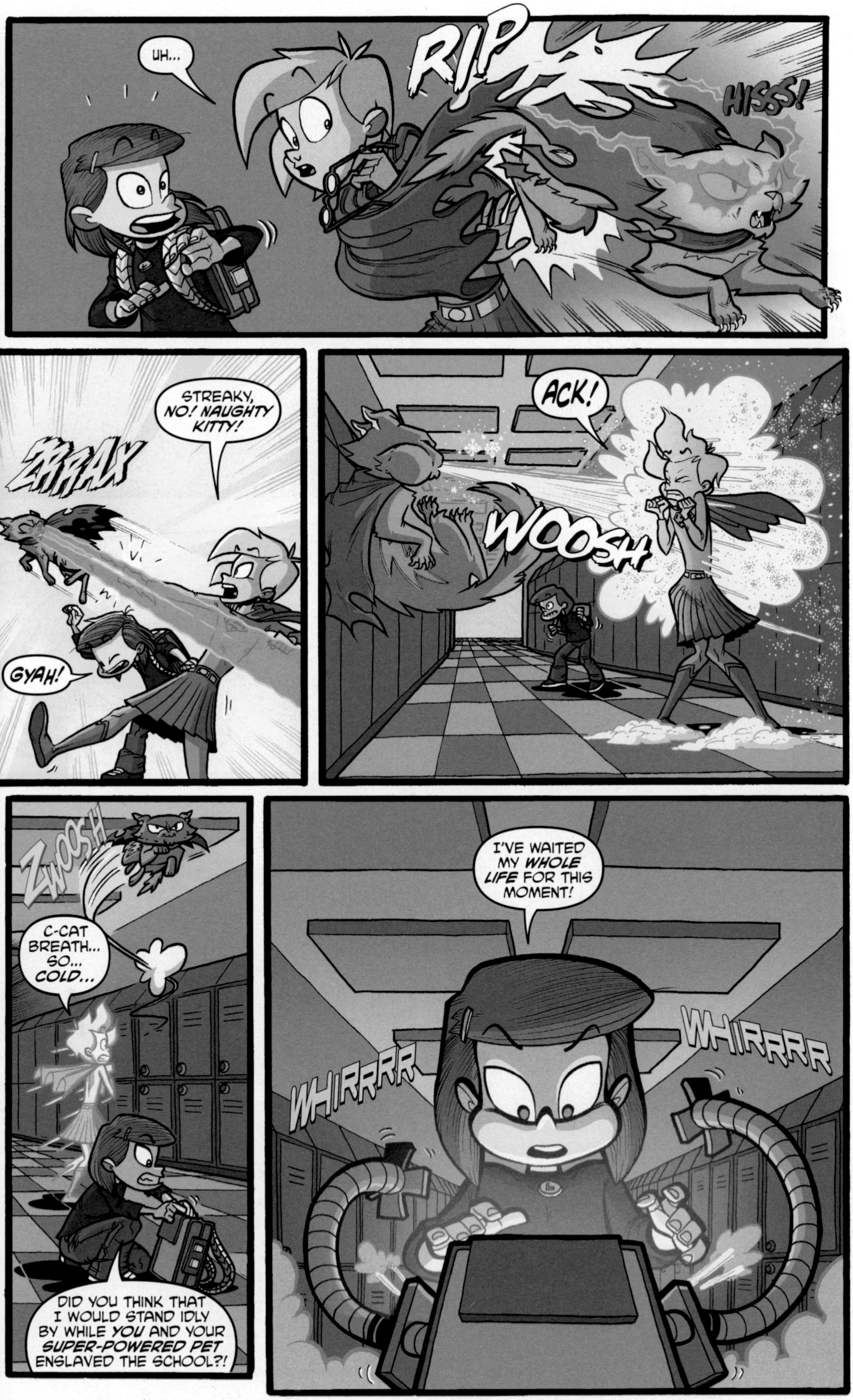
UH...
RIP
HISSS!
STREAKY, NO! NAUGHTY KITTY!
ZRRAX
GYAH!
ACK!
WOOSH
ZWOOSH
C-CAT BREATH... SO... COLD...
DID YOU THINK THAT I WOULD STAND IDLY BY WHILE YOU AND YOUR SUPER-POWERED PET ENSLAVED THE SCHOOL?!
I'VE WAITED MY WHOLE LIFE FOR THIS MOMENT!
WHIRRRR
WHIRRRR

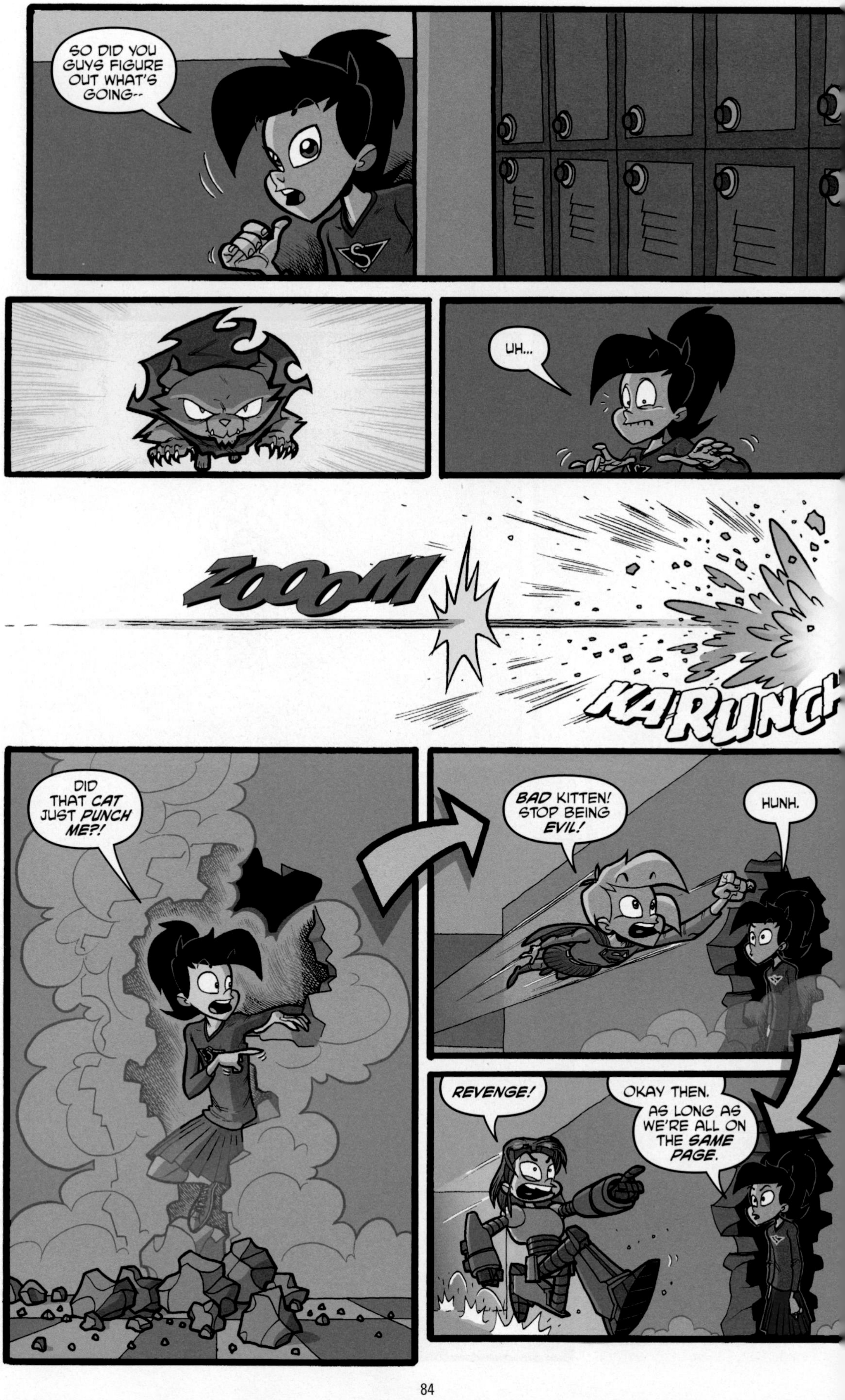
SO DID YOU GUYS FIGURE OUT WHAT'S GOING--
UH...
ZOOOM
KARUNCH
DID THAT *CAT* JUST *PUNCH ME?!*
BAD KITTEN! STOP BEING *EVIL!*
HUNH.
REVENGE!
OKAY THEN.
AS LONG AS WE'RE ALL ON THE *SAME PAGE*.

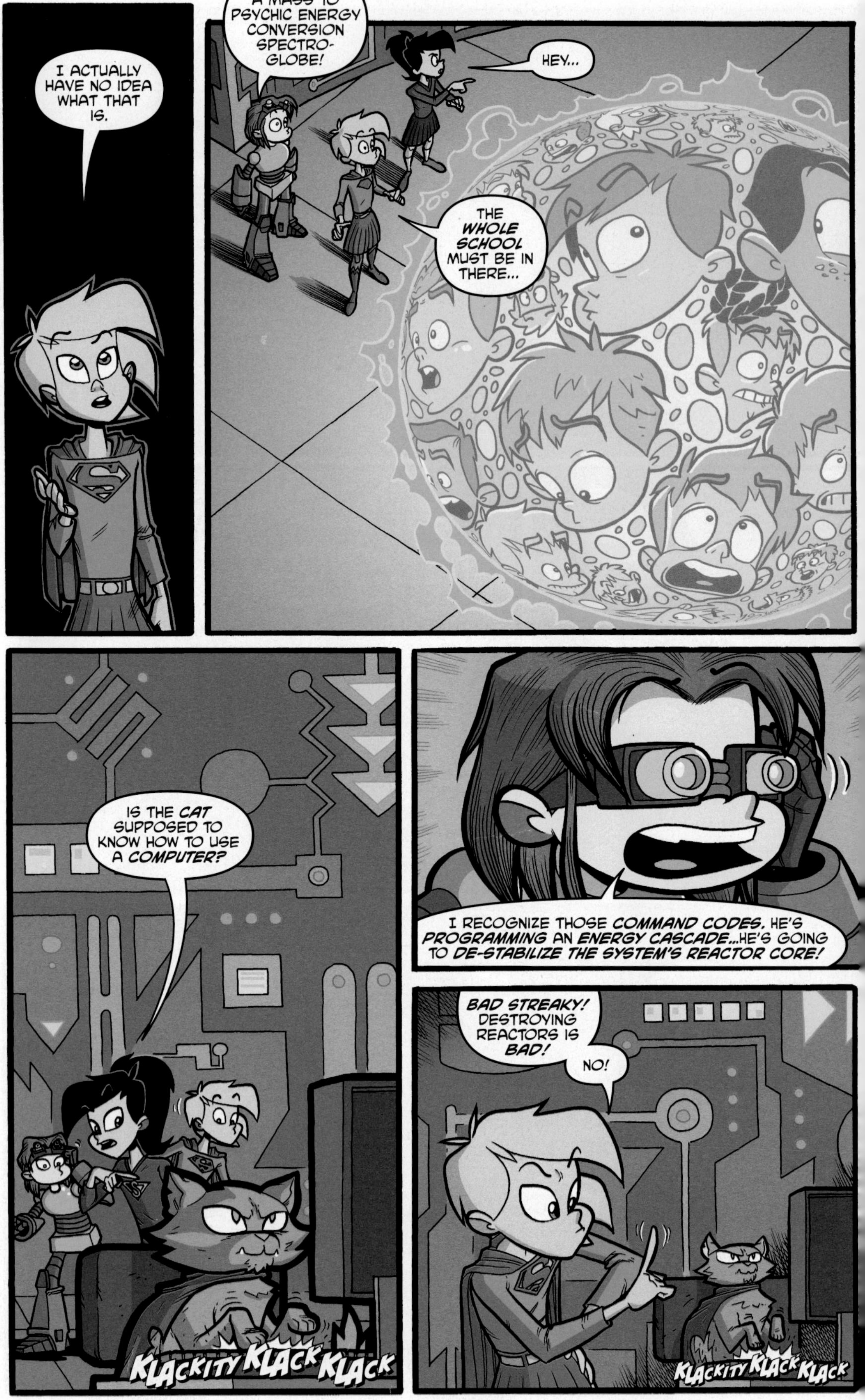
I ACTUALLY HAVE NO IDEA WHAT THAT IS.
THAT'S A MASS TO PSYCHIC ENERGY CONVERSION SPECTRO-GLOBE!
HEY...
THE *WHOLE SCHOOL* MUST BE IN THERE...
IS THE *CAT* SUPPOSED TO KNOW HOW TO USE A *COMPUTER?*
KLACKITY KLACK KLACK
I RECOGNIZE THOSE *COMMAND CODES.* HE'S *PROGRAMMING* AN *ENERGY CASCADE*...HE'S GOING TO *DE-STABILIZE THE SYSTEM'S REACTOR CORE!*
BAD STREAKY! DESTROYING REACTORS IS *BAD!*
NO!
KLACKITY KLACK KLACK

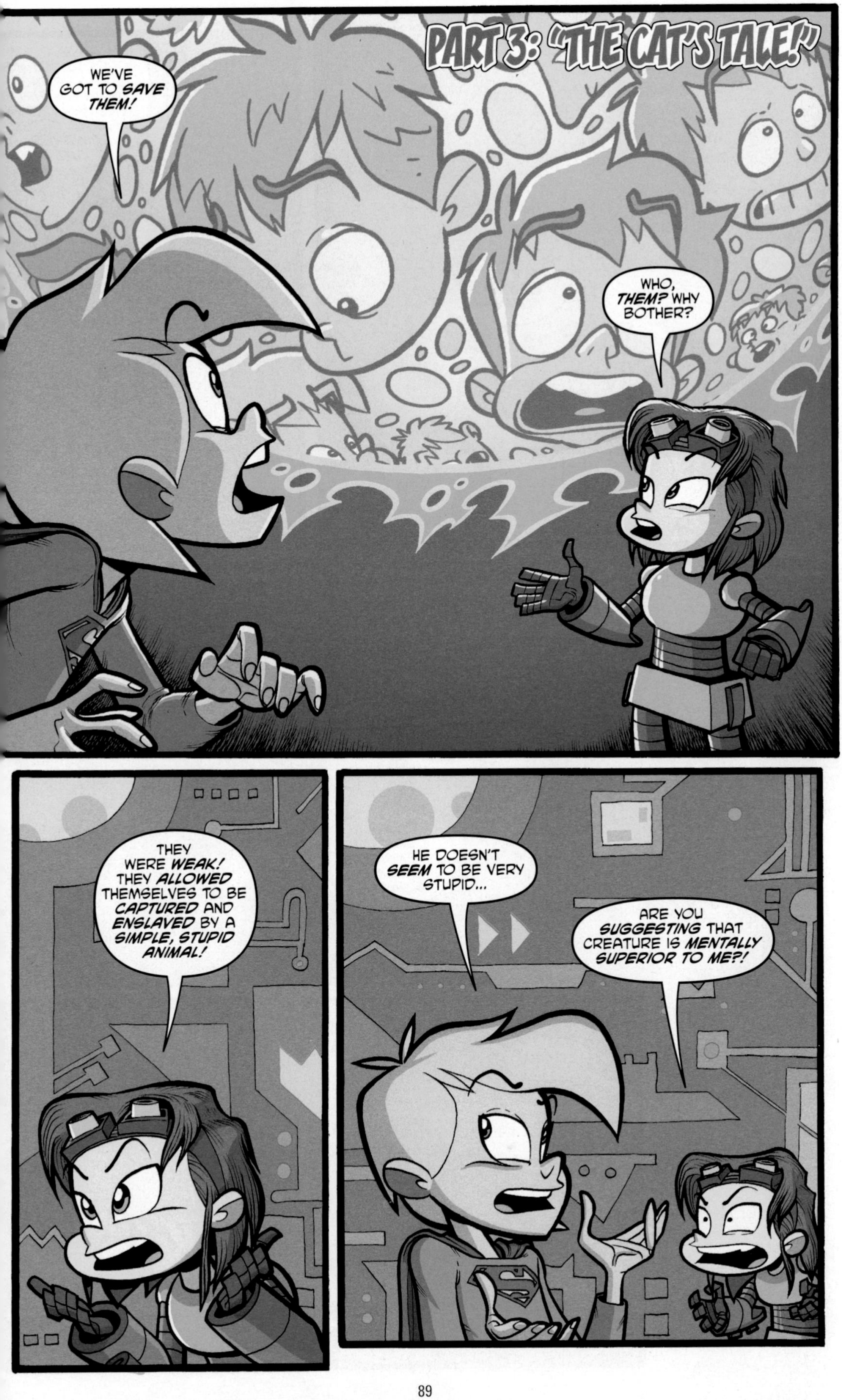
PART 3: "THE CAT'S TALE!"
WE'VE GOT TO SAVE THEM!
WHO, THEM? WHY BOTHER?
THEY WERE WEAK! THEY ALLOWED THEMSELVES TO BE CAPTURED AND ENSLAVED BY A SIMPLE, STUPID ANIMAL!
HE DOESN'T SEEM TO BE VERY STUPID...
ARE YOU SUGGESTING THAT CREATURE IS MENTALLY SUPERIOR TO ME?!

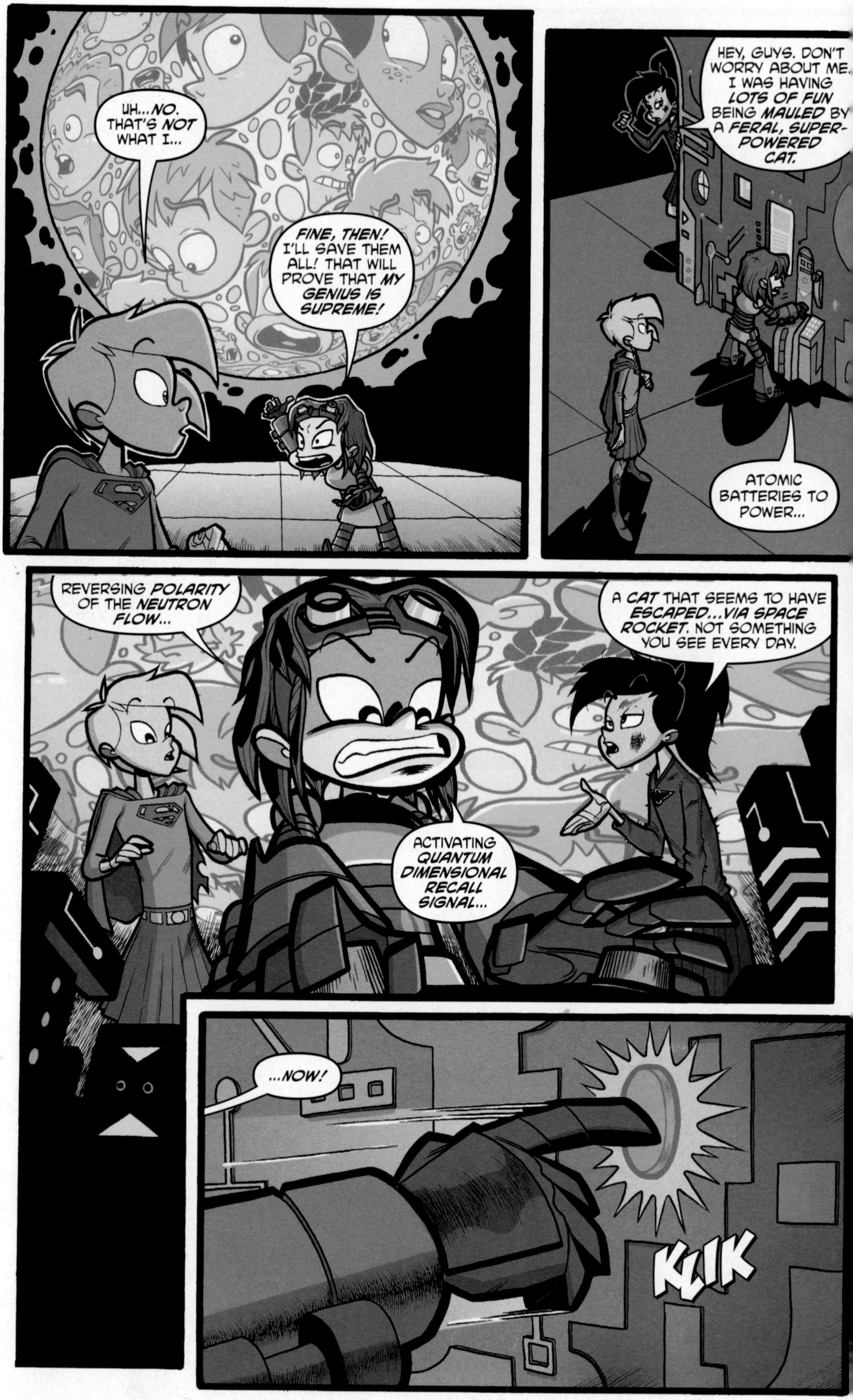
UH...NO. THAT'S NOT WHAT I...
FINE, THEN! I'LL SAVE THEM ALL! THAT WILL PROVE THAT MY GENIUS IS SUPREME!
HEY, GUYS. DON'T WORRY ABOUT ME. I WAS HAVING LOTS OF FUN BEING MAULED BY A FERAL, SUPER-POWERED CAT.
ATOMIC BATTERIES TO POWER...
REVERSING POLARITY OF THE NEUTRON FLOW...
A CAT THAT SEEMS TO HAVE ESCAPED...VIA SPACE ROCKET. NOT SOMETHING YOU SEE EVERY DAY.
ACTIVATING QUANTUM DIMENSIONAL RECALL SIGNAL...
...NOW!
KLIK

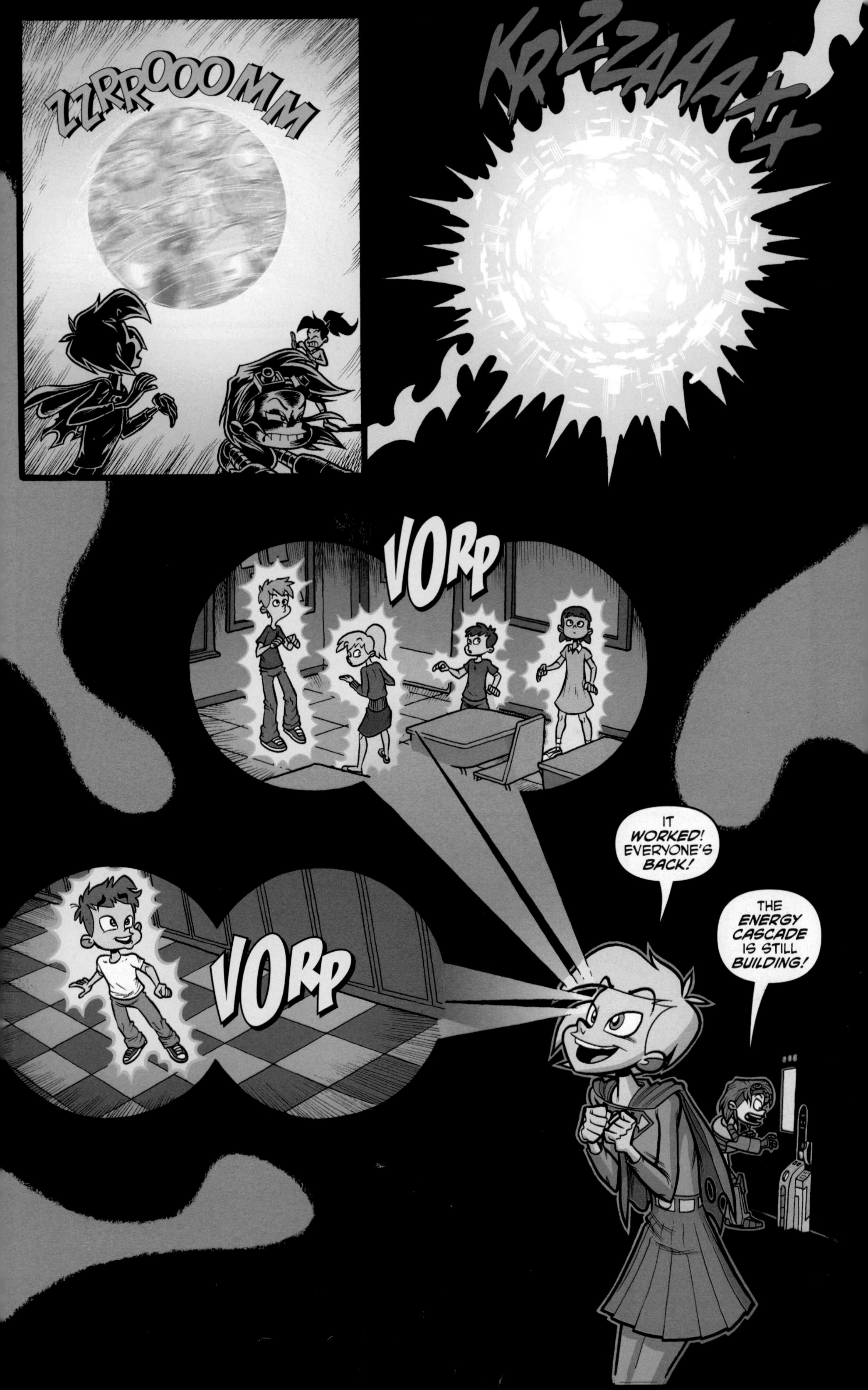
ZZRROOOMM
KRZZAAAK
VORP
IT WORKED! EVERYONE'S BACK!
VORP
THE ENERGY CASCADE IS STILL BUILDING!

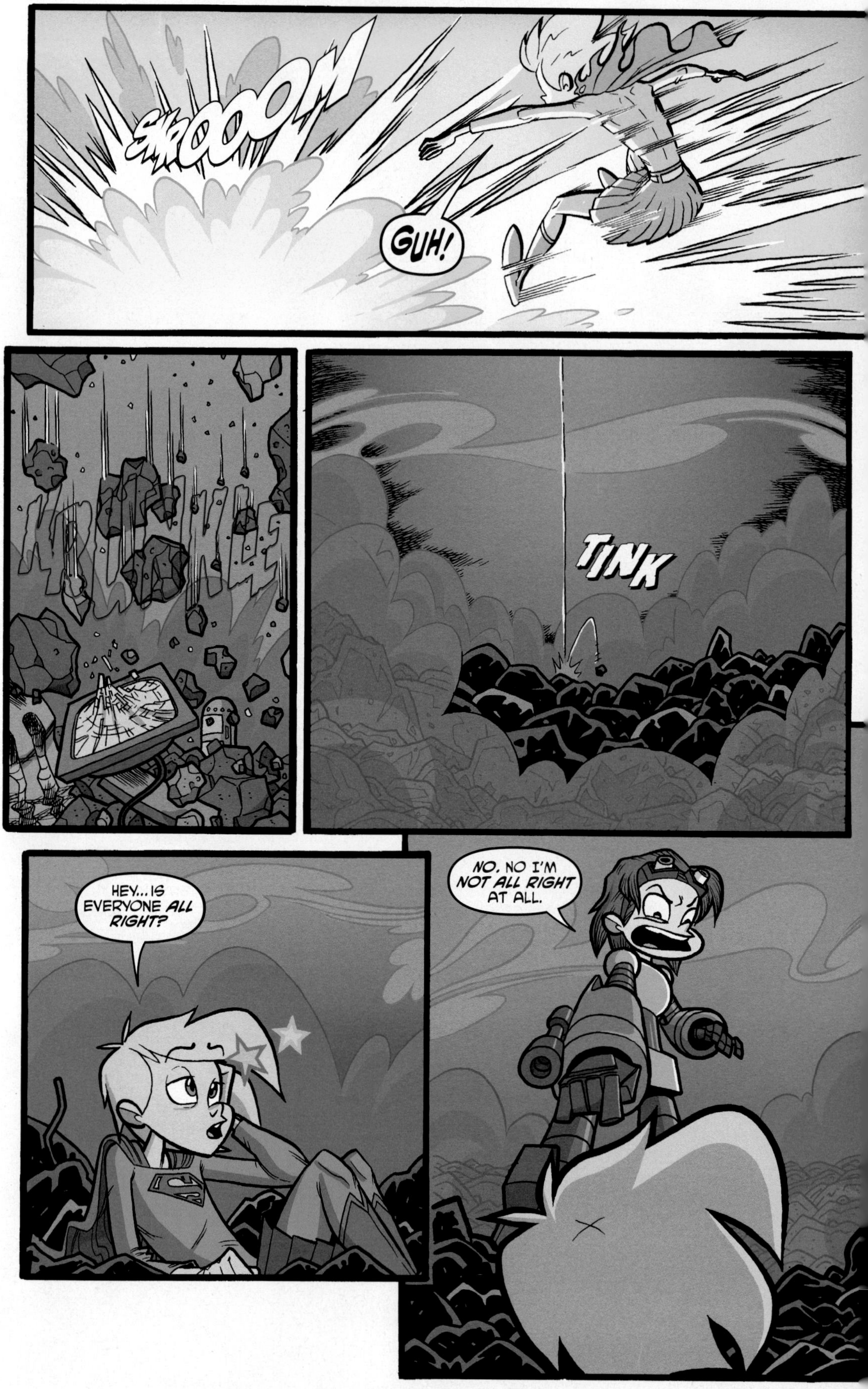
SHOOOM
GUH!
TINK
HEY... IS EVERYONE ALL RIGHT?
NO. NO I'M NOT ALL RIGHT AT ALL.

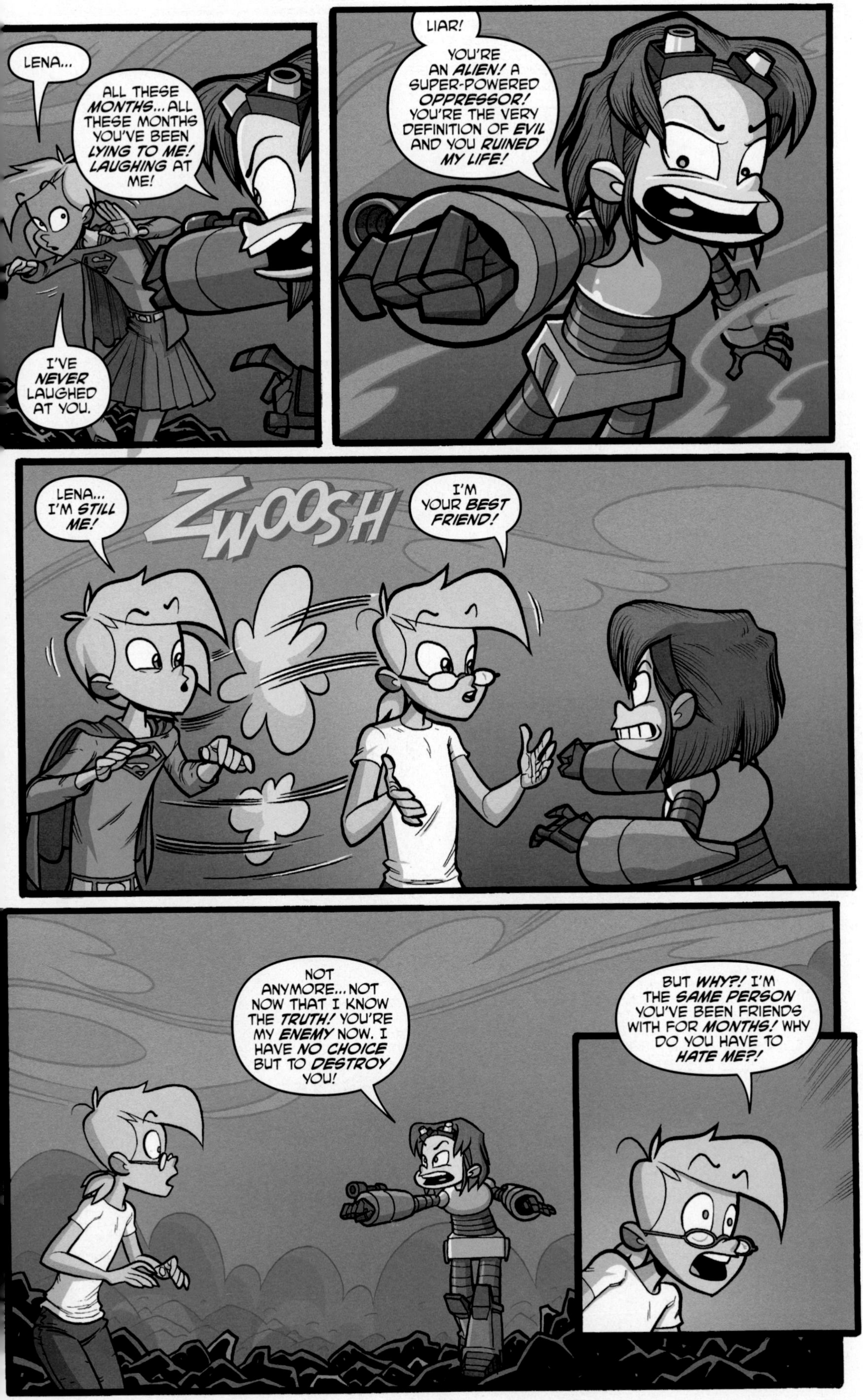
LENA...
ALL THESE MONTHS... ALL THESE MONTHS YOU'VE BEEN LYING TO ME! LAUGHING AT ME!
I'VE NEVER LAUGHED AT YOU.
LIAR!
YOU'RE AN ALIEN! A SUPER-POWERED OPPRESSOR! YOU'RE THE VERY DEFINITION OF EVIL AND YOU RUINED MY LIFE!
LENA... I'M STILL ME!
ZWOOSH
I'M YOUR BEST FRIEND!
NOT ANYMORE... NOT NOW THAT I KNOW THE TRUTH! YOU'RE MY ENEMY NOW. I HAVE NO CHOICE BUT TO DESTROY YOU!
BUT WHY?! I'M THE SAME PERSON YOU'VE BEEN FRIENDS WITH FOR MONTHS! WHY DO YOU HAVE TO HATE ME?!

BECAUSE YOUR KIND OFFENDS THE *NATURAL ORDER!* YOU FLOAT THROUGH THE *SKY* AS IF YOU *OWN* IT! YOU *CHANGE THE COURSE OF RIVERS* WITHOUT A THOUGHT TO THE CONSEQUENCES! YOUR VERY *EXISTENCE* UNDERMINES THE PURITY OF *TRUE HUMAN ACHIEVEMENT!*

SUPERHEROES ARE NOTHING BUT A BUNCH OF *GLORY-HOGGING TYRANTS*, AND I WILL NOT REST UNTIL I SEE YOU *HUMILIATED AND DESTROYED* FOR WHAT YOU DID TO MY...!

PK*OW*

GUH-YUH!

WHY DID YOU *DO THAT!?*

IT'S AN ANCIENT KRYPTONIAN *MEMORY ERASURE* PRESSURE POINT. BY TAPPING HER SKULL IN THAT *PRECISE SPOT* AT THAT *EXACT PRESSURE*, I'VE *ERASED EVERY MEMORY* THAT SHE HAD OF THE *LAST HOUR.*

THERE'S *NO SUCH THING* AS AN ANCIENT KRYPTONIAN *MEMORY ERASURE* PRESSURE POINT.

TRUE ENOUGH.

GUH... WHERE... *WHERE ARE WE...?*

LENA?

94

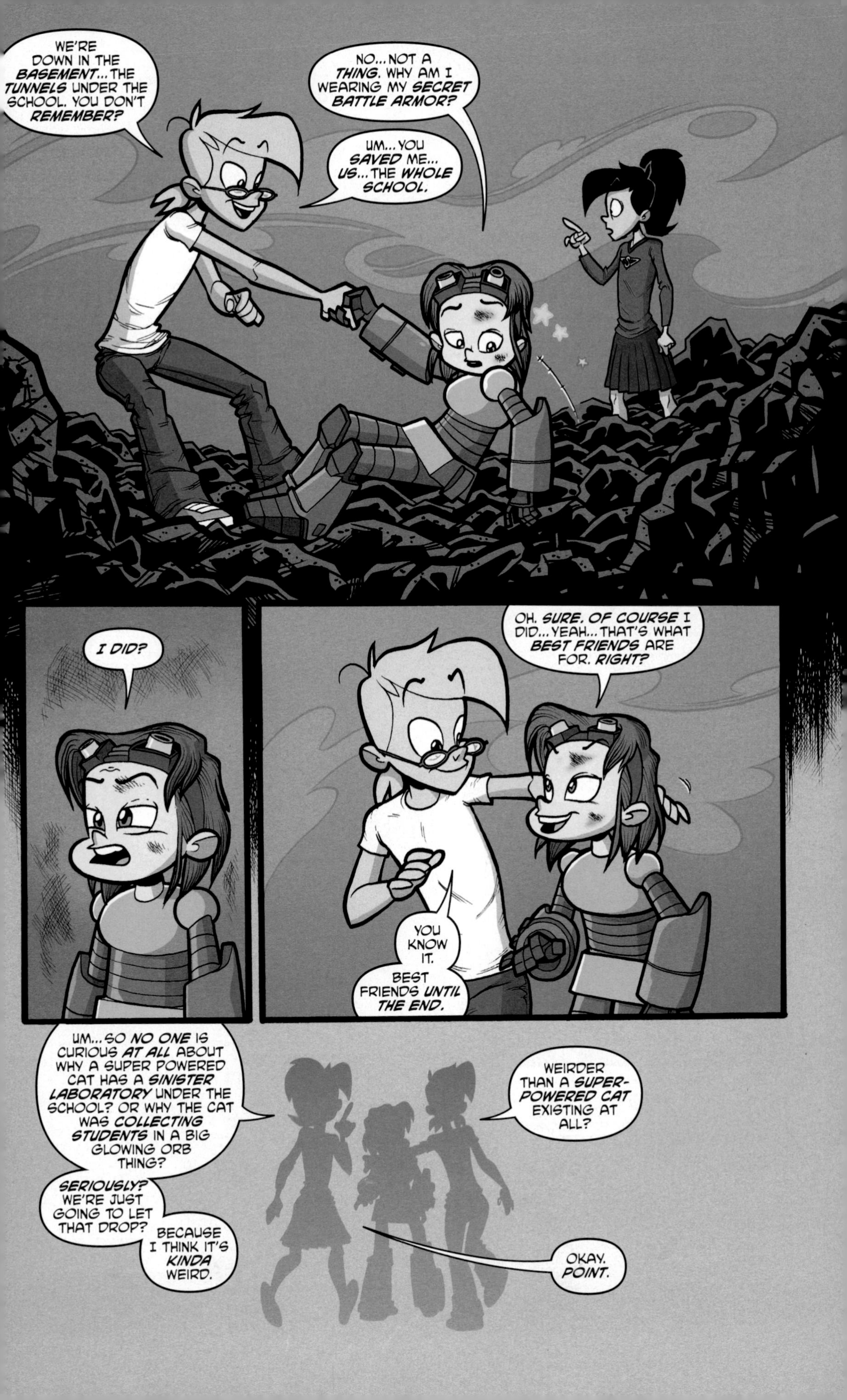
WE'RE DOWN IN THE BASEMENT... THE TUNNELS UNDER THE SCHOOL. YOU DON'T REMEMBER?
NO... NOT A THING. WHY AM I WEARING MY SECRET BATTLE ARMOR?
UM... YOU SAVED ME... US... THE WHOLE SCHOOL.
I DID?
OH. SURE. OF COURSE I DID... YEAH... THAT'S WHAT BEST FRIENDS ARE FOR. RIGHT?
YOU KNOW IT.
BEST FRIENDS UNTIL THE END.
UM... SO NO ONE IS CURIOUS AT ALL ABOUT WHY A SUPER POWERED CAT HAS A SINISTER LABORATORY UNDER THE SCHOOL? OR WHY THE CAT WAS COLLECTING STUDENTS IN A BIG GLOWING ORB THING?
SERIOUSLY? WE'RE JUST GOING TO LET THAT DROP?
BECAUSE I THINK IT'S KINDA WEIRD.
WEIRDER THAN A SUPER-POWERED CAT EXISTING AT ALL?
OKAY. POINT.

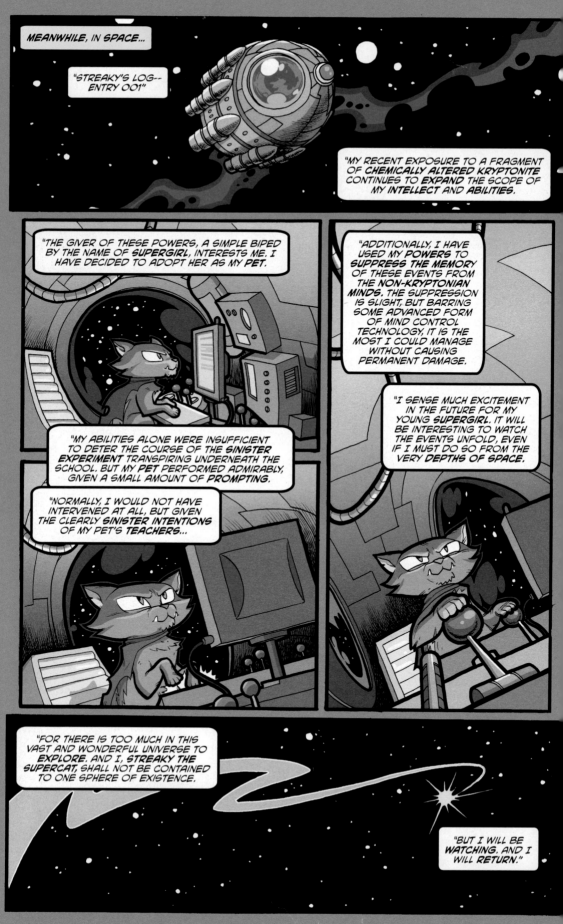

MEANWHILE, IN SPACE...

"STREAKY'S LOG-- ENTRY 001"

"MY RECENT EXPOSURE TO A FRAGMENT OF **CHEMICALLY ALTERED KRYPTONITE** CONTINUES TO **EXPAND** THE SCOPE OF MY **INTELLECT** AND **ABILITIES.**

"THE GIVER OF THESE POWERS, A SIMPLE BIPED BY THE NAME OF **SUPERGIRL**, INTERESTS ME. I HAVE DECIDED TO ADOPT HER AS MY **PET.**

"ADDITIONALLY, I HAVE USED MY **POWERS** TO **SUPPRESS THE MEMORY** OF THESE EVENTS FROM THE **NON-KRYPTONIAN MINDS.** THE SUPPRESSION IS SLIGHT, BUT BARRING SOME ADVANCED FORM OF MIND CONTROL TECHNOLOGY, IT IS THE MOST I COULD MANAGE WITHOUT CAUSING PERMANENT DAMAGE.

"MY ABILITIES ALONE WERE INSUFFICIENT TO DETER THE COURSE OF THE **SINISTER EXPERIMENT** TRANSPIRING UNDERNEATH THE SCHOOL. BUT MY **PET** PERFORMED ADMIRABLY, GIVEN A SMALL AMOUNT OF **PROMPTING.**

"NORMALLY, I WOULD NOT HAVE INTERVENED AT ALL, BUT GIVEN THE CLEARLY **SINISTER INTENTIONS** OF MY PET'S **TEACHERS...**

"I SENSE MUCH EXCITEMENT IN THE FUTURE FOR MY YOUNG **SUPERGIRL.** IT WILL BE INTERESTING TO WATCH THE EVENTS UNFOLD, EVEN IF I MUST DO SO FROM THE VERY **DEPTHS OF SPACE.**

"FOR THERE IS TOO MUCH IN THIS VAST AND WONDERFUL UNIVERSE TO **EXPLORE.** AND I, **STREAKY THE SUPERCAT,** SHALL NOT BE CONTAINED TO ONE SPHERE OF EXISTENCE.

"BUT I WILL BE **WATCHING.** AND I WILL **RETURN.**"

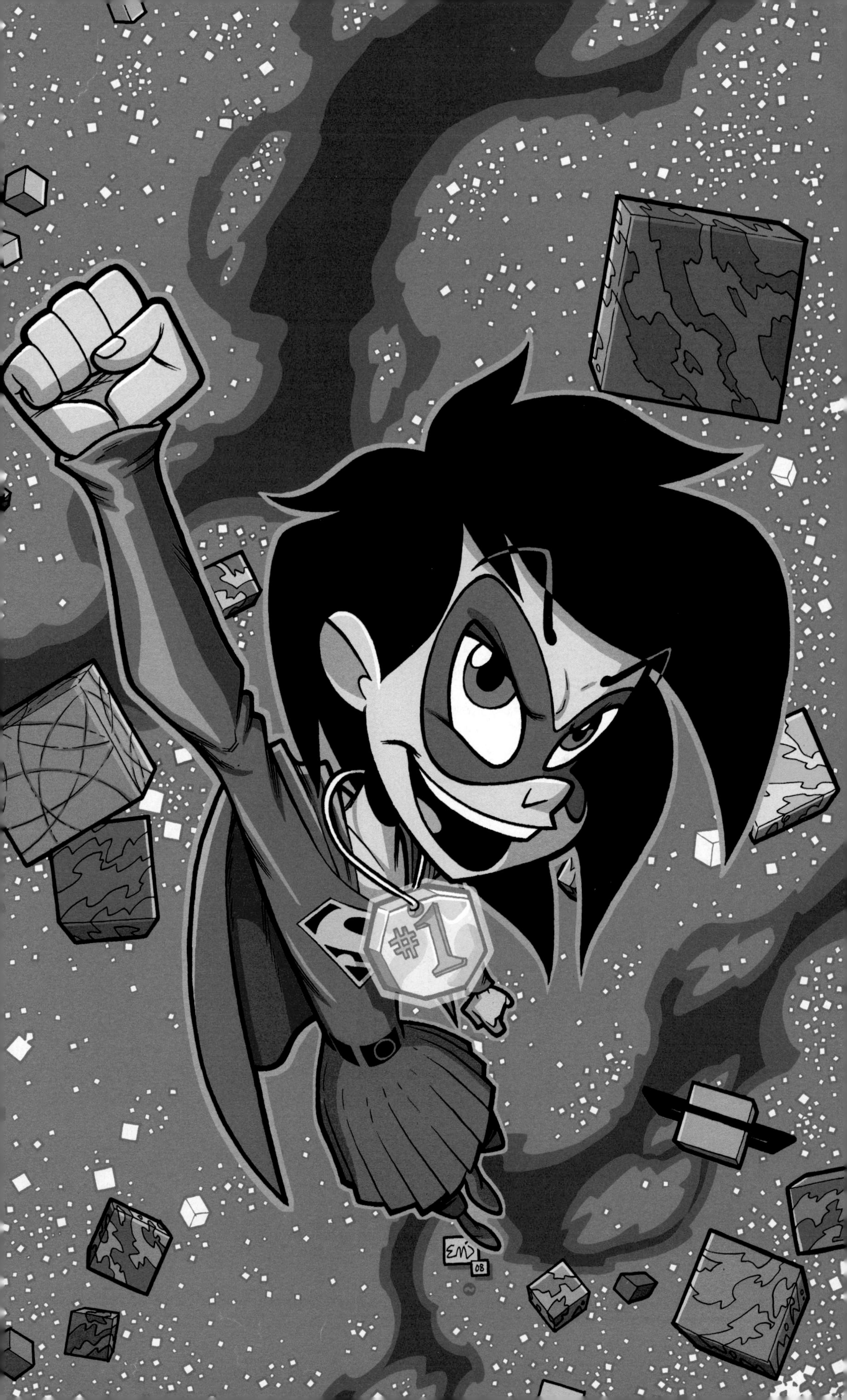
#1

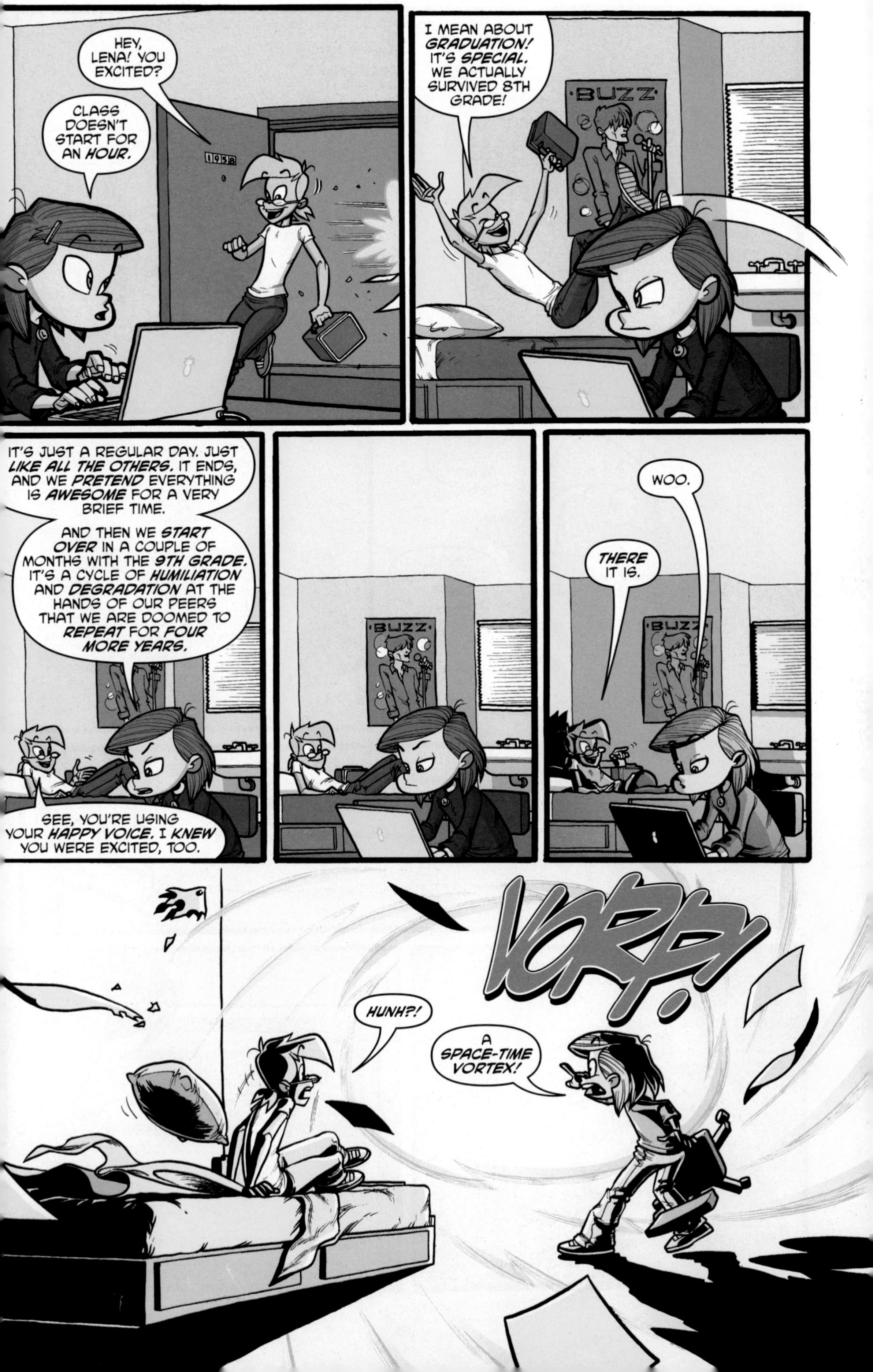
HEY, LENA! YOU EXCITED?
CLASS DOESN'T START FOR AN HOUR.
1958
I MEAN ABOUT GRADUATION! IT'S SPECIAL. WE ACTUALLY SURVIVED 8TH GRADE!
BUZZ
IT'S JUST A REGULAR DAY. JUST LIKE ALL THE OTHERS. IT ENDS, AND WE PRETEND EVERYTHING IS AWESOME FOR A VERY BRIEF TIME.
AND THEN WE START OVER IN A COUPLE OF MONTHS WITH THE 9TH GRADE. IT'S A CYCLE OF HUMILIATION AND DEGRADATION AT THE HANDS OF OUR PEERS THAT WE ARE DOOMED TO REPEAT FOR FOUR MORE YEARS.
SEE, YOU'RE USING YOUR HAPPY VOICE. I KNEW YOU WERE EXCITED, TOO.
BUZZ
WOO.
THERE IT IS.
BUZZ
VORP!
HUNH?!
A SPACE-TIME VORTEX!

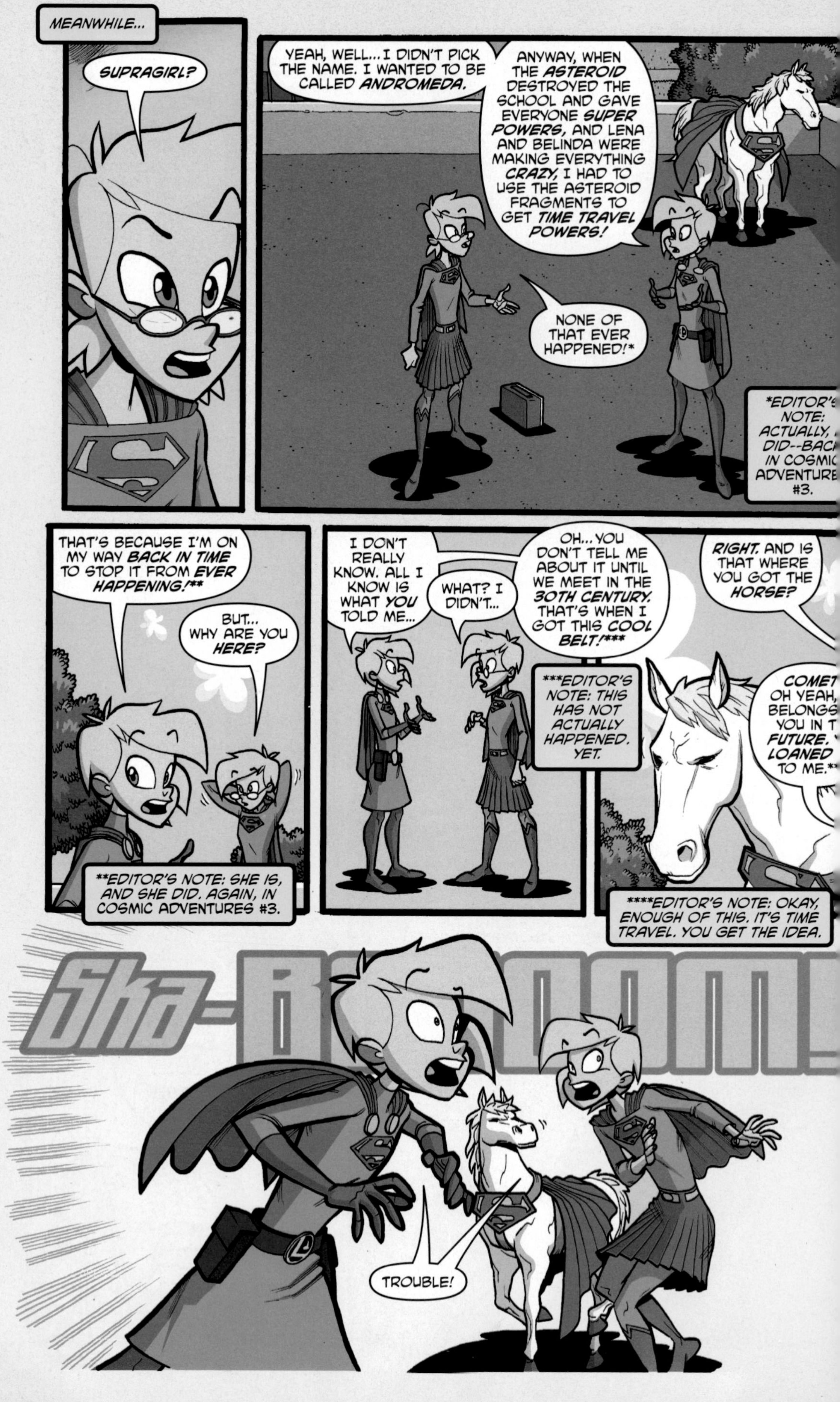
MEANWHILE...
SUPRAGIRL?
YEAH, WELL... I DIDN'T PICK THE NAME. I WANTED TO BE CALLED ANDROMEDA.
ANYWAY, WHEN THE ASTEROID DESTROYED THE SCHOOL AND GAVE EVERYONE SUPER POWERS, AND LENA AND BELINDA WERE MAKING EVERYTHING CRAZY, I HAD TO USE THE ASTEROID FRAGMENTS TO GET TIME TRAVEL POWERS!
NONE OF THAT EVER HAPPENED!*
*EDITOR'S NOTE: ACTUALLY, DID--BAC IN COSMIC ADVENTURE #3.
THAT'S BECAUSE I'M ON MY WAY BACK IN TIME TO STOP IT FROM EVER HAPPENING!**
BUT... WHY ARE YOU HERE?
**EDITOR'S NOTE: SHE IS, AND SHE DID. AGAIN, IN COSMIC ADVENTURES #3.
I DON'T REALLY KNOW. ALL I KNOW IS WHAT YOU TOLD ME...
WHAT? I DIDN'T...
OH... YOU DON'T TELL ME ABOUT IT UNTIL WE MEET IN THE 30TH CENTURY. THAT'S WHEN I GOT THIS COOL BELT!***
***EDITOR'S NOTE: THIS HAS NOT ACTUALLY HAPPENED. YET.
RIGHT. AND IS THAT WHERE YOU GOT THE HORSE?
COMET OH YEAH, BELONGS YOU IN T FUTURE. LOANED TO ME.**
****EDITOR'S NOTE: OKAY, ENOUGH OF THIS. IT'S TIME TRAVEL. YOU GET THE IDEA.
SKA-BOOM
TROUBLE!

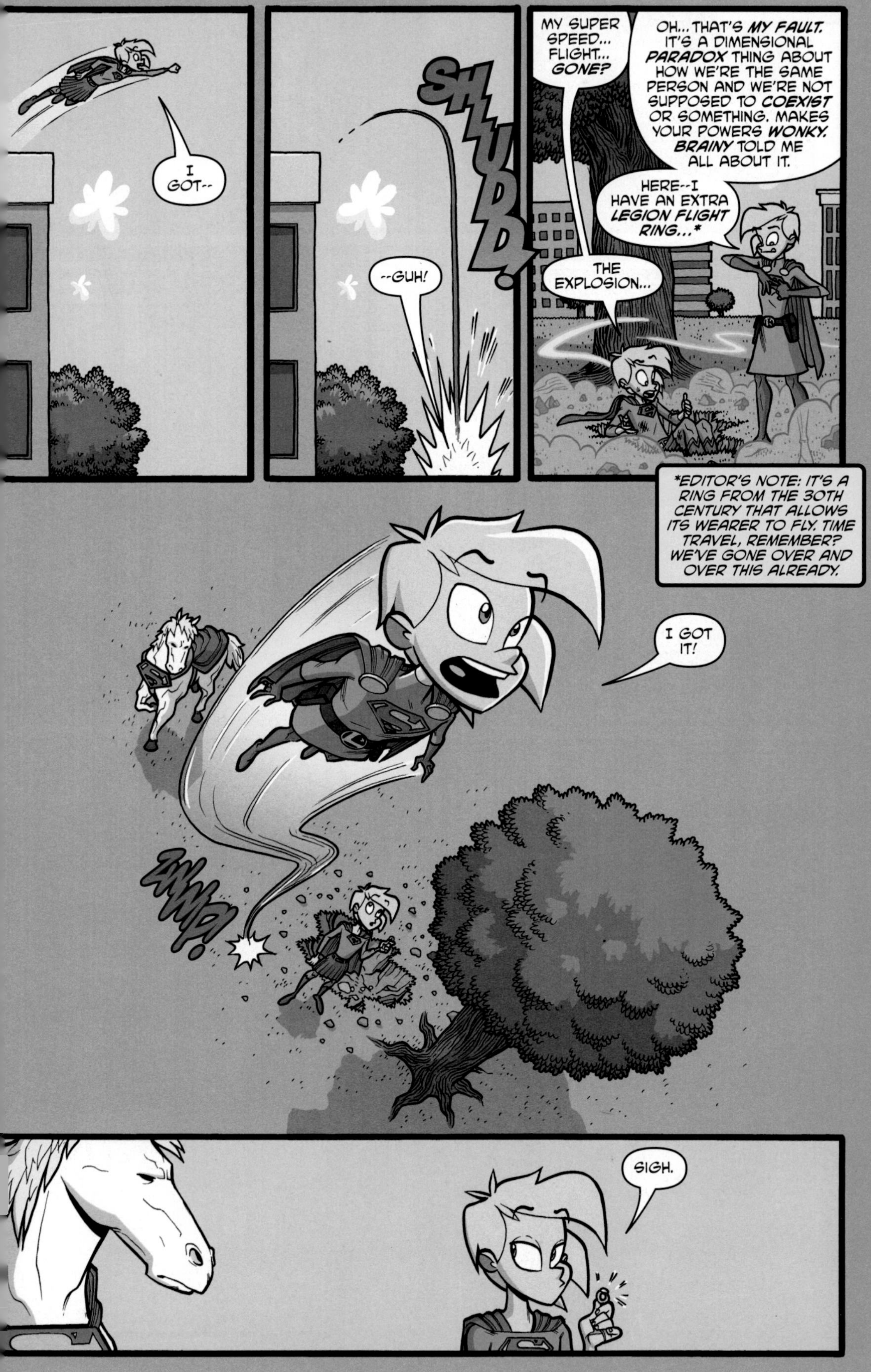
I GOT--
SHLUDD!
--GUH!
MY SUPER SPEED... FLIGHT... GONE?
THE EXPLOSION...
OH... THAT'S MY FAULT. IT'S A DIMENSIONAL PARADOX THING ABOUT HOW WE'RE THE SAME PERSON AND WE'RE NOT SUPPOSED TO COEXIST OR SOMETHING. MAKES YOUR POWERS WONKY. BRAINY TOLD ME ALL ABOUT IT.
HERE--I HAVE AN EXTRA LEGION FLIGHT RING...*
*EDITOR'S NOTE: IT'S A RING FROM THE 30TH CENTURY THAT ALLOWS ITS WEARER TO FLY. TIME TRAVEL, REMEMBER? WE'VE GONE OVER AND OVER THIS ALREADY.
I GOT IT!
WHMP!
SIGH.

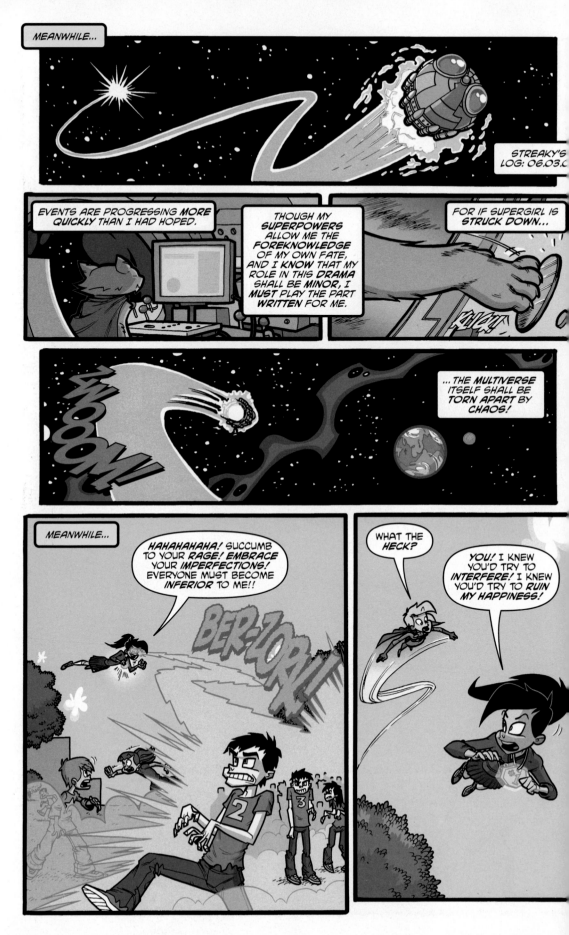

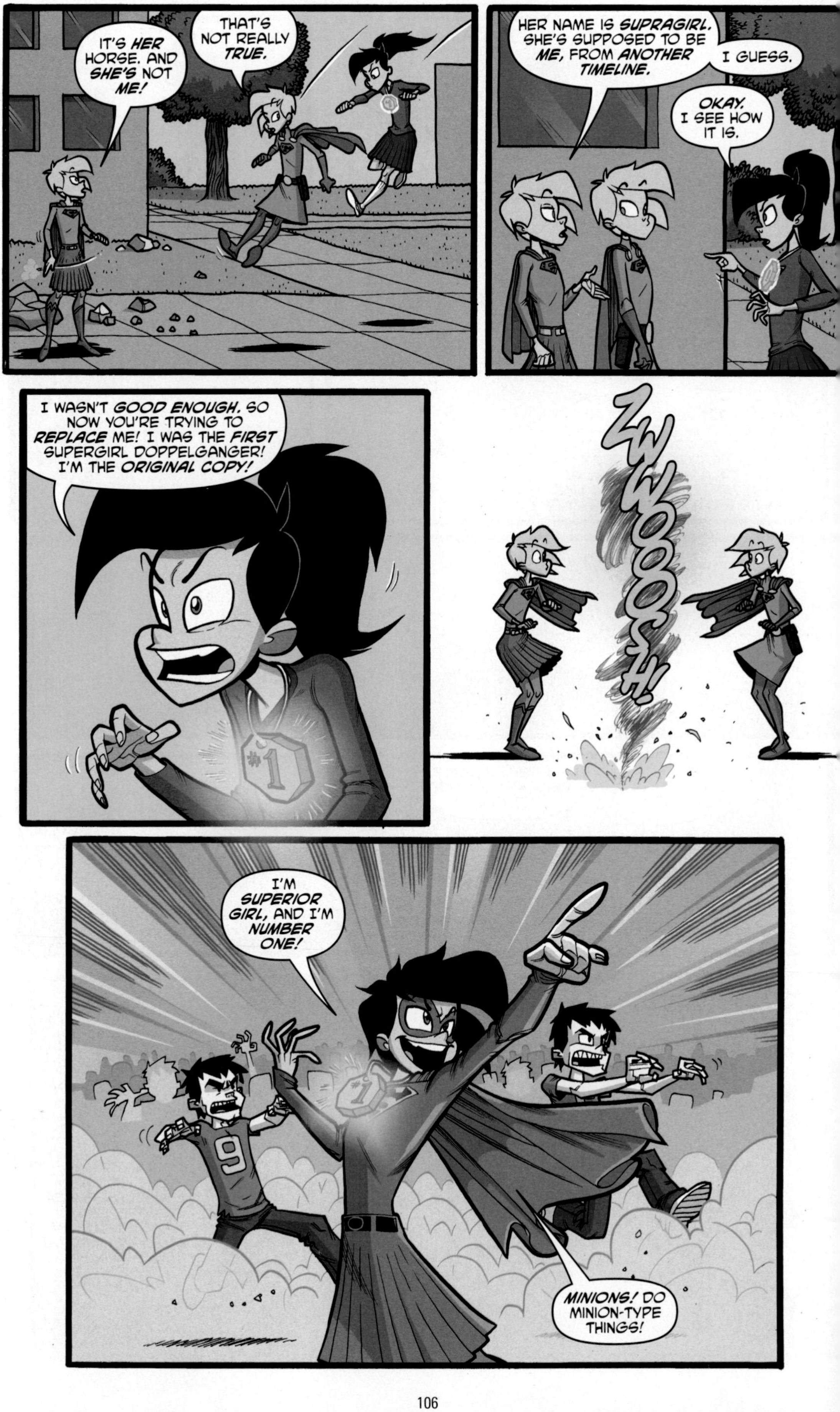

IT'S HER HORSE. AND SHE'S NOT ME!
THAT'S NOT REALLY TRUE.
HER NAME IS SUPRAGIRL. SHE'S SUPPOSED TO BE ME, FROM ANOTHER TIMELINE.
I GUESS.
OKAY. I SEE HOW IT IS.
I WASN'T GOOD ENOUGH. SO NOW YOU'RE TRYING TO REPLACE ME! I WAS THE FIRST SUPERGIRL DOPPELGANGER! I'M THE ORIGINAL COPY!
ZWOOOOCH!
I'M SUPERIOR GIRL, AND I'M NUMBER ONE!
MINIONS! DO MINION-TYPE THINGS!

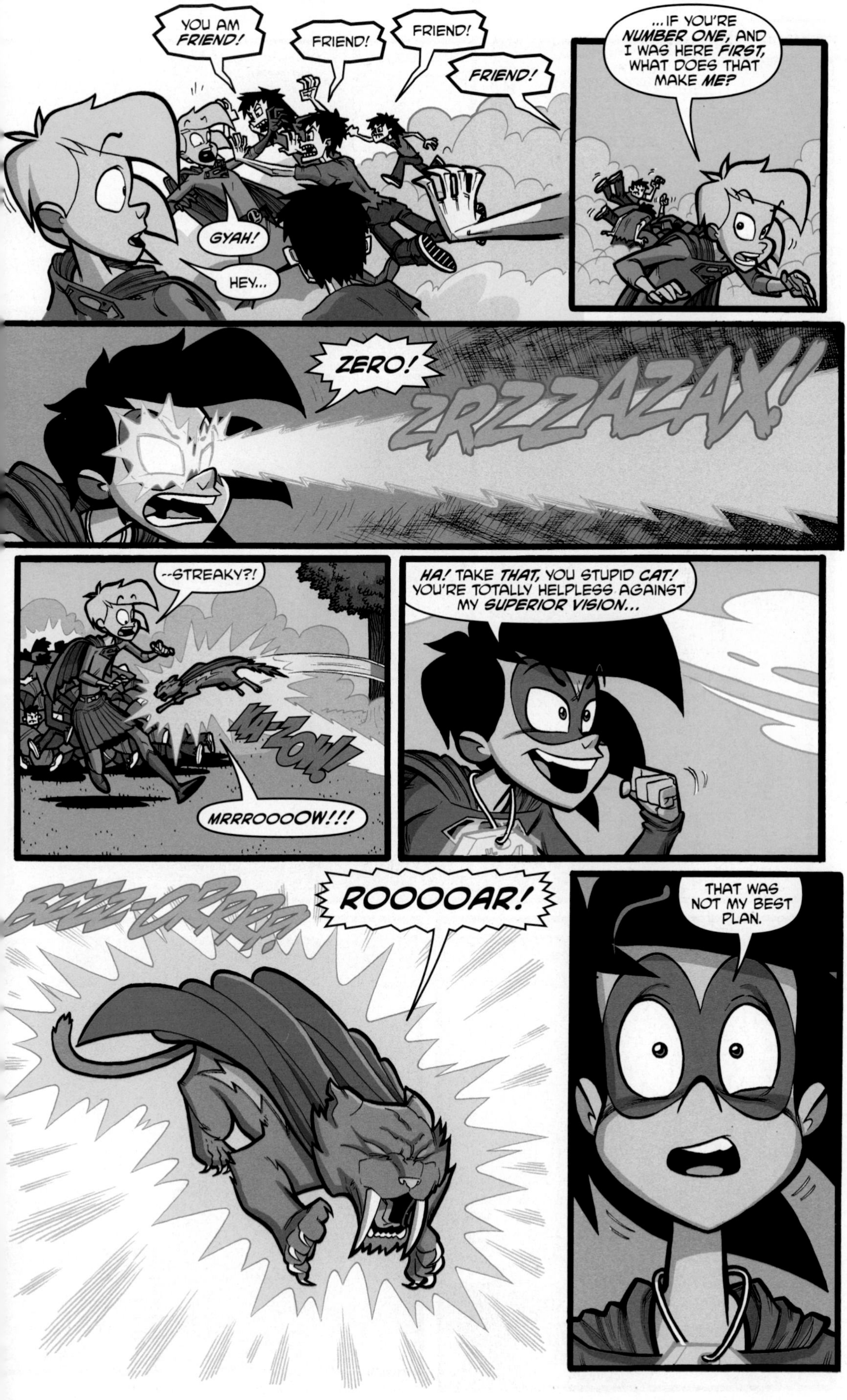
YOU AM FRIEND!
FRIEND!
FRIEND!
FRIEND!
GYAH!
HEY...
...IF YOU'RE NUMBER ONE, AND I WAS HERE FIRST, WHAT DOES THAT MAKE ME?
ZERO!
ZRZZZAZAX!
--STREAKY?!
KA-ZOW!
MRRROOOOW!!!
HA! TAKE THAT, YOU STUPID CAT! YOU'RE TOTALLY HELPLESS AGAINST MY SUPERIOR VISION...
BZZZ-ORRRR!
ROOOOAR!
THAT WAS NOT MY BEST PLAN.

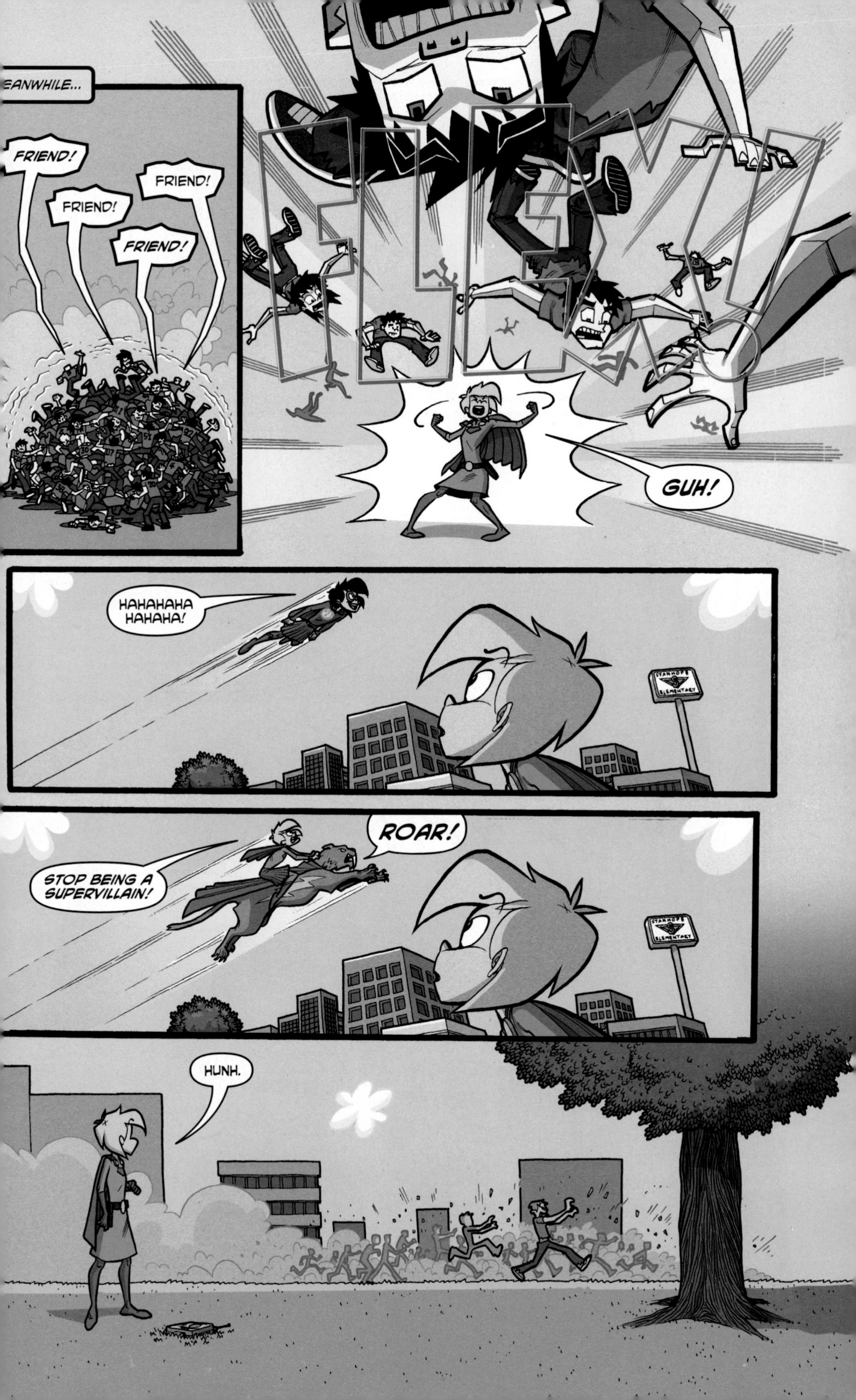
EANWHILE...
FRIEND!
FRIEND!
FRIEND!
FRIEND!
GUH!
HAHAHAHA
HAHAHA!
STOP BEING A
SUPERVILLAIN!
ROAR!
HUNH.

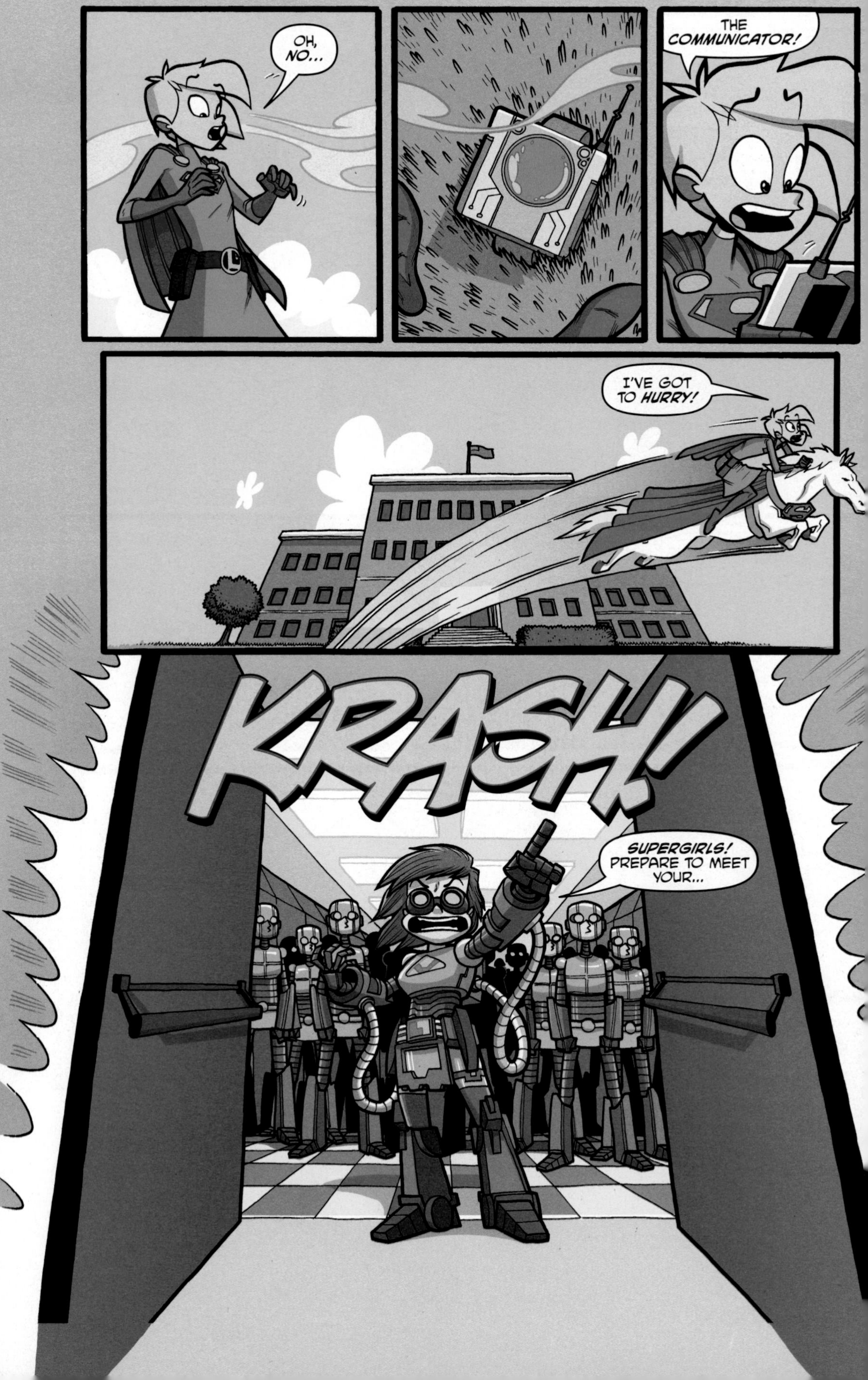
OH, NO...
THE COMMUNICATOR!
I'VE GOT TO HURRY!
KRASH!
SUPERGIRLS! PREPARE TO MEET YOUR...

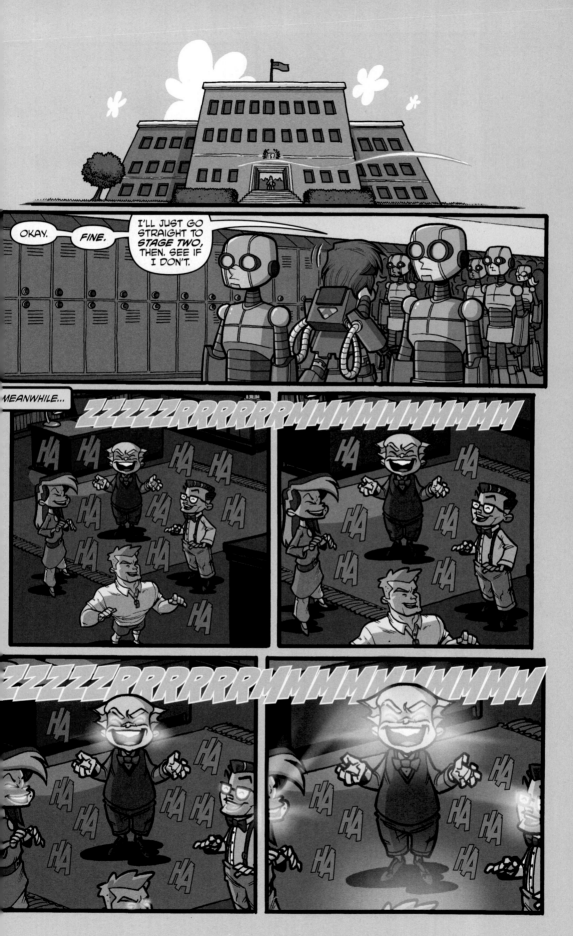

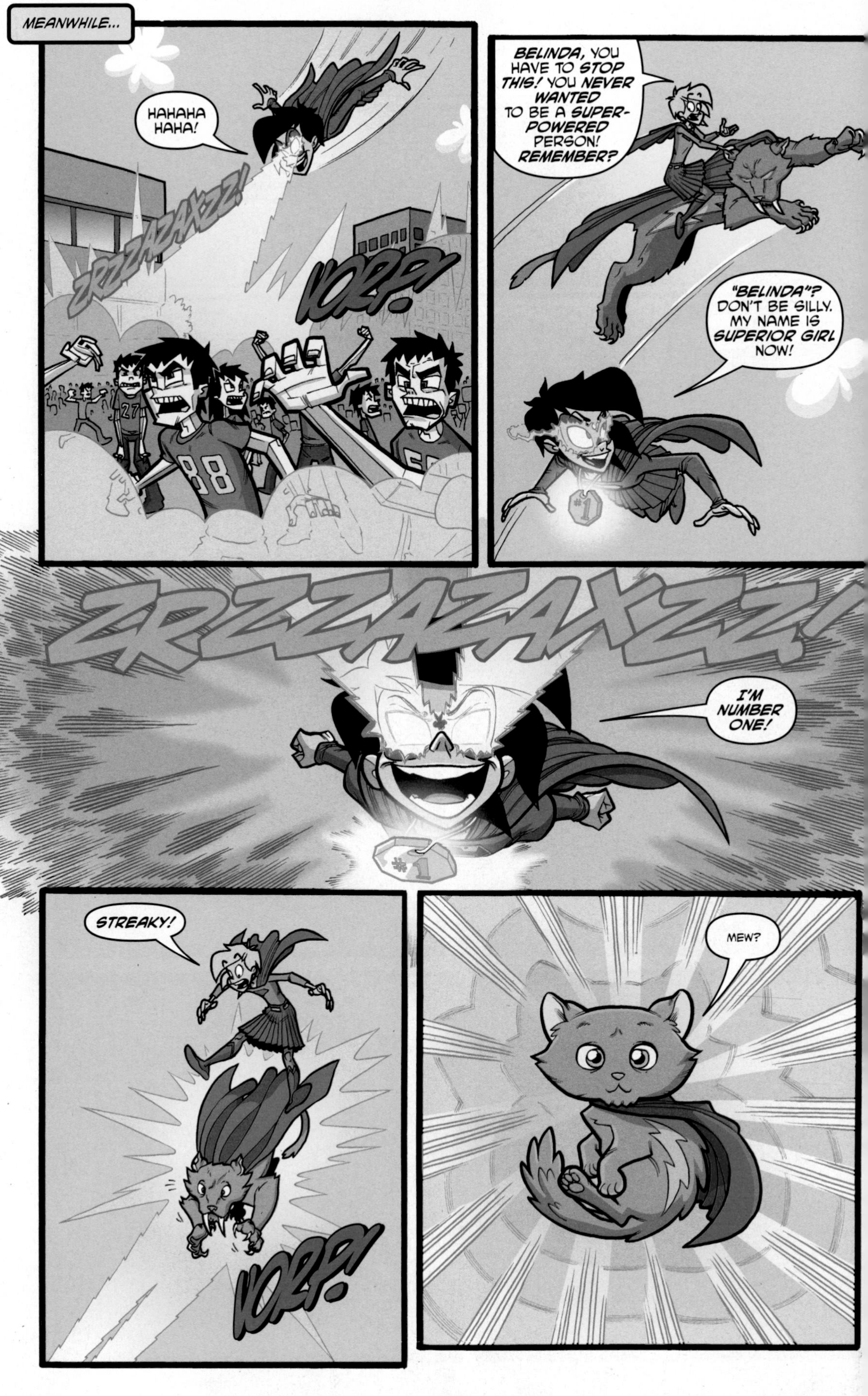
MEANWHILE...
HAHAHA HAHA!
ZRZZAZAXZZ!
VORP!
BELINDA, YOU HAVE TO STOP THIS! YOU NEVER WANTED TO BE A SUPER-POWERED PERSON! REMEMBER?
"BELINDA"? DON'T BE SILLY. MY NAME IS SUPERIOR GIRL NOW!
ZRZZAZAXZZ!
I'M NUMBER ONE!
STREAKY!
VORP!
MEW?

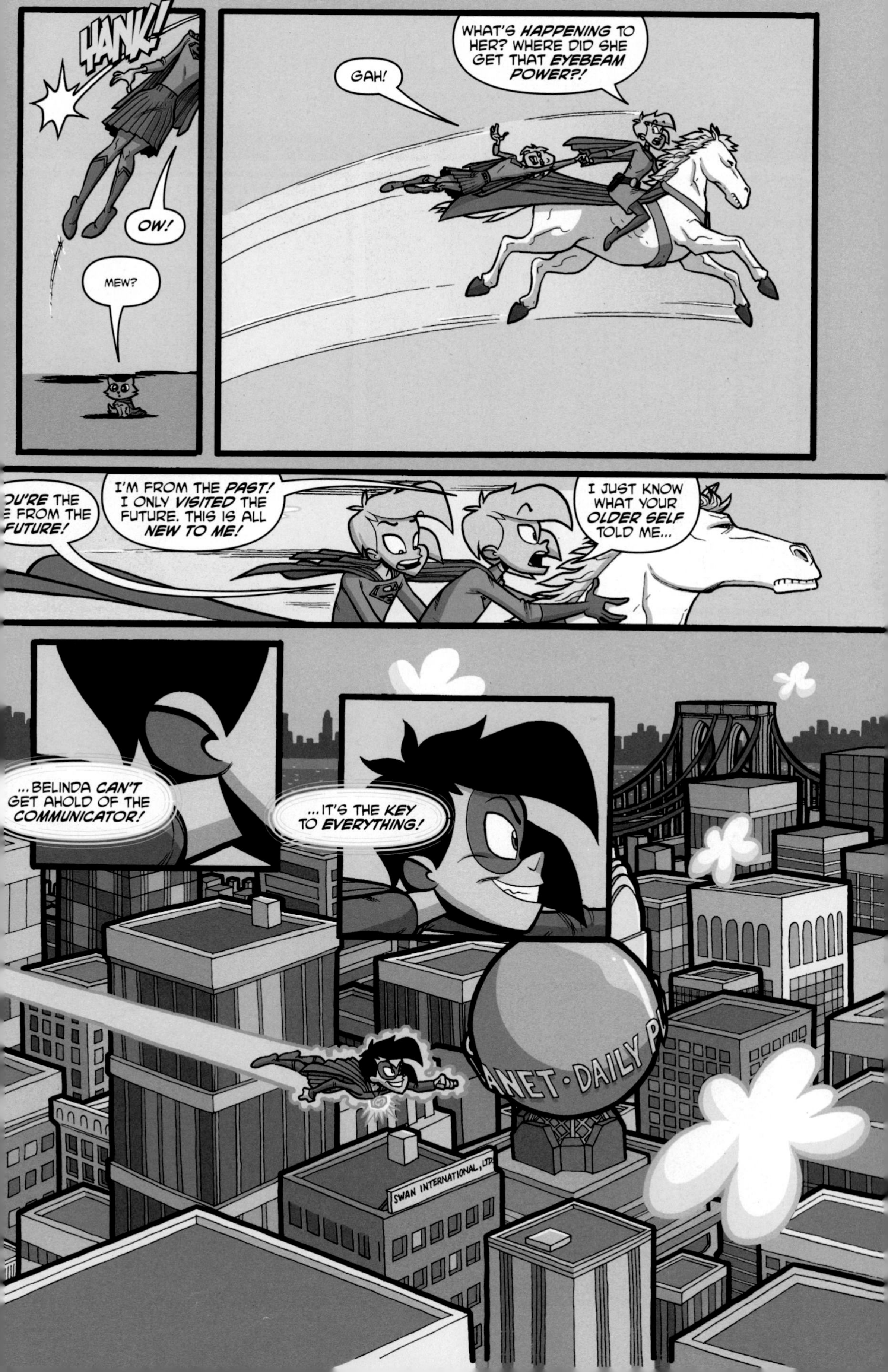
HANK!
OW!
MEW?
GAH!
WHAT'S HAPPENING TO HER? WHERE DID SHE GET THAT EYEBEAM POWER?!
OU'RE THE
E FROM THE
FUTURE!
I'M FROM THE PAST! I ONLY VISITED THE FUTURE. THIS IS ALL NEW TO ME!
I JUST KNOW WHAT YOUR OLDER SELF TOLD ME...
...BELINDA CAN'T GET AHOLD OF THE COMMUNICATOR!
...IT'S THE KEY TO EVERYTHING!
ANET · DAILY P
SWAN INTERNATIONAL, LTD.

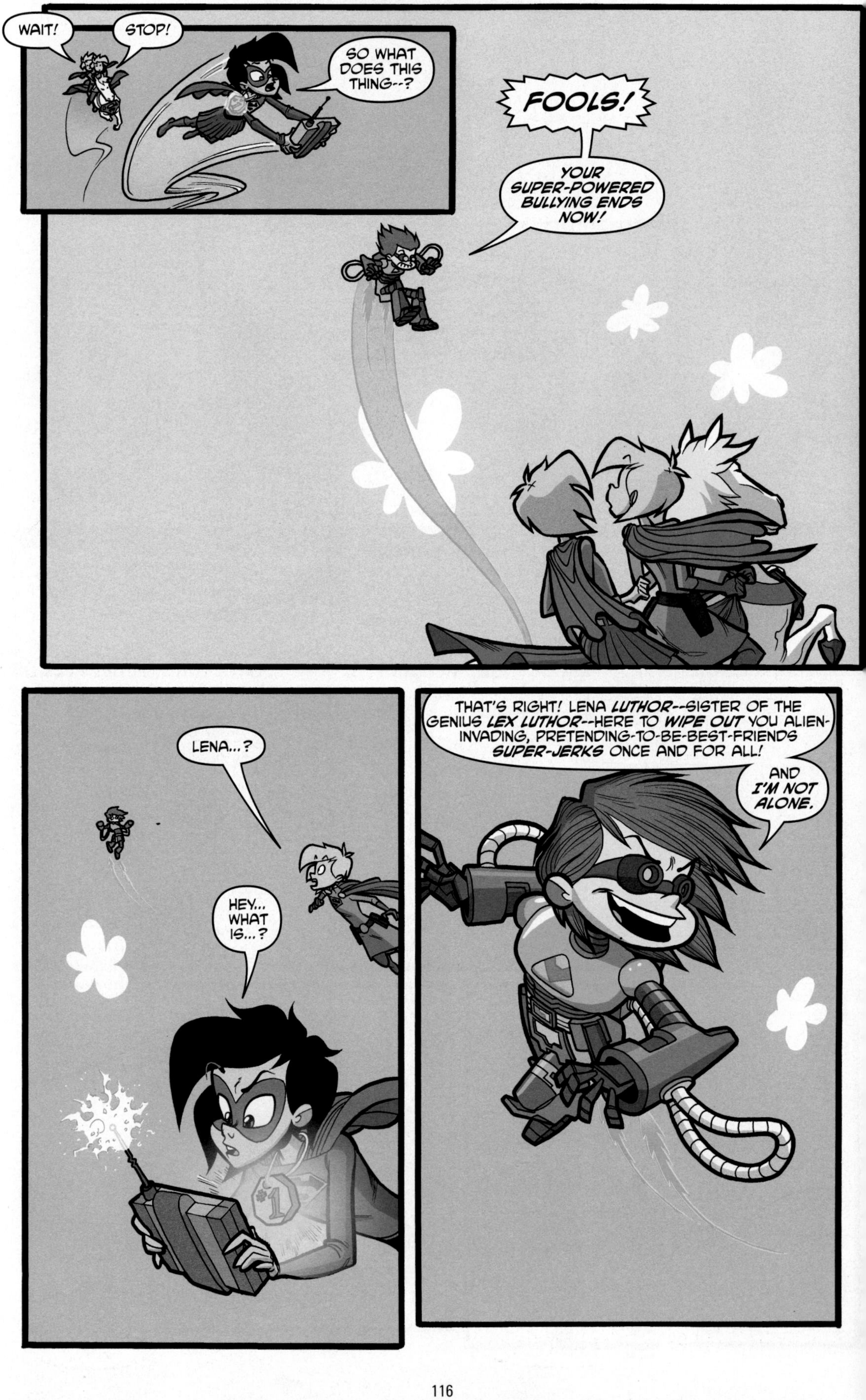
WAIT!
STOP!
SO WHAT DOES THIS THING--?
FOOLS!
YOUR SUPER-POWERED BULLYING ENDS NOW!
LENA...?
HEY... WHAT IS...?
THAT'S RIGHT! LENA LUTHOR--SISTER OF THE GENIUS LEX LUTHOR--HERE TO WIPE OUT YOU ALIEN-INVADING, PRETENDING-TO-BE-BEST-FRIENDS SUPER-JERKS ONCE AND FOR ALL!
AND I'M NOT ALONE.

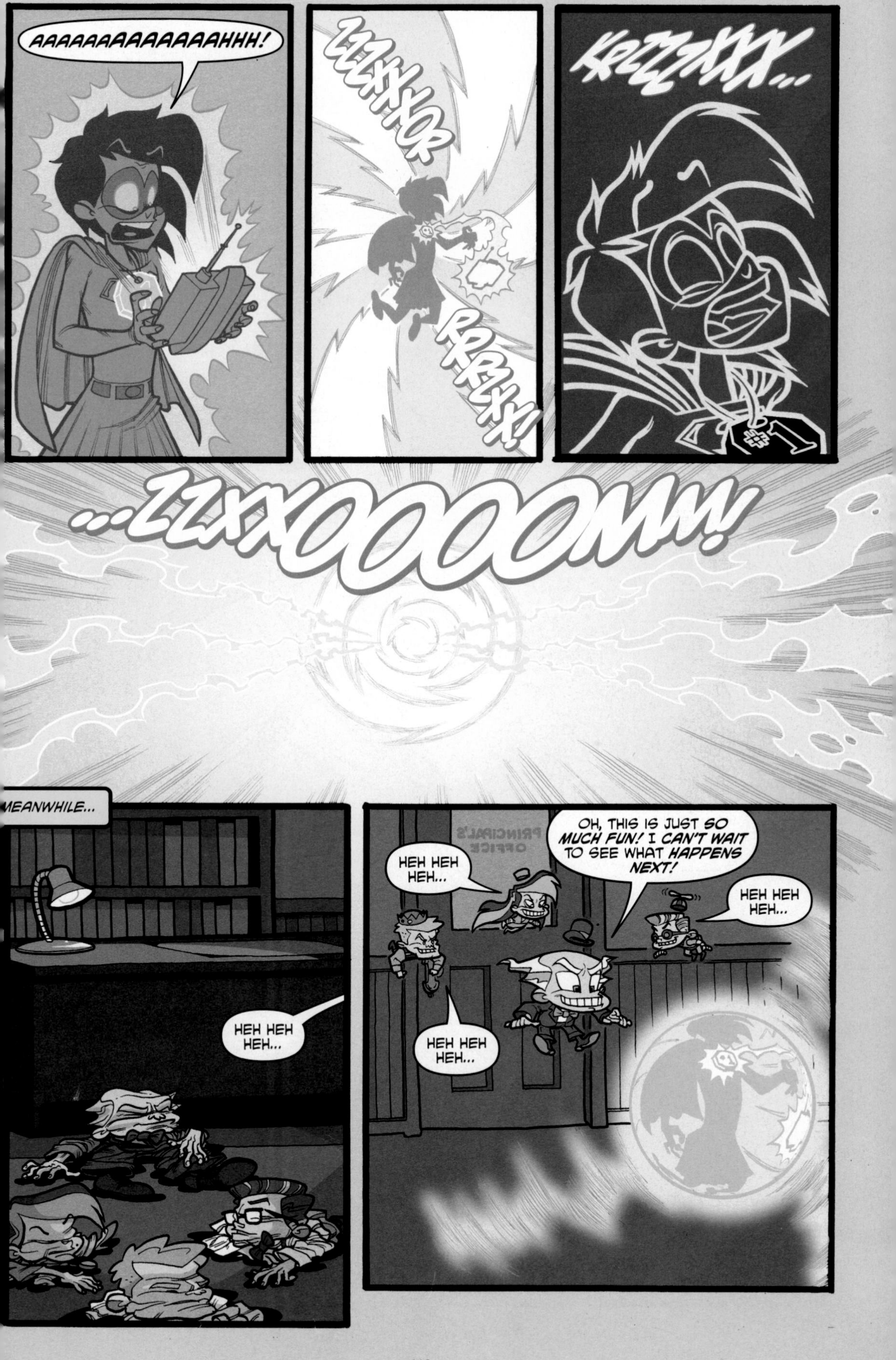
AAAAAAAAAAAAAAHHH!
ZZZXXXOR
RRRKK!
KRZZZZXXX...
...ZZXXOOOOOMM!
MEANWHILE...
HEH HEH HEH...
PRINCIPAL'S OFFICE
HEH HEH HEH...
OH, THIS IS JUST SO MUCH FUN! I CAN'T WAIT TO SEE WHAT HAPPENS NEXT!
HEH HEH HEH...
HEH HEH HEH...

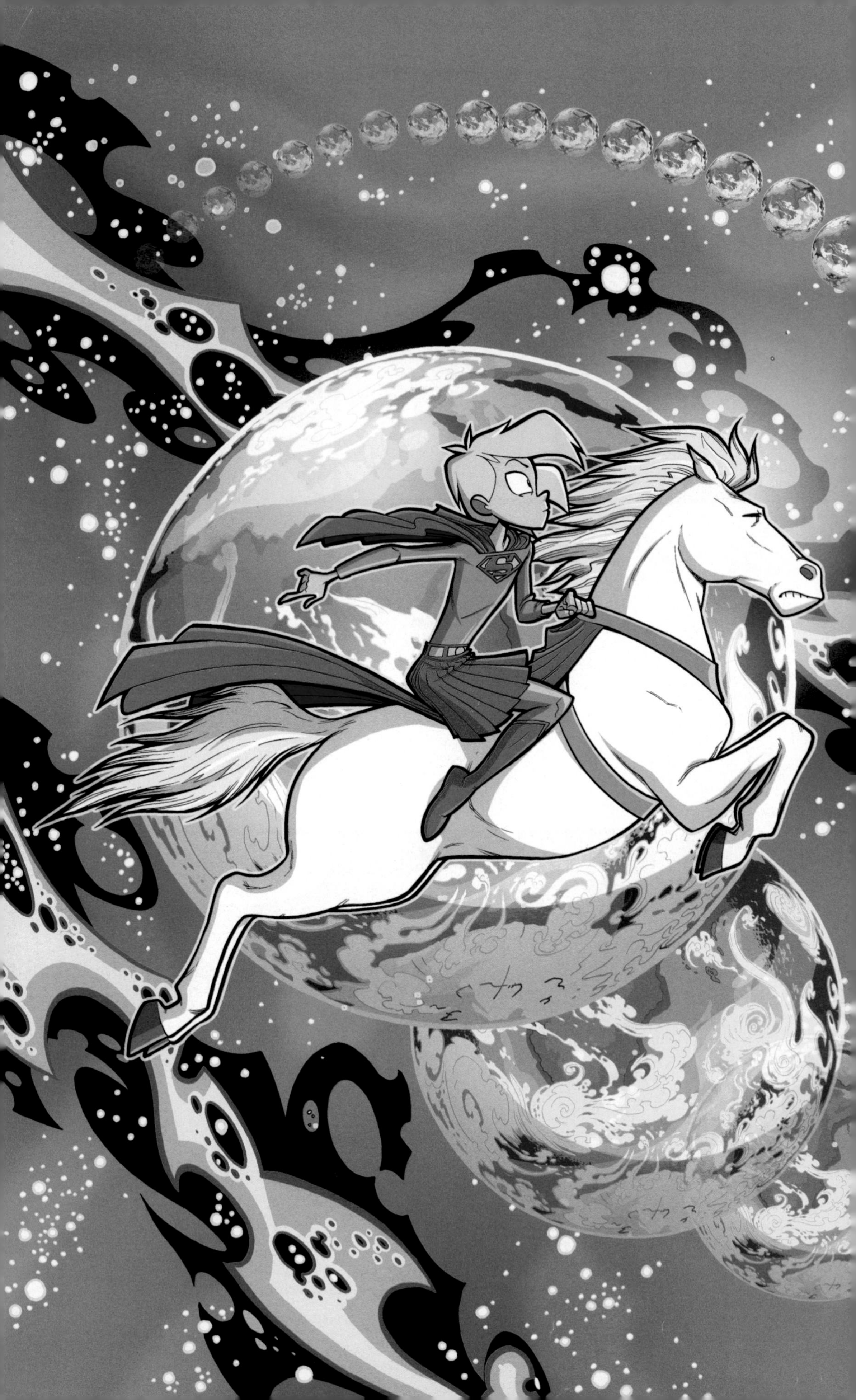

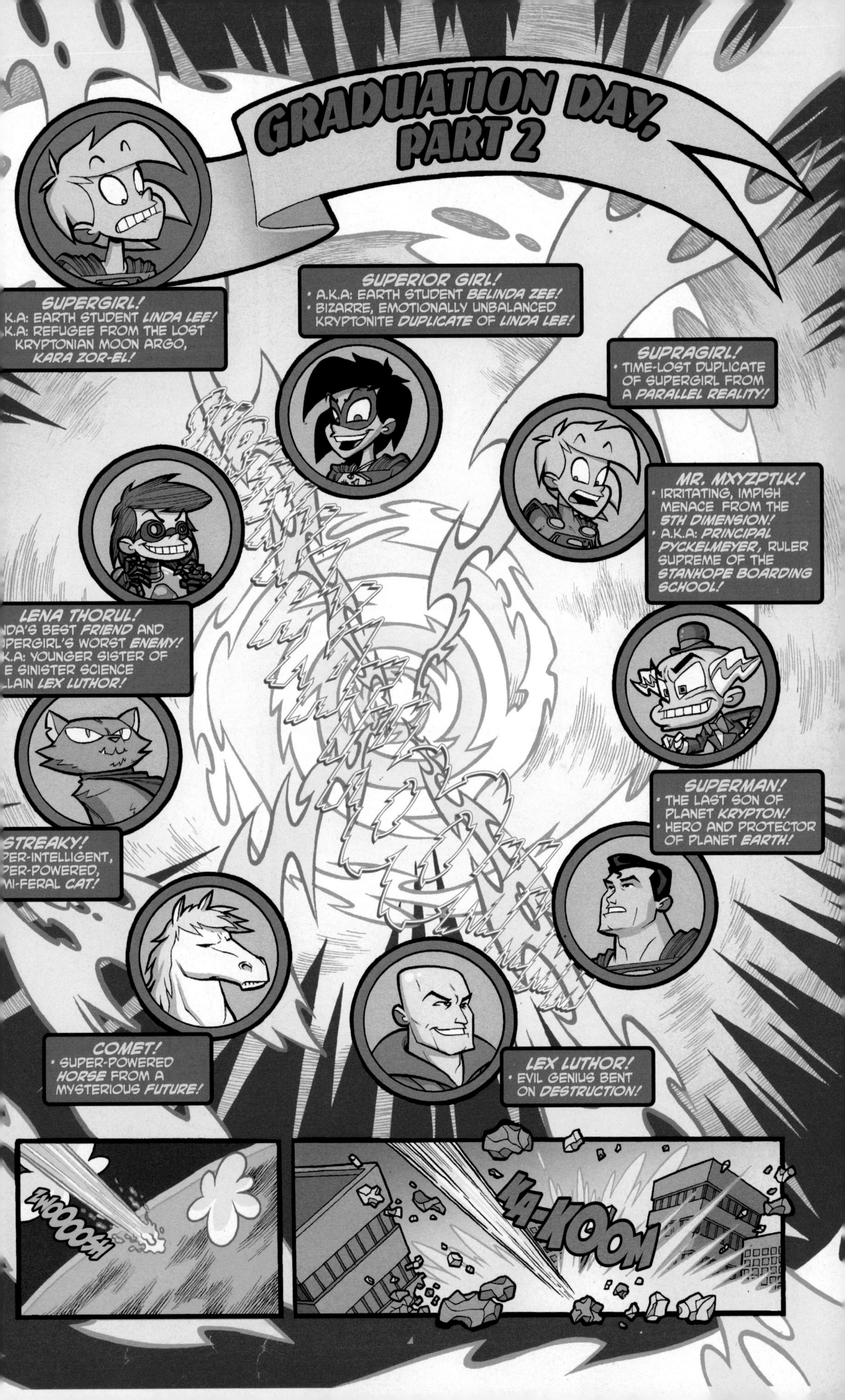
GRADUATION DAY, PART 2
SUPERGIRL!
K.A: EARTH STUDENT LINDA LEE!
.K.A: REFUGEE FROM THE LOST
KRYPTONIAN MOON ARGO,
KARA ZOR-EL!
SUPERIOR GIRL!
• A.K.A: EARTH STUDENT BELINDA ZEE!
• BIZARRE, EMOTIONALLY UNBALANCED KRYPTONITE DUPLICATE OF LINDA LEE!
SUPRAGIRL!
• TIME-LOST DUPLICATE OF SUPERGIRL FROM A PARALLEL REALITY!
MR. MXYZPTLK!
• IRRITATING, IMPISH MENACE FROM THE 5TH DIMENSION!
• A.K.A: PRINCIPAL PYCKELMEYER, RULER SUPREME OF THE STANHOPE BOARDING SCHOOL!
LENA THORUL!
NDA'S BEST FRIEND AND
UPERGIRL'S WORST ENEMY!
K.A: YOUNGER SISTER OF
E SINISTER SCIENCE
LAIN LEX LUTHOR!
SUPERMAN!
• THE LAST SON OF PLANET KRYPTON!
• HERO AND PROTECTOR OF PLANET EARTH!
STREAKY!
PER-INTELLIGENT,
PER-POWERED,
MI-FERAL CAT!
COMET!
• SUPER-POWERED HORSE FROM A MYSTERIOUS FUTURE!
LEX LUTHOR!
• EVIL GENIUS BENT ON DESTRUCTION!
ZWOOOOSH
KA-KOOM

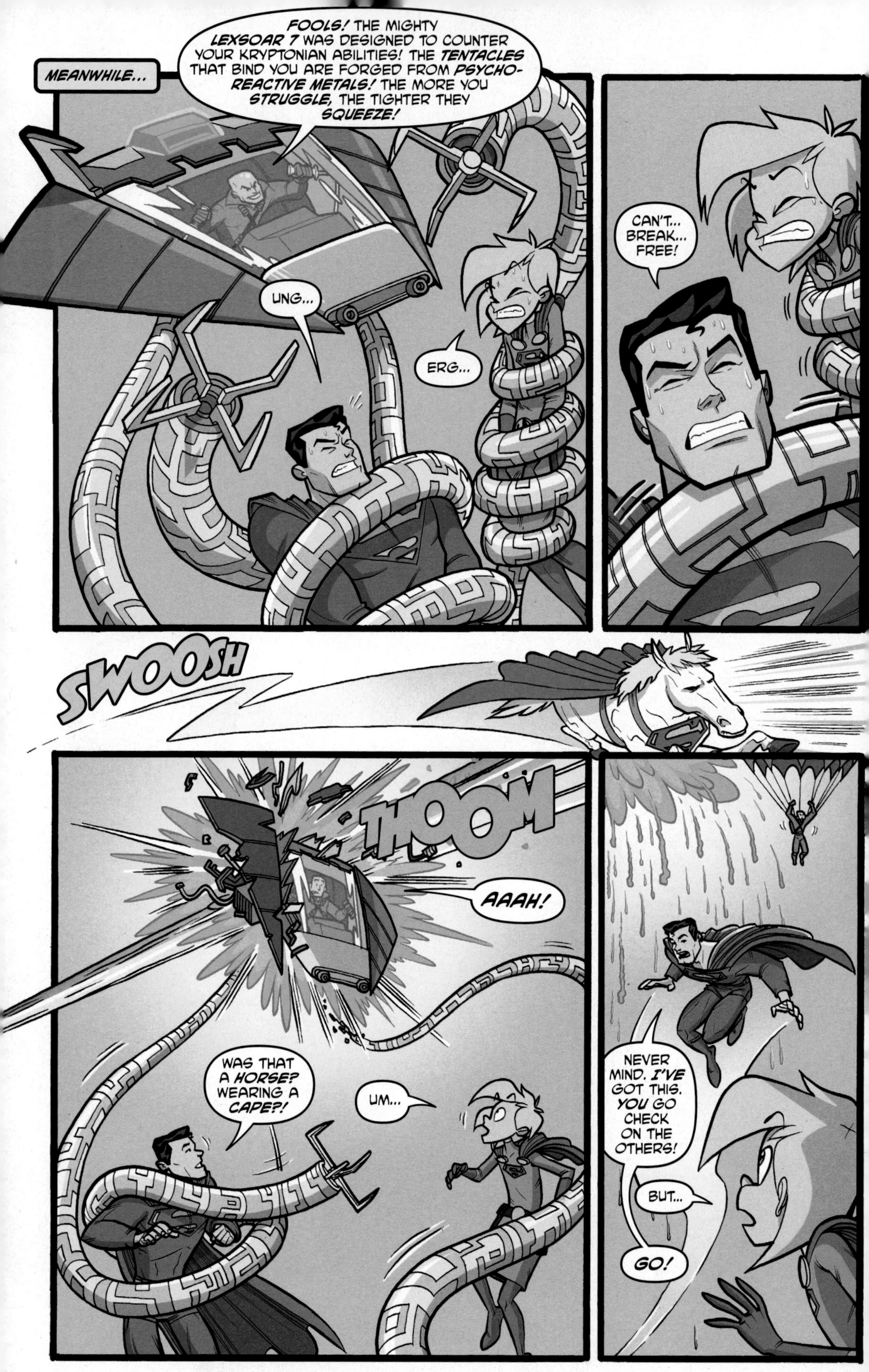
MEANWHILE...
FOOLS! THE MIGHTY LEXSOAR 7 WAS DESIGNED TO COUNTER YOUR KRYPTONIAN ABILITIES! THE TENTACLES THAT BIND YOU ARE FORGED FROM PSYCHO-REACTIVE METALS! THE MORE YOU STRUGGLE, THE TIGHTER THEY SQUEEZE!
UNG...
ERG...
CAN'T... BREAK... FREE!
SWOOSH
THOOM
AAAH!
WAS THAT A HORSE? WEARING A CAPE?!
UM...
NEVER MIND. I'VE GOT THIS. YOU GO CHECK ON THE OTHERS!
BUT...
GO!

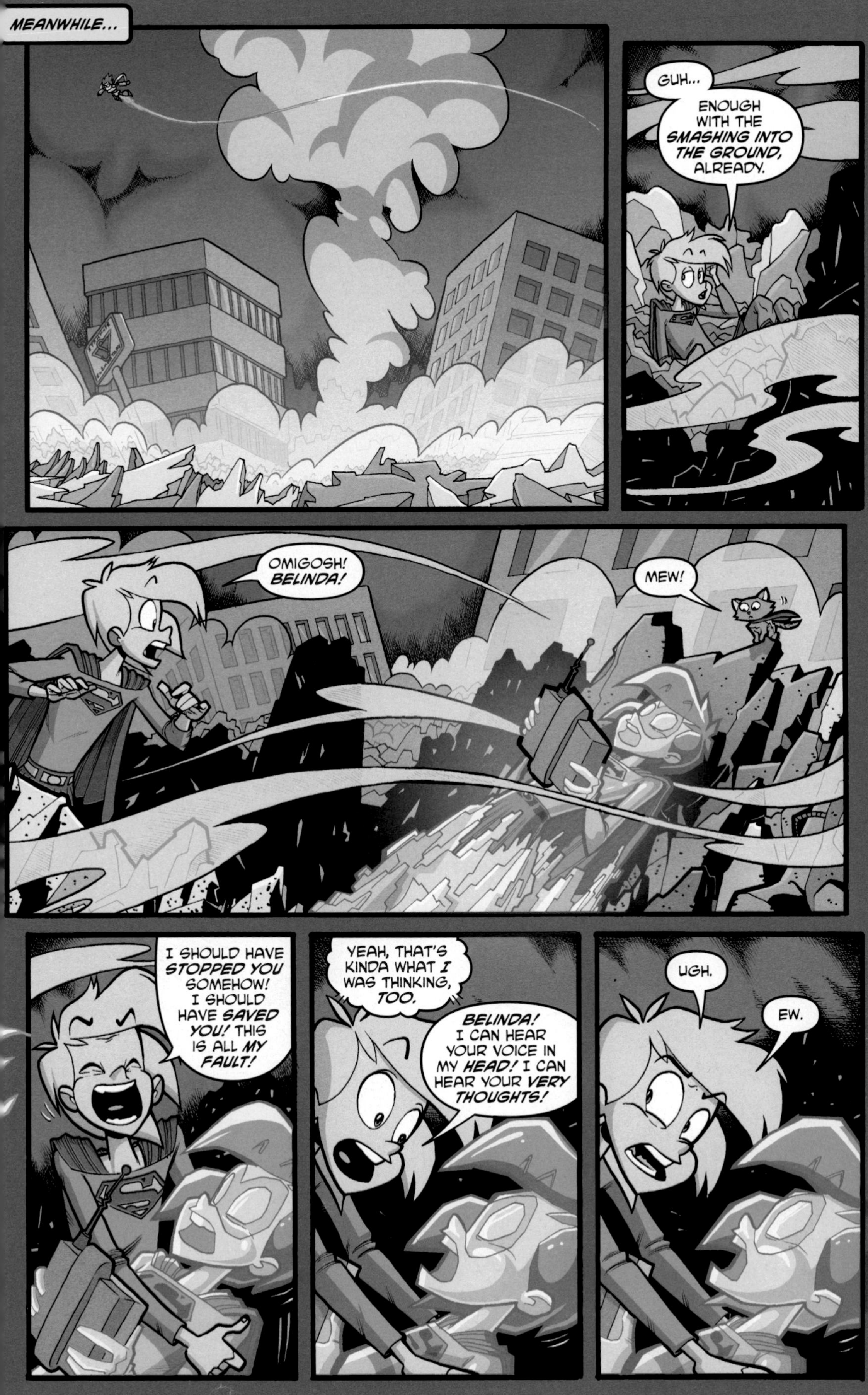
MEANWHILE...
GUH...
ENOUGH WITH THE SMASHING INTO THE GROUND, ALREADY.
OMIGOSH! BELINDA!
MEW!
I SHOULD HAVE STOPPED YOU SOMEHOW! I SHOULD HAVE SAVED YOU! THIS IS ALL MY FAULT!
YEAH, THAT'S KINDA WHAT I WAS THINKING, TOO.
BELINDA! I CAN HEAR YOUR VOICE IN MY HEAD! I CAN HEAR YOUR VERY THOUGHTS!
UGH.
EW.

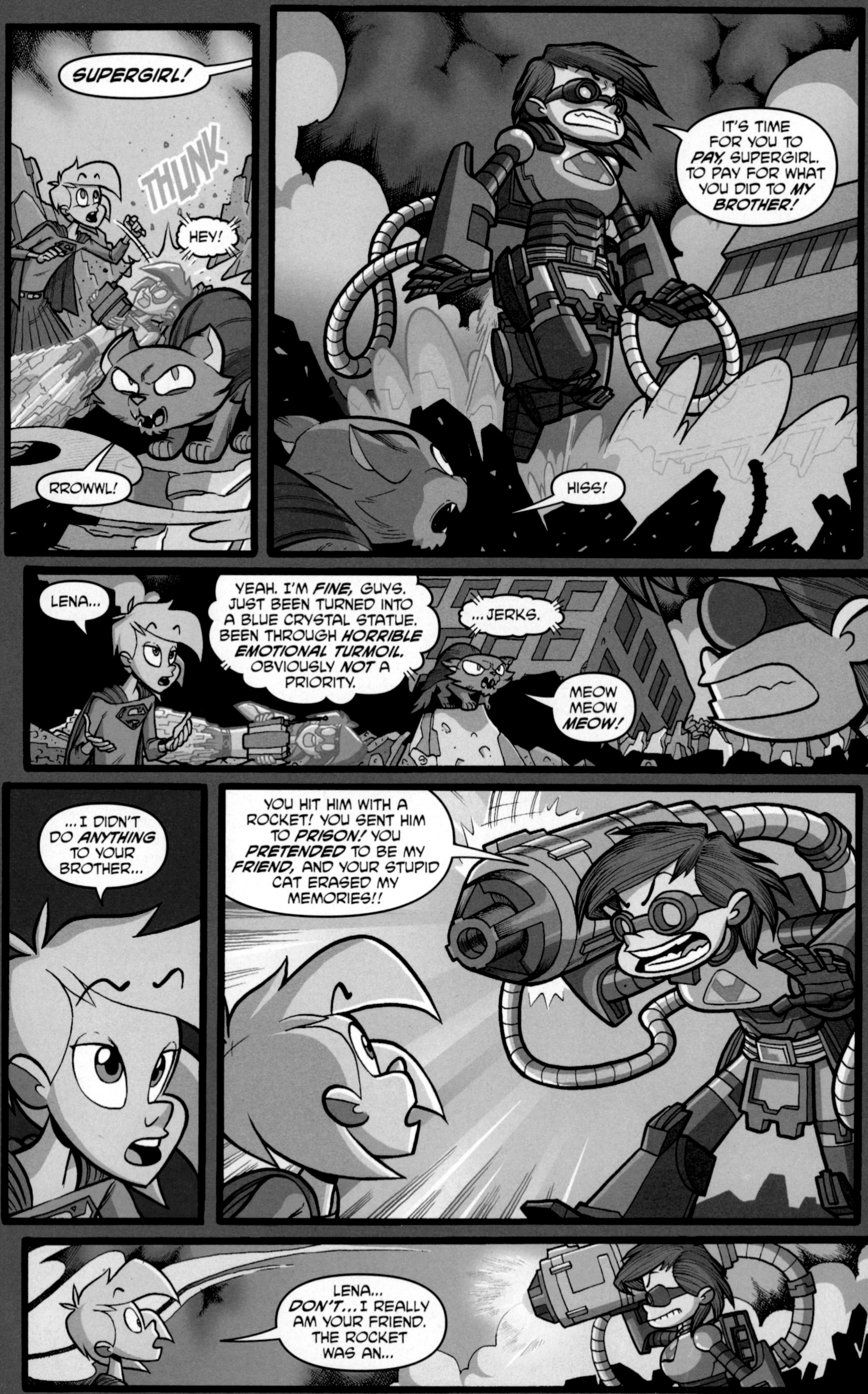
SUPERGIRL!
THUNK
HEY!
RROWWL!
IT'S TIME FOR YOU TO PAY, SUPERGIRL. TO PAY FOR WHAT YOU DID TO MY BROTHER!
HISS!
LENA...
YEAH. I'M FINE, GUYS. JUST BEEN TURNED INTO A BLUE CRYSTAL STATUE. BEEN THROUGH HORRIBLE EMOTIONAL TURMOIL. OBVIOUSLY NOT A PRIORITY.
...JERKS.
MEOW MEOW MEOW!
...I DIDN'T DO ANYTHING TO YOUR BROTHER...
YOU HIT HIM WITH A ROCKET! YOU SENT HIM TO PRISON! YOU PRETENDED TO BE MY FRIEND, AND YOUR STUPID CAT ERASED MY MEMORIES!!
LENA... DON'T... I REALLY AM YOUR FRIEND. THE ROCKET WAS AN...

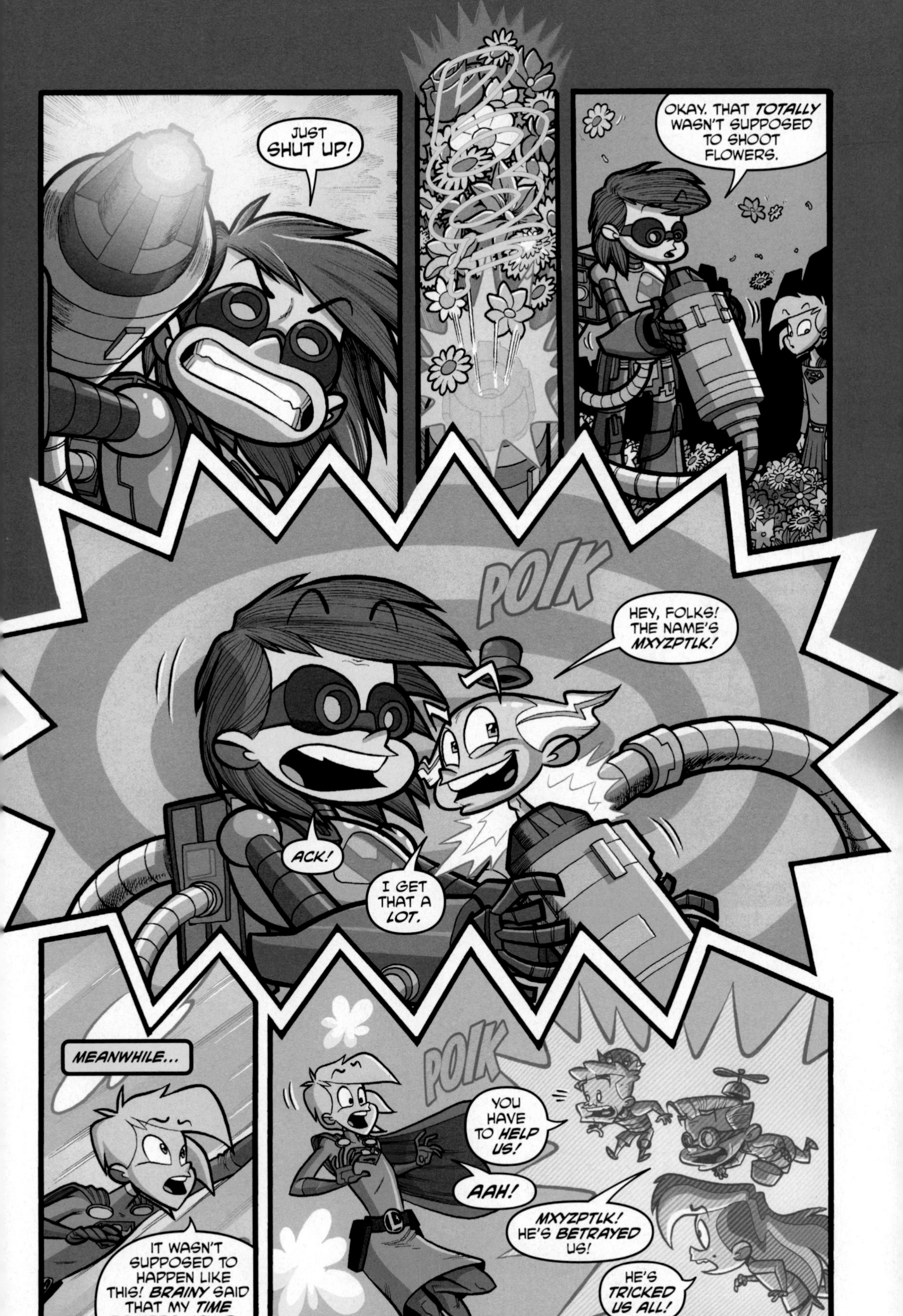
JUST SHUT UP!
OKAY. THAT TOTALLY WASN'T SUPPOSED TO SHOOT FLOWERS.
POIK
HEY, FOLKS! THE NAME'S MXYZPTLK!
ACK!
I GET THAT A LOT.
MEANWHILE...
IT WASN'T SUPPOSED TO HAPPEN LIKE THIS! BRAINY SAID THAT MY TIME POWERS WOULD...
POIK
YOU HAVE TO HELP US!
AAH!
MXYZPTLK! HE'S BETRAYED US!
HE'S TRICKED US ALL!

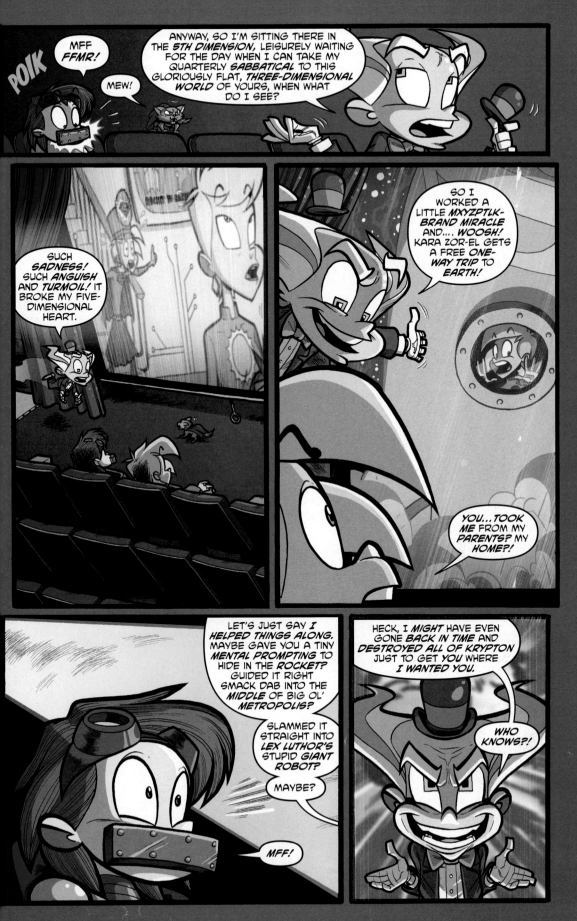

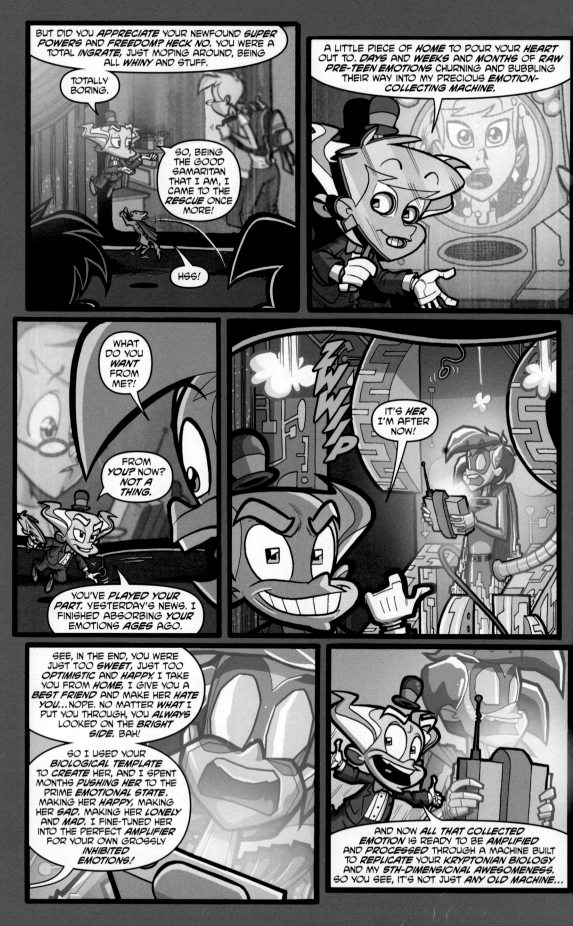

BUT DID YOU *APPRECIATE* YOUR NEWFOUND *SUPER POWERS* AND *FREEDOM*? *HECK NO*. YOU WERE A TOTAL *INGRATE*, JUST MOPING AROUND, BEING ALL *WHINY* AND STUFF.

TOTALLY *BORING*.

SO, BEING THE *GOOD SAMARITAN* THAT I AM, I CAME TO THE *RESCUE* ONCE MORE!

HSS!

A LITTLE PIECE OF *HOME* TO POUR YOUR *HEART* OUT TO. *DAYS* AND *WEEKS* AND *MONTHS* OF *RAW PRE-TEEN* EMOTIONS CHURNING AND BUBBLING THEIR WAY INTO MY PRECIOUS *EMOTION-COLLECTING MACHINE*.

WHAT DO YOU *WANT* FROM ME?!

FROM *YOU*? NOW? *NOT A THING*.

YOU'VE *PLAYED YOUR PART*. YESTERDAY'S NEWS. I FINISHED ABSORBING *YOUR* EMOTIONS *AGES* AGO.

IT'S *HER* I'M AFTER NOW!

SEE, IN THE END, YOU WERE JUST TOO *SWEET*, JUST TOO *OPTIMISTIC* AND *HAPPY*. I TAKE YOU FROM *HOME*, I GIVE YOU A *BEST FRIEND* AND MAKE HER *HATE YOU*...NOPE. NO MATTER *WHAT* I PUT YOU THROUGH, YOU *ALWAYS* LOOKED ON THE *BRIGHT SIDE*. BAH!

SO I USED YOUR *BIOLOGICAL TEMPLATE* TO *CREATE* HER, AND I SPENT MONTHS *PUSHING HER* TO THE PRIME *EMOTIONAL STATE*. MAKING HER *HAPPY*, MAKING HER *SAD*. MAKING HER *LONELY* AND *MAD*. I FINE-TUNED HER INTO THE PERFECT *AMPLIFIER* FOR YOUR OWN GROSSLY *INHIBITED EMOTIONS*!

AND NOW *ALL THAT COLLECTED EMOTION* IS READY TO BE *AMPLIFIED* AND *PROCESSED* THROUGH A MACHINE BUILT TO *REPLICATE* YOUR *KRYPTONIAN BIOLOGY* AND MY *5TH-DIMENSIONAL AWESOMENESS*. SO YOU SEE, IT'S NOT JUST *ANY OLD MACHINE*...

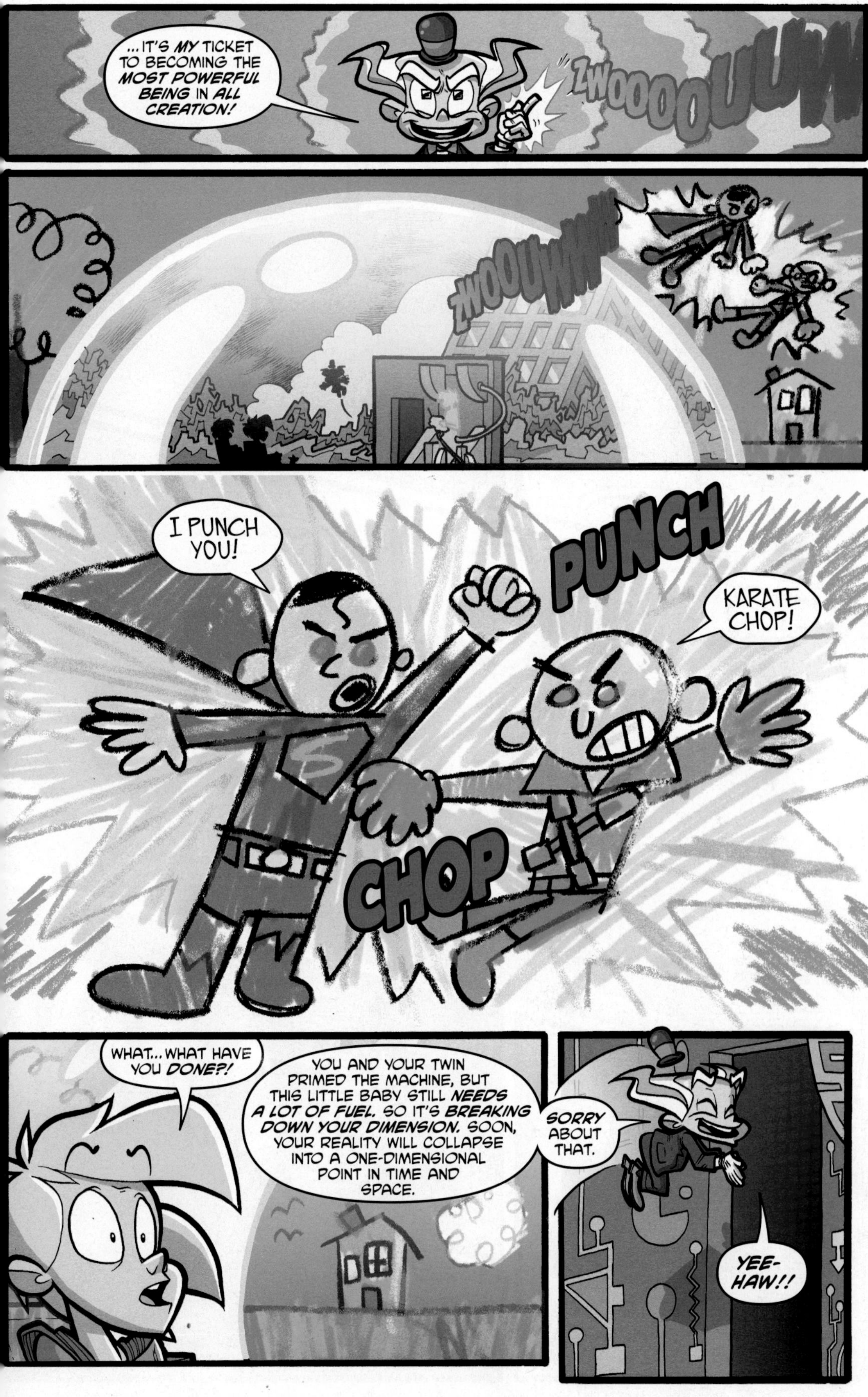
...IT'S *MY* TICKET TO BECOMING THE *MOST POWERFUL BEING* IN *ALL CREATION!*
ZWOOOOOUUWW
ZWOOUWWW
I PUNCH YOU!
PUNCH
KARATE CHOP!
CHOP
WHAT...WHAT HAVE YOU *DONE?!*
YOU AND YOUR TWIN PRIMED THE MACHINE, BUT THIS LITTLE BABY STILL *NEEDS A LOT OF FUEL.* SO IT'S *BREAKING DOWN YOUR DIMENSION.* SOON, YOUR REALITY WILL COLLAPSE INTO A ONE-DIMENSIONAL POINT IN TIME AND SPACE.
SORRY ABOUT THAT.
YEE-HAW!!

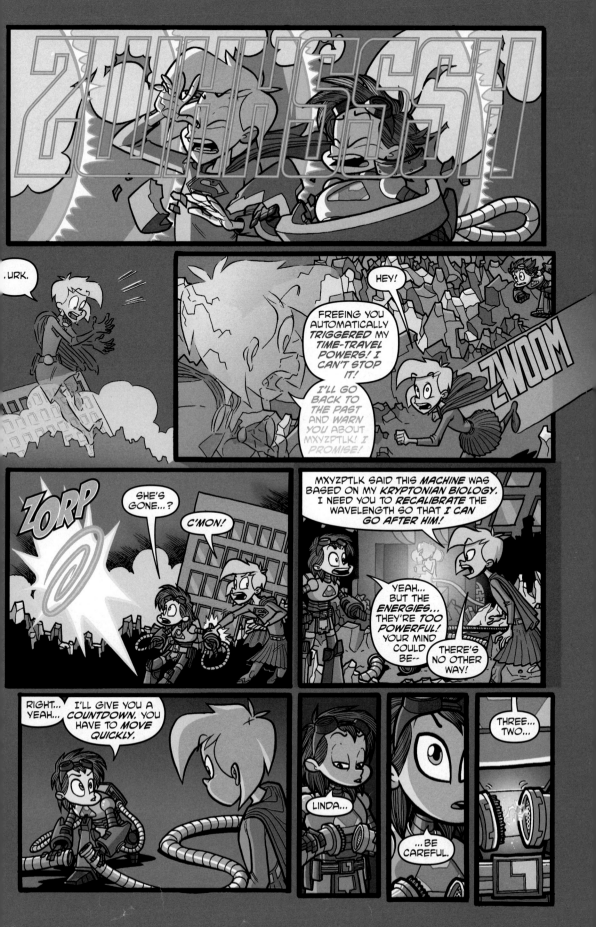

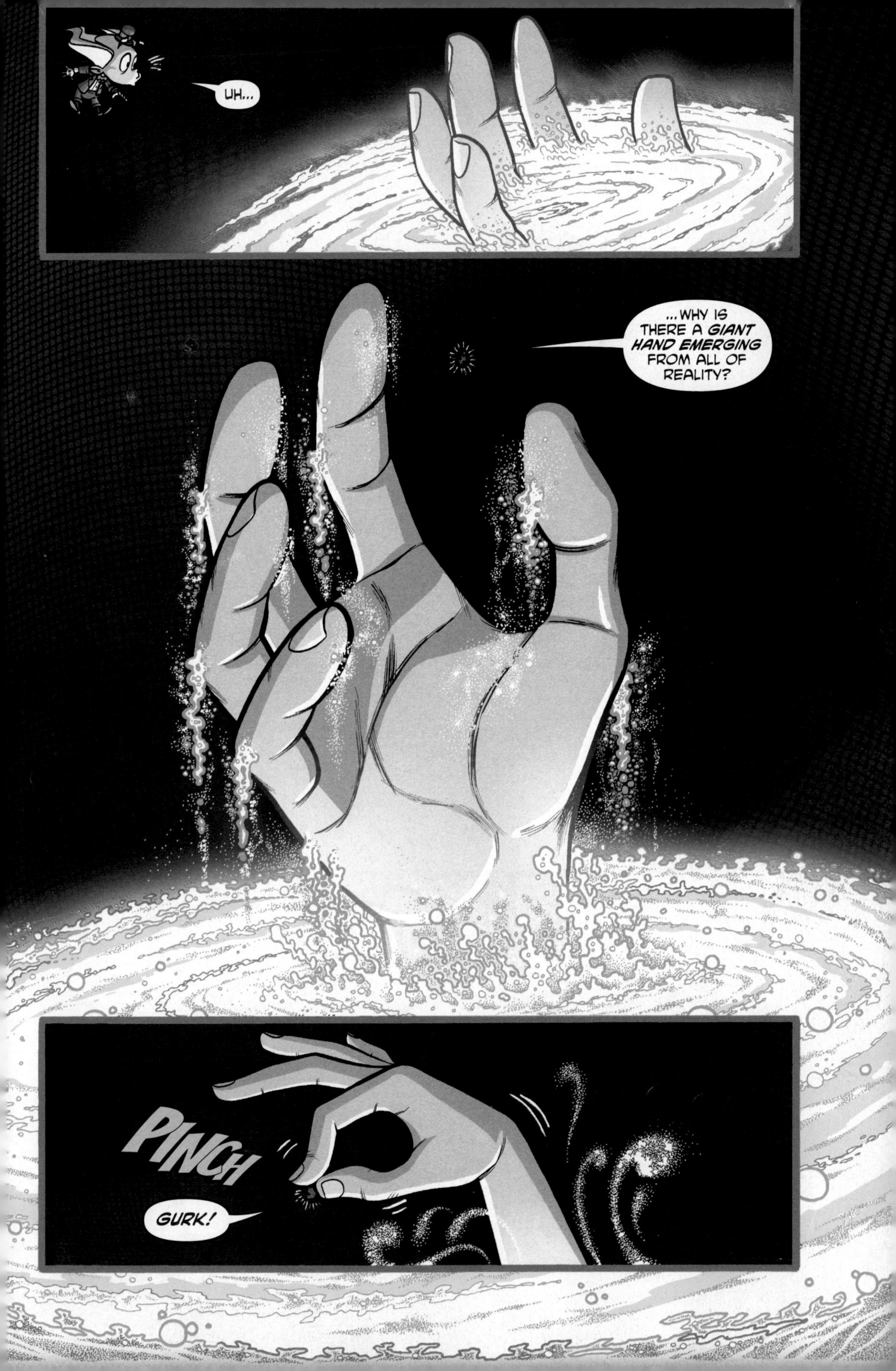
UH...
...WHY IS THERE A GIANT HAND EMERGING FROM ALL OF REALITY?
PINCH
GURK!

REDESIGNING SUPERGIRL:

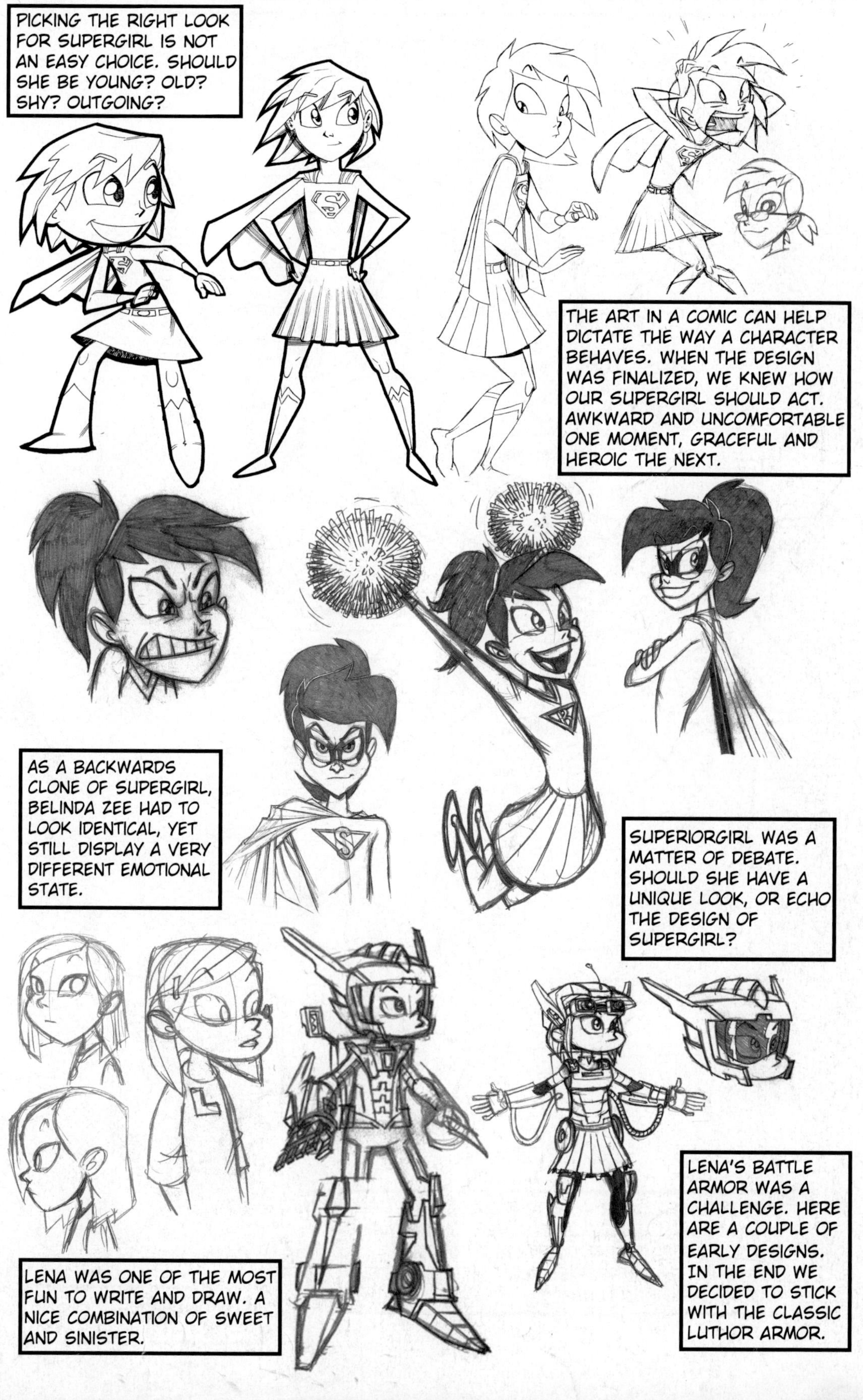

PICKING THE RIGHT LOOK FOR SUPERGIRL IS NOT AN EASY CHOICE. SHOULD SHE BE YOUNG? OLD? SHY? OUTGOING?
THE ART IN A COMIC CAN HELP DICTATE THE WAY A CHARACTER BEHAVES. WHEN THE DESIGN WAS FINALIZED, WE KNEW HOW OUR SUPERGIRL SHOULD ACT. AWKWARD AND UNCOMFORTABLE ONE MOMENT, GRACEFUL AND HEROIC THE NEXT.
AS A BACKWARDS CLONE OF SUPERGIRL, BELINDA ZEE HAD TO LOOK IDENTICAL, YET STILL DISPLAY A VERY DIFFERENT EMOTIONAL STATE.
SUPERIORGIRL WAS A MATTER OF DEBATE. SHOULD SHE HAVE A UNIQUE LOOK, OR ECHO THE DESIGN OF SUPERGIRL?
LENA WAS ONE OF THE MOST FUN TO WRITE AND DRAW. A NICE COMBINATION OF SWEET AND SINISTER.
LENA'S BATTLE ARMOR WAS A CHALLENGE. HERE ARE A COUPLE OF EARLY DESIGNS. IN THE END WE DECIDED TO STICK WITH THE CLASSIC LUTHOR ARMOR.

THIS IS AN EARLY VERSION OF THE COVER TO ISSUE 6 OF THE SERIES. ISSUE 6 WAS THE FINAL ISSUE, AND WE WANTED A COVER WHERE SUPERGIRL BASICALLY RODE OFF INTO THE SUNSET.

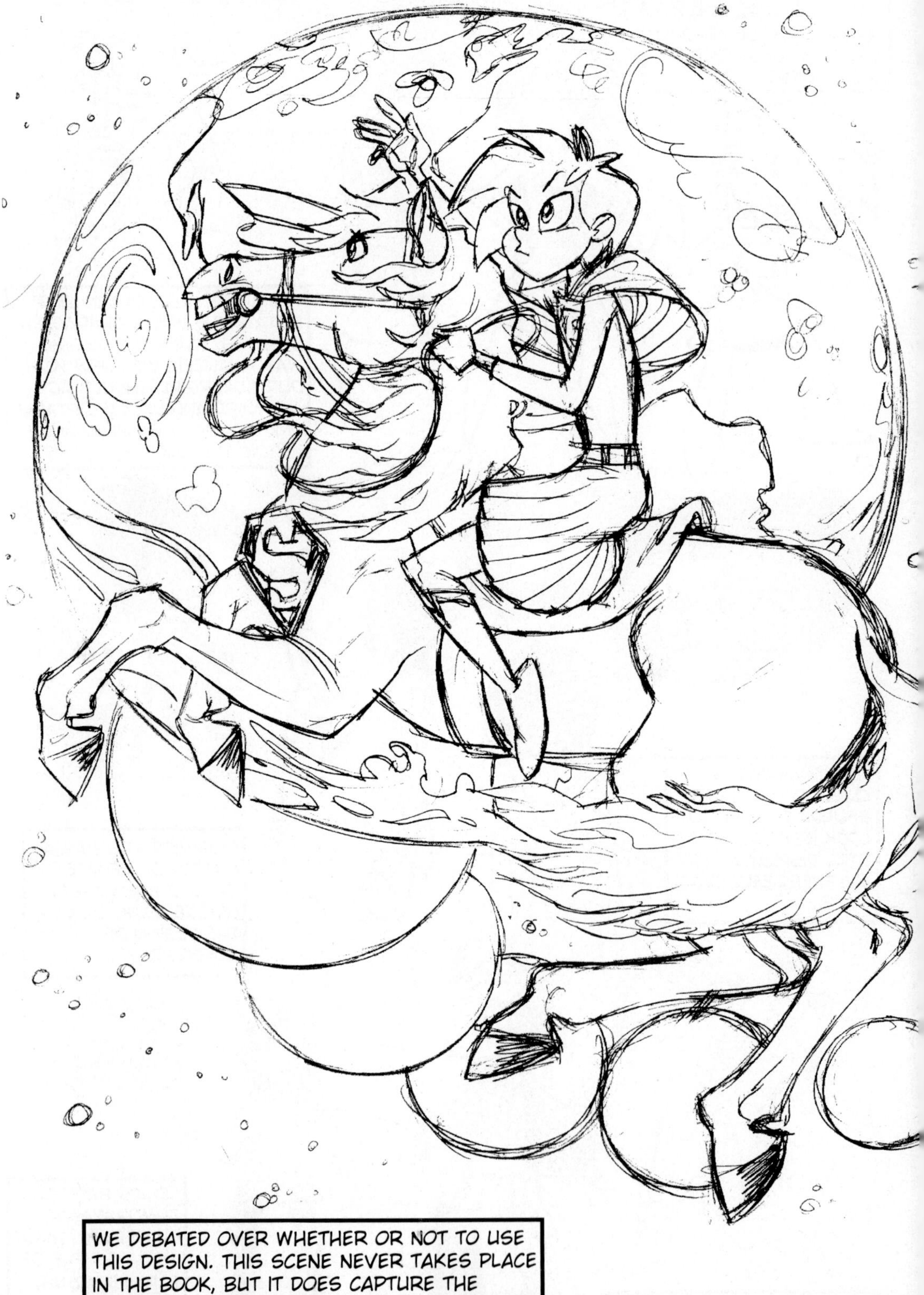

WE DEBATED OVER WHETHER OR NOT TO USE THIS DESIGN. THIS SCENE NEVER TAKES PLACE IN THE BOOK, BUT IT DOES CAPTURE THE ESSENCE OF THE SERIES AND THE CHARACTER AS WE IMAGINED HER.

IT WAS, AND STILL IS, A GOOD NOTE TO END ON.